The Politics of Mental Health and Illness

Series Editor
Bruce M. Z. Cohen
Sociology University of Auckland
Auckland, New Zealand

The Politics of Mental Health and Illness conceptualises the western mental health system as a social, economic, political, and cultural project which cannot be adequately theorised without considering wider societal and structural issues such as professional power, labelling and deviance, ideological and social control, consumption, capital, and self-governance. Engaging with both social theory and empirical evidence, and situated at the intersections of critical psychiatry, sociology, anthropology, social psychology, social work, history, media studies, and the health and education sciences, the series offers academics, researchers, postgraduate students, and practitioners new and innovative monographs and edited collections with which to contest and challenge the taken-for-granted understandings of psychiatry and the mental health system currently progressed in western society. Research topics for the collection may include: aspects of the medicalisation and/or pharmaceuticalisation of everyday life; psy-professional power and knowledge production; psychopolitics and the expansion of talk therapies; the biomedical model and the future of psychiatric nosology; the marketisation of mental health discourse; social media and self-diagnosing behaviour; capitalism and psychiatric violence; and specific analyses of psy-professionals and their practices from a variety of locations (including prisons, workplaces, addiction clinics, the military, schools, the home, and general hospitals). As the first book series to explicitly encourage critical contributions in the area of mental health and illness, we welcome scholarship from a wide range of different theoretical and empirical perspectives.

If you would like to discuss a book idea prior to submitting a proposal please contact the Series Editor, Dr Bruce M. Z. Cohen, via the Commissioning Editor, Beth Farrow (beth.farrow@palgrave.com).

Jon Hook • Frank Gruba-McCallister
Editors

The Revolutionary Psychologist's Guide to Radical Therapy

palgrave
macmillan

Editors
Jon Hook
Counter-Psych, Chicago, IL, USA

Frank Gruba-McCallister
Counter-Psych, Chicago, IL, USA

ISSN 2731-5266　　　　　　ISSN 2731-5274　(electronic)
The Politics of Mental Health and Illness
ISBN 978-3-032-02398-8　　ISBN 978-3-032-02399-5　(eBook)
https://doi.org/10.1007/978-3-032-02399-5

© The Editor(s) (if applicable) and The Author(s), under exclusive license to Springer Nature Switzerland AG 2025

This work is subject to copyright. All rights are solely and exclusively licensed by the Publisher, whether the whole or part of the material is concerned, specifically the rights of translation, reprinting, reuse of illustrations, recitation, broadcasting, reproduction on microfilms or in any other physical way, and transmission or information storage and retrieval, electronic adaptation, computer software, or by similar or dissimilar methodology now known or hereafter developed.

The use of general descriptive names, registered names, trademarks, service marks, etc. in this publication does not imply, even in the absence of a specific statement, that such names are exempt from the relevant protective laws and regulations and therefore free for general use.

The publisher, the authors and the editors are safe to assume that the advice and information in this book are believed to be true and accurate at the date of publication. Neither the publisher nor the authors or the editors give a warranty, expressed or implied, with respect to the material contained herein or for any errors or omissions that may have been made. The publisher remains neutral with regard to jurisdictional claims in published maps and institutional affiliations.

Cover credit: Malte Mueller

This Palgrave Macmillan imprint is published by the registered company Springer Nature Switzerland AG.
The registered company address is: Gewerbestrasse 11, 6330 Cham, Switzerland

If disposing of this product, please recycle the paper.

[Jon Hook]: To David Lethbridge, whose underrated work gave me an initial shove. To all my teachers for their guidance on what not *to do.*
[Frank Gruba-McCallister]: To my daughter, Deirdre, and son, Brian. And for a more just society for children everywhere.

Whilst in ordinary life every shopkeeper is very well able to distinguish between what somebody professes to be and what he really is, our historians have not yet won even this trivial insight. They take every epoch at its word and believe that everything it says and imagines about itself is true.
Karl Marx, the German Ideology, 1845

Only by denying can one live. Assertion is bondage. To question and deny is necessary. It is the essence of revolt and without revolt there can be no freedom.
Nisargadatta Maharaj, I Am That, 1973

Preface

I recall while in high school back in the early 1970s first encountering the work of the critical theorist, Erich Fromm. I was at "the" bookstore in Chicago, Kroch and Brentano, and purchased his book, *The Revolution of Hope Toward a Humanized Technology*. I still have in my possession and it had quite an impact on me. At the time, I was struggling with feelings of alienation and inadequacy which I assumed were rooted in something being wrong with me. What struck me as radical in reading Fromm that first time was his assertion that the cause of psychological distress was not something inside of people, but actually the result of adverse social conditions rooted in injustice. In particular, Fromm was visionary in his critique of corrupting impacts of capitalism. By weaving his Marxist perspective with his training as both a sociologist and psychoanalyst, Fromm presented a truly integral and complex analysis of the ways in which social structure and practices shape human beings. Throughout his corpus of work he detailed the diverse ways in which capitalism exerts negative impacts through its promotion of widespread commodification, its creation of extreme inequality and related forms of injustice, and its degradation of the environment. All of these points have since been well substantiated by theorists and research across diverse disciplines, as will be detailed in various chapters in this book.

Fromm described the beliefs and values espoused by capitalism as constituting what he called a necrophilic or death-affirming orientation. This necrophilous worldview is organized around a malignant form of narcissism in which individuals have a highly inflated self-image and exaggerated self-interest. At the same time, they regard others as inferior, dangerous, and immoral. This orientation places an emphasis on having rather than being. Individuals who adopt it display a sadistic desire to completely dominate and control other human beings, viewing them as mere things. This leads them to inflict suffering on them and even to kill them. This emphasis on having is also channeled into unchecked greed and the extreme need to acquire of material possessions. The neglect of being leads to a spiritual vacuum and an absence of compassion toward oneself and others. In addition, based on his work on the psychological and social dynamics involved in Nazi Germany, it is not surprising that Fromm (1941) saw parallels between fascism and unbridled capitalism. Both exert a corrupting influence on human character.

There is little question that Fromm is a truly pivotal figure in radical approaches to psychology and was prophetic in his warning about the dire consequences of neoliberalism and fascism. The destruction wrought by these two ideologies can still be witnessed in many events unfolding today, making his thinking as relevant as ever.

I recall when I first read his work that I experienced a welcome sense of validation of experiences and feelings that up to that time I was unable to either describe or understand. Growing up in a blue collar family and a working class neighborhood, I had begun to become aware of the ways in which significant economic stresses and certain forms of oppression and discrimination had harmed me and those close to me. However, being still very young and immature, I had only started on a journey that would unfold and evolve in the years ahead. As I moved through my education in clinical psychology and early career, I became increasingly attracted to and influenced by existential and transpersonal theory. These both seemed compatible with a number of ideas from Fromm. However, at the same time I succumbed to the excessive individualism characteristic of mainstream psychology. My focus was on looking for and fixing things wrong "inside" those who I treated. Sadly, I forgot some pivotal lessons from Fromm.

Working with a clinical population dealing with significant loss, I became interested in exploring the nature of human suffering and launched into an intensive study of this. At first, I did not appreciate the degree to which suffering was due to social injustice. However, as I moved from clinical practice to teaching and training, I found myself coming back to the seminal work of Fromm. This led me to delve more into studying the role of psychology to promote social justice. This included becoming versed in the work of a number of critical psychologists, very much in the tradition of Fromm. Inspired by this work, I made advocacy of social justice a significant part of my teaching and training. I also initiated efforts to revise program curricula in my administrative position in order to train students in socially responsible practice. This culminated in my writing a book arguing that neoliberalism and the oppression it causes are the most significant causes of human suffering.

Nonetheless, the need for the kind of radical psychology espoused by Fromm remains. More than 50 years have passed since the publication of *The Revolution of Hope*. The socialist revolution called for by Fromm to establish a society that fosters human flourishing has not come to pass. Indeed, neoliberalism has become even more virulent and fascism and right-wing extremism more prevalent. Moreover, the dangers posed by unbridled technology rooted in greed raised by Fromm continue to threaten human well-being and even survival. The latest iteration of this is the looming impact of artificial intelligence in replacing actual human connection. In calling for a revolution, Fromm raised a question of paramount importance, "What does it mean to be human?" Any true revolution must take this question seriously as the fundamental cause of human suffering is the many ways in which dehumanization occurs. Radical psychologists must embrace exploring this question and forthrightly condemn any form of dehumanization. More importantly they must work tirelessly to oppose it by promoting individual and collective liberation. This book is devoted to these goals—goals that Erich Fromm taught us to cherish and aspire to.

Kalamazoo, MI, USA　　　　　　　　　　　　　　　　　　　　Jon Hook
Park Ridge, IL, USA　　　　　　　　　　　　　Frank Gruba-McCallister
September 13, 2024

Acknowledgements

We would like to express our gratitude to our contributors for lending knowledge, experience and passion to the collection of chapters to this Handbook. Also much thanks to Dr. Bruce Cohen, the editor of "The Politics of Mental Health and Illness" series for his encouragement, guidance and support for this Handbook. Finally, thanks to our colleagues at Palgrave for their assistance and advice in preparing this Handbook.

December, 2024   Jon Hook
                                                              Frank Gruba-McCallister

Praise for *The Revolutionary Psychologist's Guide to Radical Therapy*

"In contemporary culture, we are in desperate need of new, radical approaches to psychotherapy that take seriously the social and political aspects of suffering. Hook and Gruba-McCallister provide us with an indispensable resource toward this end. Filled with contributions from many liberatory and radical psychotherapy scholars, The Revolutionary Psychologist's Guide to Radical Therapy engages essential topics from epistemological violence to capitalism to social justice. This is a critically important read for all therapists striving to empower a more just society."
—Louis Hoffman, PhD, Executive Director, *Rocky Mountain Humanistic Counseling and Psychological Association*, Author, *Case Formulation in Existential-Humanistic Therapy*, Editor, *Rising Voices: Poems Toward a Social Justice Revolution*

"The psy-disciplines have been justifiably criticized for their complicity with existing power structures. Yet, throughout their history, alternative movements and counter-narratives have emerged to challenge one-dimensional psychological thinking and doing. The authors, who recognize the entanglements of societal, interpersonal, and individual realities in psychotherapy, articulate radical concepts and methods to demonstrate that psychologists are not bound to uphold the status quo. This book offers a timely and necessary interruption in a field too often marked by a lack of collective hope and critical reflexivity and envisions a praxis at the intersection of the personal and political."
—Thomas Teo, PhD, Professor of Psychology, *Historical, Theoretical, and Critical Studies of Psychology, Department of Psychology, York University*

"This brilliant volume offers a searing critique of mainstream psychotherapy's entanglement with capitalist ideology. Yet it goes far beyond critique, reclaiming therapy as a vehicle for emancipation rather than a tool for ensuring conformity with neoliberal norms. With precision and moral urgency, it reveals how therapeutic practice routinely individualizes and depoliticizes social suffering, while charting a path toward radical renewal. "World bad, you bad" becomes a galvanizing call for justice and human flourishing. Every progressive professional should read this book."
—James Davies, PhD, Reader in Social Anthropology and Mental Health, *University of Roehampton*, Psychotherapist

"Literature on radical forms of psychotherapy and healing is scarce and often either overly theoretical without practical application, or overly technical without theoretical depth. The Revolutionary Psychologist's Guide to Radical Therapy attends to these limitations. It is an essential text for anyone seeking not only to alleviate distress but also to address the sociogenic roots of human suffering. The authors offer rigorous philosophical, ethical, and clinical reflections on the social causes of distress and the psychologist's role in responding to them—alongside concrete strategies for doing this work both within and beyond the clinic."

—José G. Luiggi-Hernández, PhD, MPH, Clinical Psychologist; Assistant Professor of Medicine, *University of Pittsburgh*, Contributing Author, *Decolonial Psychology: Towards Anticolonial Theories, Research, Training, and Practice*

"The Revolutionary Psychologist's Guide to Radical Therapy is a compelling and timely collection that challenges the status quo of mainstream psychotherapy by addressing the impact of systemic oppression on mental health. Editors Jon Hook and Frank Gruba-McCallister bring together a diverse group of voices to advocate for a radical approach that integrates theory, practice, and social context. This book offers not just a critique of current practices but also practical strategies and transformative visions for therapists committed to personal and social liberation. It is a crucial resource for practitioners and activists seeking to dismantle oppressive systems and promote genuine healing."

—Robert K. Beshara, PhD, MFA, Associate Professor of Psychology, *Northern New Mexico College*, Editor of *A Critical Introduction to Psychology and Critical Psychology Praxis*

Contents

Part I Introduction   1

1 The Good, the Bad, and the Radical   3
   Jon Hook

Part II Theory   15

2 Compassion and Justice: Integrating the Two
   Roles of Radical   17
   Frank Gruba-McCallister

3 (Anti)Capitalist Therapeutics: Analyzing Psychotherapy's
   Role within Capitalism and Proposing a Critical-
   Liberation Psychotherapy (CLP) Alternative   31
   Micah Ingle and Zenobia Morrill

4 Radical Epistemologies for Radical Psychologists   53
   Oliver Yimeng Xu and Laura Smith

Part III Practice   73

5 The Radical Circle: Toward a Psychological Counter-Hegemony   75
Jon Hook

6 Personal and Social Liberation: Necessary Foundations for Radical Therapy   97
Frank Gruba-McCallister

7 Transformative Therapies for Holistic Liberation   115
Sebastienne Grant

8 Psychoanalysis, Revolution, and the Red Clinic   135
Ian Parker

9 Working as a Therapist in an Unjust Mental Health Care System   149
Joel Vos

Part IV Context   177

10 For the Breathless to Breathe: Frantz Fanon's Clinic   179
Leswin Laubscher

11 Working as a Therapist with Victims of Social Injustice   203
Joel Vos

12 Radical Youth Work: A Community Based Approach to Working with Youth, Young Adults and Families   229
Weston Robins

Part V	Sublation	249
13	Self-death as a Symbol of Radical Freedom *Farhan Shah*	251
14	How to Ruin Your Clients: Mindfulness as Cruelty *Glenn Wallis*	263
15	Facing the Abyss: Daoist Contemplative Psychology as Old/New Paradigm *Louis Komjathy* 康思奇	281
Part VI	Concluding Thoughts	307
16	To Arms! Psychotherapy as Class Warfare *Jon Hook*	309
Index		333

Notes on Contributors

Sebastienne Grant is an associate professor in the PhD Integral and Transpersonal Psychology program at California Institute of Integral Studies. They hold a PhD in Psychology: Consciousness and Society from the University of West Georgia. Their psychological orientation is grounded in an integration of critical, humanistic, existential, Buddhist, and transpersonal perspectives. Their work broadly focuses on the intersections of individual and societal wellbeing, social justice, prosociality, and self and subjectivity. Most recently they have been delving into the benefits of compassion and service practices in nurturing individual and societal wellbeing.

Frank Gruba-McCallister is currently retired after having taught and served in academic administration for over thirty-three years at the Illinois School of Professional Psychology-Chicago, Adler University, and the Chicago School of Professional Psychology-Chicago. Prior to teaching, Gruba-McCallister provided clinical services primarily to individuals in a medical setting and in private practice. While the Vice President of Academic Affairs at Adler he oversaw the revision of all degree programs to support the newly adopted mission of the school to educate socially responsible practitioners. This innovation was recognized by the Clinical Psychology Doctoral program receiving the 2007 American Psychological

Association's Board of Education Affairs Award for Innovative Practices in Graduate Education in Psychology. He has published and done professional presentations in the areas of humanistic/existential psychology, spirituality, health psychology, critical psychology, and the role of psychology in advancing social justice. His book, Embracing Disillusionment: Achieving Liberation Through the Demystification of Suffering, also published by University Professors Press explores the significant adverse impact of oppression on physical and psychological well-being, the role of neoliberal ideology in oppression.

Jon Hook is a doctoral candidate in Counseling Psychology at Western Michigan University. Jon is a clinician and researcher whose work explores the intersections of psychotherapy process and outcome, political radicalism, ludology, and contemplative studies. He is also the founder of *Counterpsych*, a newsletter, podcast, and seminar group dedicated to fostering a counter-hegemony in psychotherapy through critical discourse and transformative practice. Outside of psychology, Jon Hook is a published role-playing game designer and the creator of *SURREALPUNK*.

Micah Ingle is part-time faculty in Psychology at Point Park University and the University of West Georgia. His research areas of interest include humanistic, critical, and liberation psychologies, with a particular focus on hermeneutics, phenomenology, and psychology's intersection with the sociopolitical. Micah serves as Communications Chair for Division 32 of the American Psychological Association (Society for Humanistic Psychology), as well as Division 24 (Society for Theoretical and Philosophical Psychology). He also works as a Science News Writer for Mad in America. His current research aims to critique the western individualizing medical model grounded in neoliberal capitalism, as well as to cultivate alternatives via humanities-oriented group and community work.

Louis Komjathy 康思奇 (Xiūjìng 修靜 [Cultivating Stillness]; Wànruì 萬瑞 [Myriad Blessings]) is a leading scholar-practitioner of Daoism and an ordained Daoist priest (dàoshì 道士) in the Huàshān 華山 lineage of Quánzhēn 全眞 Daoism. He hold a Ph.D. in Religious Studies from Boston University in 2005, specializing in Daoism and comparative religious studies. In 2006, Louis trained as a Daoist recluse in Chéngdū, Sìchuān, where he was ordained into the Huàshān lineage, later living and practicing in the monasteries of Láoshān 嶗山 and Huàshān 華山. A prolific author, Louis has published extensively on Daoism, including seminal works such as *Entering Stillness: A Guide to Daoist Practice* (2022), *Primer for Translating Daoist Literature* (2022), the *Handbooks for Daoist Practice: Twentieth Anniversary Edition* (2023), and *Dàodé jīng: A Contextual, Contemplative, and Annotated Bilingual Translation* (2023). His forthcoming book, *Traces of a Daoist Immortal: Chén Tuán of the Western Marchmount*, will be published in 2024. He was also prominently featured in *Dream Trippers: Global Daoism and the Predicament of Modern Spirituality* (2017). Louis is the founding co-director of the Daoist Foundation, where he serves as a senior teacher and spiritual director. He lives and works as an independent scholar-educator and translator in the wooded ravines of Ravinia, Illinois.

Leswin Laubscher is an associate professor in the clinical psychology department at Duquesne University, Pittsburgh, and extraordinary professor at the University of the Western Cape, South Africa. He is the author of *Levinas for Psychologists* and co-editor of *Fanon, Phenomenology and Psychology* (Routledge).

Zenobia Morrill is an assistant professor in the Clinical Psychology Department of William James College. In 2023 she was the recipient of the Sigmund Koch award, from Division 24 of the American Psychological Association, for her early career contributions to psychology. Her research areas include psychotherapy process, critical and liberation psychology, and qualitative inquiry. Previously, she served as a research officer to the United Nations' Special Rapporteur on the right to health. In addition to being a professor, Zenobia is also a licensed practicing psychologist and Senior Research Associate of the Center of Psychological Humanities and Ethics at Boston College. She is an editorial board member of the *Psychology and Other* book series and has served as an executive member on several APA division boards including the Society for Theoretical and Philosophical Psychology (STTP), the Society for Qualitative Inquiry in Psychology (SQIP), and the Society for Humanistic Psychology (SHP).

Ian Parker is a psychoanalyst and revolutionary Marxist in Manchester, Honorary Secretary of the College of Psychoanalysts, UK, and on the Board of the Red Clinic. His books include (with David Pavón-Cuéllar) Psychoanalysis and Revolution: Critical Psychology for Liberation Movements (1968 Press, 2021).

Weston Robins is the president and founder of Eternal Strength, Executive Director of Cosmic Lamb 501(c)3, owner of Weston J. Robins, LLC (private practice), and Professor of Psychology and Counseling at the University of West Georgia and the University of North Georgia. He holds a Ph.D. in Consciousness and Society from the University of West Georgia, with his research focused on critical psychology, family systems, and radical approaches to youth work. Robins is dedicated to disrupting traditional mental health paradigms through innovative, person-centered, and humanistic care. He integrates creative, relational approaches rooted in the philosophies of Deleuze and Guattari, Gregory and Nora Bateson, and the Anti-Psychiatry movement. Eternal Strength has become a dynamic hub for youth, families, and communities, offering mentoring and experiential care. He is currently building a certifiable methodology for radical youth work that weaves together existential, psychodynamic, and psychospiritual philosophies. Robins has published a book with Routledge Psychology, collaborated with global initiatives like Unpsychology, and remains committed to teaching and mentoring the next generation of mental health professionals. His work reflects a profound belief in the transformative power of connection creativity, and care in fostering individual and systemic growth. He strives to create a world where youth and families are empowered to thrive authentically and unapologetically.

Farhan Shah is a Norwegian philosopher with a doctoral degree from the University of Oslo, Norway. He is also an advisor at the Center for Process Studies, US, and research advisor at the Center for Open and Relational Theology at Nampa, US. Shah`s research interests include the topic of self-death and death-wishes as a human possibility, radicalization, religion and spirituality, the existential philosophical-theology of Muhammad Iqbal, eco-philosophy, existential health and non-pathological and non-clinical approaches to human despair and (self) destructivity.

Laura Smith is Professor of Psychology and Education in the Counseling Psychology Program at Teachers College, Columbia University, and she is the Chair of the Department of Counseling and Clinical Psychology. Laura was formerly the founding director of the Rosemary Furman Counseling Center at Barnard College and the Director of Psychological Services at the West Farms Center in the Bronx, where she provided services, training, and programming within a multifaceted community-based organization. Laura's scholarly interests include critical approaches to whiteness and antiracism, the influence of racism and classism on psychological theory and practice, and the relationship between social inclusion and emotional well-being. Outside psychology, she loves buildings, maps, animals, and New York City.

Joel Vos is a psychologist, philosopher and psychological therapist. He works as a senior researcher and senior lecturer at the Metanoia Institute in London. He is Director of IMEC International Meaning Events and Community, a consultant and board member to several mental health services. He has been advisor to politicians, social movements and political activists. In the past he has worked at the University of Roehampton and the New School of Psychotherapy and Counselling in the United Kingdom, and at Leiden University in the Netherlands. Joel has published over 160 articles and chapters. His recent books include Doing research in psychological therapies: a step-by-step guide (Sage), The Psychology of COVID-19 (Sage, 2021) and Mental Health in Crisis together with Ron Roberts and James Davies (Sage, 2019). Other books include Meaning in Life: An evidence-based handbook for practitioners (Bloomsbury, 2019) and The Economics of Meaning in Life (University Professors Press, 2020). His recent research focuses on psychological therapies, meaning in life, existential topics, social movements, critical psychology, and social justice. Read more on his personal website joelvos.com

Glenn Wallis holds a Ph.D. in Buddhist Studies from Harvard University, where his training focused on Sanskrit, Pali, and Tibetan Buddhist literature. His work explores how classical Buddhist philosophy and practice can remain relevant in contemporary life, drawing from his experience in Vipassana, Dzogchen, and Soto Zen traditions. Wallis has written extensively on Buddhism, radical education, and anarchism, blending academic rigor with public accessibility. His recent works include *A Critique of Western Buddhism: Ruins of the Buddhist Real* and *Non-Buddhist Mysticism: Performing Irreducible and Primitive Presence*, which exemplify his critical approach to Buddhist studies and his concept of "buddhofiction." He also founded the *Speculative Non-Buddhism* blog, a platform for essays reflecting this direction. Before transitioning to independent scholarship, Wallis taught at several universities, including the University of Georgia, Brown University, and the Rhode Island School of Design. His latest book, *Nietzsche NOW! The Great Immoralist on the Vital Issues of Our Time*, extends his critical inquiry into broader philosophical questions.

Oliver Yimeng Xu is a doctoral student in counseling psychology at Teachers College, Columbia University. As a member of the Racism, Class, and Inclusion Laboratory (Inclab), he researches the epistemological assumptions foundational to racial hierarchies and how they structure psychological research methods. His doctoral research focuses on Asian American mental health, specifically the unique challenges that second-generation Asian Americans face in relation to model minority imperatives. Oliver previously worked as a biochemical researcher at Columbia University Medical Center and holds an MS in environmental engineering. Outside of academia, Oliver is a semi-professional ballroom dancer and a community leader in the collegiate ballroom dance scene in New York City.

List of Figures

Fig. 9.1	Visualization of the therapist's systematic critical self-reflection and reflexivity (Based on Vos, 2023)	153
Fig. 9.2	Example of a vicious cycle in mental health care	166
Fig. 9.3	Social model of mental health care (Vos et al., 2019)	172
Fig. 11.1	Cycle of social injustice	222
Fig. 11.2	Example of breaking the cycle of social injustice	225
Fig. 15.1	Dimensions of (religious) praxis	287

List of Tables

Table 9.1	Examples of safety-creating actions	151
Table 11.1	Systematic-pragmatic-phenomenological-analysis of social justice	206
Table 15.1	Classical Daoist technical terms designating "apophatic meditation"	289

Part I

Introduction

1

The Good, the Bad, and the Radical

Jon Hook

2024 is a strange and contradictory chapter in human history. Optimists point to the unprecedented advancements in technology, longevity, global wealth, and culture. Indeed, by many measures we are witnessing the best conditions humanity has ever known. At the same time, all of this has been achieved at enormous human cost and it is all currently at risk. Democracy's foundations are cracking under a resurgence of fascism, imperialist conflicts once more flirt with nuclear oblivion, and environmental disaster escalates pressing us ineluctably toward global economic depression and perhaps even mass extinction. It is between these two polarities that the suffering masses enter the therapy clinic. Therapy seekers are not arriving in increasing numbers merely because they're suffering, but because they feel their lives—however comfortable or precarious—are not what they could be.

One way mainstream psychology deals with this chasm between our lived experience and actual potential is through an approach best

---

J. Hook (✉)
Counter-Psych, Chicago, IL, USA

described as "World good, you bad." In this view, the present system is either hunky dory or non-existent, and it is the individual who is ungrateful, defective, ill, or in need of yet another coping mechanism. Every therapy from the driest, coldest forms of CBT to the warmest gooiest humanistic therapies falls into this bucket. For these psychologists, vast realms of learning such as human history, culture, anthropology, politics, and economy are reduced to mere footnotes on the thoughts and feelings of the abstract individual. This is the reactionary side of psychology, and its narratives predominate the field. Conversely, from the small and so-called progressive wing comes what we may call the "World bad, you good" approach, which laments the world's evils and praises those they impact as holy victims. Yet even the beating heart of psychology offers little beyond a condemnation of various diffuse identities, uncontrollable political forces, and unnamable enemies. You are cajoled into waging the culture war, so long as you ignore the material conditions that produce it. You are invited to cope with more sensitive slogans painted in timely palettes, with the implication that rescue will finally arrive when we all come together and properly grieve.

Despite their surface appearances, these approaches are equally one-sided. Reactionary psychologists ignore history and politics altogether, while progressive liberal psychologists understand little about them. Together they walk hand in hand to fulfill that most important of all liberal maxims that when it comes to the material world the best thing to do is nothing at all. If we were to combine these two approaches, then we might really get somewhere. Call it the "World bad, you bad" approach—where despair reigns across every dimension. Hate the world, hate yourself, and get on with it already. At this precarious moment in history, and between the two sides depicted here, the imperative for radical therapy emerges.

Somehow we must simultaneously embrace the march toward the heights of human flourishing and guard against devolution into the twin miscarriages of compliance and despair. It is for this reason that this is not a book about coping, though it may offer some intimations. Nor is this a book about grievance, though you may find much to grieve with. Instead, this is a book about the infinite unfolding of human potential, the capitalist system that so arbitrarily holds this unfolding back, and what, in fledgling steps, we might do about it. There can be no doubt as to the hubris of this aim, but history is made by steps more courageous than careful, and no foundational work of psychology is worth reading if it does not at least gesture toward the complete development and final freedom of all humankind.

In generating what may be the first major anti-capitalist psychotherapy text in 30 years, Frank and I have cast the widest net possible and brought together as many radical thinkers as could be convinced to contribute. The authors come from a diverse array of perspectives, both in and outside of applied psychology, and are positioned within numerous left-wing traditions. Though these traditions may at times be as disagreeable with one another as they are with the capitalists, they share a commitment to calling out psychotherapy as a soft power maintaining the capitalist system—and, in turn, a practice that perpetuates the human misery it is designed to resolve. Unlike so many academic books on the topic, you will not find a mere flowery description of the myriad issues with psychotherapy but suggestions and guidance on bridging the gap between the world we know and the world we aspire to. Our cadre of authors presents numerous conceptions of radicalism—its many sides, paths, and tensions. What unites them is the understanding captured by Karl Marx who said, "To be radical is to grasp the root of the matter. But, for man, the root is man himself" (1844). That is, we share the view that human behavior and human relations in the real world must be grasped, not mere abstractions, theories, or concepts.

For Marx, of course, the root social relationship that must be pulled up is class exploitation. Capitalism necessitates that the vast majority of humanity, the working class, rent their bodies and minds to the owning class. It is this arrangement that prevents the infinite unfolding of human potential, and that enables and empowers social oppression. Liberal critics of Marx and so-called "post-Marxists" claim that this view is reductive and economistic, but this is an opportunistic fabrication. Marx's real critique of capitalism was never merely about obtaining economic justice, but about the myriad forms of psychological turmoil capitalist alienation generates and the psychological well-being it impairs. Marx and Marxists have historically sought a system in which we may, "overthrow all relations in which man is a debased, enslaved, abandoned, despicable essence." With economic exploitation as its basis, capitalism generates numerous forms of social oppression, like patriarchy and white supremacy, to justify the composition of the ruling class and class exploitation. Socialism does not usher in an instant utopia by uprooting class exploitation, but gradually by putting political and economic power back into the hands of regular working people. What's more it is only socialism, a true economic democracy, which can avoid global crises like climate change. As inspiring as this notion is, these have never been empty ideas.

Marx is one of the few philosophers and scientists whose words seem to leap off the page and onto the world stage. The application of Marxism has led more people out of debased relations than any movement in history, and this work is clearly not yet done. It is now the task of the contemporary radical to pick up this mantle of anti-capitalism and to simultaneously understand and transform the world. In the context of mental health, the radical therapist must continuously draw dialectical connections between the sufferer's material exploitation and their social oppression; between an individual's psychic suffering and the external conditions that sustain it. Radical therapy is then the revolutionary praxis aimed at the liberatory resolution of the bio/psycho/social contradictions within the ensemble of social relations. It intervenes at the individual and social levels—both theoretical and practical, therapeutic and political, immanent and transcendent. It may take on a hundred forms, but it operates to promote liberation and agitates against capitalism, full stop.

Radical therapy is a field that has lain fallow over several decades and hence it is overripe for taxonomy. Therefore, you will not find this to be a meticulous manual but rather something closer to a rough field guide. This book is broken into four themed sections—Theory, Practice, Context, and Sublation—with each contributor offering something like a first report from the frontier.

Theory lays the conceptual groundwork for radical therapy by interrogating psychology's current role in upholding capitalist and oppressive systems. The contributors examine the personal, social, and historical forces that shape psychotherapy, emphasizing that the discipline can either reinforce the status quo or cultivate genuine liberation. Collectively, they propose that rigorous self-reflection, direct engagement with marginalized communities, and a new epistemological vision are central to forging an authentically radical therapy practice. Each chapter offers distinct theoretical standpoints and tools for realizing this liberatory potential. Contributors present the theory of radical therapy by asserting its necessity in contrast to mainstream psychotherapy.

In the first chapter of the text, Frank Gruba-McCallister situates radical therapy in two core values, compassion and justice, which correspond to the "contemplative" and "prophetic" roles of the therapist. He argues that radical therapists must engage in self-examination to uncover the internalized ideological distortions imposed by a harmful status quo. Compassion involves connecting with clients' suffering, while justice compels therapists to speak out against oppressive social structures. Liberation requires praxis: reflecting on oppressive conditions and transforming them through collective action. Ultimately, the goal is "economic democracy" consistent with socialist values that foster community, solidarity, and human flourishing.

Furthering the need for a definitively anti-capitalist approach to healing, Micah Ingle and Zenobia Morrill critique mainstream psychotherapy's complicity in propping up capitalist values, particularly through shaping an atomized, "productive" sense of self. They use Foucault's concept of social construction to reveal how capitalist therapy discourses mold individuals to adapt to oppressive systems rather than transform them. To counter this, the authors propose "Critical-Liberation Psychotherapy" (CLP), which emphasizes interconnected, community-driven approaches and foregrounds collective empowerment. CLP reimagines the therapeutic relationship as a site for mutual exploration and social resistance. It offers a blueprint for an anti-capitalist therapy that deconstructs the status quo and fosters new modes of liberatory selfhood.

Finally, Oliver Yimeng Xu and Laura Smith take us one step deeper into the foundations of the dominant psychological worldview in their exploration of how mainstream psychology's epistemology—rooted in positivism and hyper-scientific methods—reinforces oppressive power structures. Drawing on Foucault, they show that "truth" in psychology is produced within sociopolitical contexts that often privilege White or capitalist interests. The authors champion reflexive, community-engaged research approaches that unmask and subvert these power dynamics. Liberation psychology, critical race theory, and transdisciplinary humanities all figure prominently as alternative knowledge frameworks. By redefining how psychology knows what it knows, they argue, we open the door to radical, justice-oriented practices that reject epistemic violence.

Theory, in the most fundamental sense, is useful only in how it is enacted. Hence, Part III, "Practice," explores how radical therapists can tangibly apply theory to transform individuals, therapy settings, and broader social structures. Each contributor tackles concrete challenges—from dismantling hegemonic forces in treatment to fostering liberatory therapeutic methods—and offers strategies for re-envisioning the clinical environment. The chapters collectively provide a roadmap for practitioners committed to systemic change, emphasizing the intimate link between personal healing and social emancipation.

In the first chapter of this section, I offer what amounts to a letter to young and early career radicals in psychology, revealing how mainstream psychology's professional "psyauthorities" uphold capitalist ideology and crush dissent among aspiring therapists. Building on Antonio Gramsci, I show how these authorities function within the professional managerial class to define "normality" and preserve class power—far from promoting effective therapeutic training. As a response, I propose the formation of "Radical Circles": small, decentralized groups that quietly organize for systemic change even under oppressive structures. Drawing on the genesis of this very book, I illustrate how such circles offer a concrete means for radical therapists to resist and reshape the profession.

Frank Gruba-McCallister's second contribution offers solid advice to those who have formed radical circles, merging critical psychology with existential and transpersonal insights to help us understand suffering as both social and deeply personal. With reference to Heidegger, Fromm, and Tillich, he insists that genuine healing must tackle capitalism's warped individualism alongside humanity's natural interdependence. To Gruba-McCallister, real therapy involves blending compassion, justice, and active social engagement to free both individuals and communities from ongoing harm.

Continuing that thread of radical action that follows holistic understanding of the human condition, Sebastienne Grant explores the intersecting roles of spirituality, decolonial thought, critical race theory, and activism in creating "transformative psychologies." Rather than simply mitigating symptoms, she urges therapists to use compassion, peer collaboration, and transcendence as catalysts for collective change. With echoes of Buddhist concepts of interconnectedness, Grant envisions therapy less as an adjustment tool and more as a bridge between personal healing and structural reform.

Bringing these considerations out into the world of therapeutic practice, Ian Parker highlights his work in the "Red Clinic" in the UK. To begin, he traces the early history of psychoanalysis among leftist circles before detailing its subsequent co-optation under capitalism. To reclaim its emancipatory core, Parker presents the "Red Clinic," as a concrete project that fuses psychoanalytic praxis with unambiguously anticapitalist aims. Mapping out twenty-two programmatic points, he demonstrates how clinicians in real world clinics can uphold political integrity while still offering safe and transformative therapeutic spaces.

Finally, Joel Vos confronts the everyday ethical pitfalls of practicing therapy within an unjust, profit-centered mental health system. Anchored in the notion of "social injustice," he guides clinicians to adopt reflective strategies that preserve their moral compass amid systemic demands. Practical tools—ranging from conscious boundary-setting to coalition-building—are laid out for therapists determined to fight burnout while still pressing for systemic improvements.

Theme three, "Context", situates practice within specific social, cultural, and communal spheres. Each contributor situates their work amid broader political and historical backdrops, providing concrete examples of how oppression, violence, and injustice require equally systemic therapeutic responses. From Fanonian clinical methods to social-justice interventions and community-based youth outreach, these chapters underscore that healing does not happen in isolation. Instead, it emerges within relational networks—where personal agency meets collective action, and theory merges with grassroots praxis.

The exploration of context begins with Leswin Laubscher who outlines the timeless embodiment of struggle that was Franz Fanon. Laubscher revisits Fanon as a radical guide whose clinical innovation sprang directly from his lived experiences of anti-Black racism, colonial injustice, and the necessity for meaningful liberation. Engaging Fanon's lesser-known psychiatric writings, Laubscher highlights how Fanon wove existential phenomenology with an unflinching critique of colonial structures to reform the asylum as a space of social therapy. By centering patients' real conditions—sociopolitical oppression and bodily alienation—Fanon championed a dialectic of healing and political activism. His legacy, Laubscher insists, reminds us that the "radical" in Fanon was not just theoretical but anchored in daily, fiercely humane clinical practice.

Following Fanon, Joel Vos extends a pragmatic framework for clinicians confronting pervasive inequality. Taking a phenomenological approach, he lays out the cyclical nature of injustice, where oppressive systems intersect with internalized victimhood or denial, forming feedback loops that deepen suffering. Vos's cycle-of-injustice model guides therapists toward re-engaging clients in the communal dimensions of trauma recovery. By integrating a critical-liberation perspective, therapists can turn social injustice into a catalyst for activism, policy reform, and the authentic pursuit of justice. In practice, this demands reflexivity, empathy, and a willingness to champion clients' social as well as personal transformation.

While Vos details how therapy can dismantle injustice at a structural level, Weston Robins describes how to do so in tandem with young people themselves. Channeling a "radical youth work" ethos, he demonstrates how non-hierarchical, creative collaboration becomes a powerful antidote to the dehumanizing aspects of the mental health industry. Rooted in community-building and mutual liberation, the Eternal Strength Center melds ideas from Batesonian systems thinking and poststructural philosophies to spark youth-led social change. Robins' approach draws on the tradition of anti-psychiatry and emphasizes the critical synergy of adult allies and youth forging alliances based on love, activism, and co-creative freedom.

Our exploration of the field of Radical Therapy enters its furthest reaches and its widest conclusions in the book's final section where existence and being are themselves problematized and interrogated. Rather than use the word "Transcendence," I have opted to name this section "Sublation". Sublation, in Marxist use, means the resolution of contradictions into a higher synthesis that both includes and negates these contradictions. By refusing solutions that merely help individuals adapt, each of the chapters in this section embraces "Sublation" by integrating the contradictions of suffering and freedom and examining how therapy might merge radical negation into a generative possibility. The therapeutic act becomes something far beyond coping strategies: it enters the domain of existential risk, expansive being, and spiritual ruination.

This three-chapter arc begins with Farhan Shah's exploration of the phenomenon of suicide, wrested from its sole classification as psychopathology and recast as a deeply human capacity for self-negation. In challenging the so-called "zero vision" approach to suicidality, Shah interrogates the structural injustices, neoliberal illusions, and moral paternalism that ignore existential dimensions of despair. From his viewpoint, therapy must move beyond mere risk assessment and medical diagnoses if it is to acknowledge people's free agency over their own being. Such a stance shatters the taboo around suicide, recasting it as a radical critique of oppressive systems and an urgent call for social responsibility.

Next, Glenn Wallis calls out mainstream "Mindfulness, Inc." as a willing accomplice to neoliberal capitalism. In glib, corporate-friendly mindfulness-based intervention culture, the therapeutic promise of calm acceptance upholds exploitative norms. Yet, ironically, mindfulness as an ancient tradition contains an undertow of disenchantment—an unsparing confrontation with the Real—that can rip complacent illusions apart. Radical therapy, in Wallis's telling, emerges when practitioners harness this element of "cruelty," rousing clients from their sedation under passive consumerist ideology. With great bombast, therapy becomes about *shattering* comfort rather than managing it, offering a deeper liberation that unsettles personal and collective illusions alike.

Finally, Louis Komjathy brings us a view of spiritual transformation from Daoism, a dialectical spiritual tradition that has thus far eluded capture by neoliberalism. For Komjathy, Daoist apophatic meditation is an expansive dissolution of self in cosmic emptiness. Rather than remedy or self-improvement, it fosters a letting go of all habituations—including capitalist subjecthood. Daoist quiet-sitting ultimately reveals an imminent "Otherness" that the standard "body-scan" or "focus-on-the-breath" packaging of mindfulness has systematically muted. From this vantage, meditative therapies cultivate *deconditioning*, unleashing the potential of emptiness and stillness to undermine social conformities and awaken new modes of being.

Like all works of true radicalism, the book ends with a call to action. In the concluding chapter, I contend that far from being a neutral science, psychotherapy is the new religion of late-stage capitalism descended from religious healing movements like Phineas Quimby's Mind Cure. Like premodern clergy whose homilies rationalized feudalism all while invoking the revolutionary words of Jesus Christ, we therapists have become psychic technicians on the payroll of the capitalists all while talking of social justice. In this regard, mainstream psychotherapy is a cudgel of the ruling class. Echoing Marx' view on religion, I conclude that psychotherapy is not the problem to be solved, but our toxic society. In simplest terms, we must grasp this cudgel and turn it around by treating society within the individual. I offer necessary, but not sufficient guidelines for budding radical therapists, admonishing them to fight the capitalists and commit the ultimate transgression of living a good life.

The design of this book is not so much to convince anyone of socialism as it is to present a clear, open, and explicit description of what anti-capitalist therapeutics can look like. Contrasted with the opaque manipulations of liberal psychologists, we echo Marx and Engels who said that "The Communists disdain to conceal our views and aims" (1848). Those who find these aims disagreeable are free to offer an alternative political vision and defend the therapeutics of that worldview. Alas, few psychologists will be conscious enough to rise to this challenge.

As for those interested in the genuine progress of humanity, none can say where the endpoint will be. What we do know is that we are at a point in history where we must begin to draw new lines. Lines that connect the suffering of every worker to the social and material relations that create their pain. Lines that crisscross to expose the web of lies and alienation that hold us in the spider's hands. Lines that stretch toward an unseen horizon. But we must not limit ourselves to one-sided struggles. We must also draw circles—circles that integrate and contain, overlapping to form a holistic understanding of our shared interdependencies. Circles where no contradiction is isolated, and where the force of others is contained within the struggle of one.

The day may soon come when in North America writing a book like this or even reading it is akin to signing one's own death warrant, but the sooner we stand together, the sooner we will be free. There will be times when the struggle feels impossible, but take heart—domination is fragile, and oppression is the mask of fear. The frontiers of resistance are everywhere, in every small act of refusal. At this time of great upheaval, we call on every radical therapist to not merely criticize but to integrate, assemble, and agitate. To unlearn and relearn. To at long last embody the struggle toward the infinite unfolding of human potential.

Reference

Marx, K. (1844). A contribution to the critique of Hegel's philosophy of right. Deutsch-Französische Jahrbücher (A. Blunden & M. Carmody, Eds.). Marx/Engels Internet Archive. https://www.marxists.org/archive/marx/works/1843/critique-hpr/Marx, K., & Engels, F. (1848). The communist manifesto. In Marx/Engels Internet Archive. Translated by S. Moore in cooperation with F. Engels. Retrieved from https://www.marxists.org/archive/marx/works/1848/communist-manifesto/

Part II

Theory

2

Compassion and Justice: Integrating the Two Roles of Radical

Frank Gruba-McCallister

Dual Values, Roles and Ways of Knowing for Radical Therapists

The theologian, Matthew Fox (1972), following on the etymological meaning of radical as "root," describes its two meanings. The first is a psychological meaning of "being rooted" that he connects with what he calls a contemplative role and compassion. The second is a social meaning of "uprooting" that he connects with a prophetic role and justice. Both of these roles come out of spiritual traditions, but have relevance to radical therapy aimed at personal and collective liberation from capitalist ideology (Gruba-McCallister, 2025).

Contemplative practice is aimed at freeing persons of illusions and attachments that distort their self-understanding and contaminate their knowledge of the true nature of existence, with the ultimate goal of achieving union with a transcendent Reality (Underhill, 1915). These

F. Gruba-McCallister (✉)
Counter-Psych, Chicago, IL, USA

© The Author(s), under exclusive license to Springer Nature Switzerland AG 2025
J. Hook, F. Gruba-McCallister (eds.), *The Revolutionary Psychologist's Guide to Radical Therapy*, The Politics of Mental Health and Illness,
https://doi.org/10.1007/978-3-032-02399-5_2

practices quiet the mind and body, enhance attention, decrease reactivity to external events, and cultivate a non-judgmental stance. The contemplative role of radical therapists takes several forms related to two different ways of knowing. The first is based on the recognition that it is the personhood of the radical therapist that plays a significant role in promoting liberation. *The transformative potential of therapy and transformation of those who seek help begins in the transformed heart, mind, and spirit of the therapist.* This means uncovering how their heart, mind, and spirit "…have been deformed by lust for power, by our fear of mutually accountable relationships, by our self-destructive tendency toward an alienated life" (Palmer, 1993, p. 108), as well as how this deformity is rooted in the internalization of a toxic ideology.

Radical therapists need to be deeply rooted in themselves by engaging in sincere and rigorous self-examination in order to identify biases, preconceptions, and values. Contemplative practice is akin to the phenomenological practice of bracketing (Ihde, 1986) devoted to identifying prejudices that color our experience, and temporarily suspending them. The resolute focusing of awareness and suspension of judgment facilitate uncovering illusions and what is taken for granted. The source of these distortions must not be restricted to personal factors and the workings of self-deception. In line with critical psychology (Schraube & Osterkamp, 2013), the goal is to uncover the equally destructive social roots of illusions. These are rooted in the dominant ideology or what Gramsci (1971) called *hegemony*. This is the worldview held by the ruling class consisting of core dogmas, accepted wisdom, and sanctioned values inculcated in subordinate classes. It serves a political function as it is posed as common sense and thus objective, universal, veridical and incapable of change. As a result, it sanctions and maintains social practices and structures responsible for inequity, oppression, and other forms of injustice.

The work of liberation for radical therapists thus begins with themselves (Gruba-McCallister, 2025). This is first because one cannot be a guide to others in the process of liberation without making this journey themselves. Discovering the personal as well as social causes of suffering within themselves by virtue of their shared humanity and their common internalization of hegemonic beliefs and values enables radical therapists to help others do likewise. This does not mean that they must successfully

2 Compassion and Justice: Integrating the Two Roles of Radical

complete this journey. The process of liberation is dynamic and constantly unfolds over the course of one's life. There will always be progress and setbacks and experiencing these makes it easier to recognize and accept them in others. The other reason is asking others to engage in this journey, with its rewards and perils, without demonstrating that one has done so themselves will be experienced as insincere. It is more important for radical therapists to show rather than tell in advocating for change. Affirming the essential social nature of human beings by means of acknowledging our shared condition opposes the exaggerated individualism promoted by capitalism.

As Palmer (1993) observes, different forms of knowing are actually ways of being. He writes, "The shape of our knowledge becomes the shape of our living; the relation of the knower to the known becomes the relation of the living self to the larger world… The way we interact with the world in knowing it becomes the way we interact with the world as we live in it" (p. 21). Contemplation is a form of *direct knowledge* in which no separation is made between subject and object. The relation between them is mutual and interdependent. There is an intimate and immediate connection with the other that is not capable of being described in words. The highest attainment of this is, in spiritual terms, the unitive or mystical experience. Experiencing a deep sense of connection and interdependence is the basis of compassion (Williams, 2008). This leads to a radically transformative experience of mind and heart (*metanoia*) that expands the boundaries of the self and so enables individuals to feel a deep connection with others. This value is essential to radical therapy. Compassion means being able to suffer with others without regard to preference or merit and without reservation due to fear or self-interest. One does not respond with apathy or indifference, but validates the experience of others' suffering and seeks to remove its causes wherever possible (Soelle, 2001). Compassion expressed in direct thought is a means of fully entering into the worldview of others. This enables radical therapists to accurately identify not only the personal obstacles to well-being, but more importantly the ways in which the internalization of an unjust hegemony causes harm based on marginalization, exploitation, oppression, and violence. Compassion provides the moral foundation for the pursuit of justice (Gruba-McCallister, 2019).

Internalized Oppression and the Role of Mystification in Maintaining Hegemony

In order to be able to extend compassion to others, one must first be able to extend compassion to oneself. This does not mean that therapists ignore or condone beliefs or values in themselves or others contrary to human flourishing. To validate one's experience is different from agreeing with it. Nor does it mean condemning themselves or others for harboring such beliefs or values. Actually this tendency to disparage oneself often serves a neglected political purpose designed to prevent awareness of harmful impacts of hegemony. This has been described as *internalized oppression* (David, 2014) and helps to explain how individuals consent to their oppression and feel disempowered to oppose it.. This has been found to have a number of adverse psychological effects, including negative self-image, self-doubt, passivity, and helplessness.

Paolo Friere (1970) who developed critical pedagogy provides insight into the development of internalized oppression. He observes that the oppressed develop an internalized duality in which they regard their oppressors as a model of humanity and thus adopt their standards, prescriptions, and beliefs. At the same time, they see themselves as falling short of humanity and wrongly believe that they are deserving of their failures and unhappiness. They likewise assume a fatalistic attitude of being incapable of changing their circumstances, which becomes self-defeating.

Clearly, radical therapists need to be thoroughly informed both about the process by which hegemony is internalized and the ways in which this impairs well-being. More importantly, they need again not to restrict this understanding to what is going on inside of individuals and recognize the powerful impacts of social, economic, and political forces outside of them. On a psychological level, clear consideration must be given to the incredible capacity for self-deception among human beings (Gruba-McCallister, 1993, 2019). There is extensive and detailed literature in psychology on the unconscious, defense mechanisms, cognitive distortions, and other explanations of self-deception. Human beings have a powerful need for control and stability rooted in neurological and biological processes that are advantageous to evolution (Goleman, 1985). Humans' vulnerability and uncertainty lead them to experience anxiety or fear of annihilation when faced with a situation that threatens their world-view and exceeds their sense of control. Such experiences are denied or distorted in order to fit with existing beliefs and values. This gives rise to fictions and illusions that, particularly when they are extremely and rigidly adhered to, ultimately become self-defeating and, as a result, have harmful consequences. Moreover, fear inhibits the capacity to exercise critical thinking that impairs the ability of individuals to become aware of and challenge these illusions (Gruba-McCallister, 1993, 2019). Experience is taken at face value and believed unquestioningly. Individuals assume the way things appear is the truth. This makes it clear that the undoing of self-deception by expanding consciousness and promoting self- reflection is an integral part of radical therapy.

However, what makes therapy truly radical is extending this process of unveiling in order to challenge illusions that have their origin in social processes, particularly *mystification* (Gruba-McCallister, 2019). Mystification refers to ways in which consciousness is conditioned by material and social conditions established by those in power to maintain hegemony. Examples of mystification include strategies aimed at denying or invalidating individuals' experience (Laing, 1967), using language to confuse people and disguise manipulation, as in propaganda (Watts, 1966), and employing powerful metaphors to frame issues in line with the dominant ideology (Lakoff, 2002). Augoustinos (1999) cautions against focusing solely on the individual level:

> The individual is viewed as failing to perceive reality accurately and failing to recognize his or her true self and group interests. Such approaches fail to acknowledge that reality construction is not an isolated cognitive task involving the direct and unmediated perception of the world. People are constantly and actively engaged in a complex and socially situated process of constructing reality, but they do this by using the cultural and ideological resources that are available to them…These resources are shaped by existing material and power relations and are embedded in the very nature of people's lived social relations and practices. (p. 302)

As societal beings, the way in which individuals develop their world-view cannot be abstracted from the social, cultural, political, and economic contexts into which they are born and continue to be embedded. All of these contexts are shaped by the dominant ideology which currently is neoliberalism (Harvey, 2005). Because this ideology is so pervasive and permeates every aspect of life, it is taken for granted or invisible. However, it exerts considerable power over how human being feel, think, and behave.

Erich Fromm (1955, 1968) writing on the disastrous impact of capitalism turning people into mindless and passive consumers described the profound way in which ideology is internalized. In his concept of *social character* (Fromm, 1941), he asserted that in order for a society to survive it must mold the character of its members so that they want to do what they have to do. This enables a small minority of the powerful to rule over and exploit the majority by inculcating them with unconscious beliefs and motivations that reflect the internalization of social dictates and norms. As a result, he describes people as half-asleep because most of their view of reality consists of fictions or half-truths. They mistakenly believe these to be an expression of the personal desires or goals. In actuality, they are carrying out implanted social directives that benefit the powerful often at their expense. Their compliance is enforced by means of implanting fear that something bad will happen to them if fail to obey and the belief that success and rewards will come if they conform. Indoctrination also succeeds because, as social beings, humans do not wish to be isolated, alienated, or rejected by their social group.

Critical Consciousness as a Model of Liberatory Radical Therapy

If this process were thoroughly effective, the efforts of radical therapy to promote liberation would be futile. Fortunately, this is not the case. Disillusionment inevitably occurs and provides the opportunity to move from non-critical, unreflective stance characteristic of direct knowledge to a more analytic, critical and evaluative stance characteristic of *discursive thought*. Discursive thought is based on reason, logic, and objectivity.

2 Compassion and Justice: Integrating the Two Roles of Radical

It allows individuals to exercise detachment that distances them from what is being scrutinized, to categorize and name it, and—most importantly—to consider alternatives. Friere (1970) describes this critical step in achieving liberation *critical consciousness*. His work on this process provides an essential roadmap for radical therapy. First, there is the discovery by the oppressed of contradictions inherent in an oppressive ideology. Next there is a validation of the experience of the oppressed that undoes denial and mystification by the powerful. This enables the problem to be named. This is followed by encouraging the oppressed to sit with the suffering caused by this discovery in order to learn from it. This relies upon the practice of compassion.

The last step of this process speaks to the second meaning of radical, underlining the role of the radical therapist as prophet. The problem becomes reframed as a form of injustice that needs to be uprooted and replaced with a more just alternative ideology. In other words, mere insight or understanding is insufficient to enable genuine change. As Friere (1970) emphasizes, liberation requires *praxis* which is the interweaving of reflection and action. Saying "No" and simply critiquing the status quo is not enough to achieve liberation. Victims of injustice must collectively take active measures to bring about a counter-hegemony that allows for true human flourishing. This serves to clarify the meaning of prophet in the context of radical therapy. It does not refer to being some fortune teller warning of future doom. Instead it is better defined with reference to prophets in the Judaic tradition who responded to the call of God to speak out forthrightly against the "sins of a nation" and command them to stand up for the lowly and dispossessed. As Eagleton (2003) asserts, prophets are individuals who courageously condemn corruption, greed, and abuses of power rooted in an unjust ideology; warn of the calamitous consequences if the current order remains unchanged; and demand radical reform to restore justice. This too is the responsibility of radical therapists.

Radical therapists must understand that compassion is empty without a commitment to justice (Gruba-McCallister, 2019, 2025). These values are inextricably linked. Acting in ways that lead victims of injustice to blame themselves for their misfortune and accommodate themselves to a toxic ideology makes therapists complicit in their oppression. Neglecting or obscuring the ways in which people suffer due to adverse social influences is equally harmful. Compassion does not merely open the mind and heart of radical therapists to the true magnitude of suffering of the oppressed, but to a realization that so much of that suffering is due to malevolent human actions rooted in greed, hatred, and selfishness. A sense of righteous anger and moral indignation expresses recognition of the need to not merely respond to others' anguish, but to work resolutely to abolish its causes. The spiritual writer, Nouwen (1972) recognizes these interdependent roles (using the term "mystic" to represent the contemplative role):

> Therefore every real revolutionary is challenged to be a mystic at heart, and he who walks in the mystical way is called to unmask the illusory quality of human society. Mysticism and revolution are two aspects of the same attempt to bring about radical change. No mystic can prevent himself from becoming a social critic, since in self-reflection he will discover the roots of a sick society. (p. 19)

The Prophetic Role: Interrogating and Critiquing the Status Quo

A central principle of critical clinical psychology (Coles & Mannion, 2017), in contrast to mainstream practice, is the requirement that therapists engage in ongoing interrogation and critique of existing unjust power structures and practices in society. It recognizes that the psychology itself is value-based and unable to separate itself from issues of power so that it must likewise be subject to criticism. Prilleltensky (2008) proposes the concept of *psychopolitical validity* to emphasize that the practice of psychology is inescapably value-laden and has the danger of upholding existing power relations that lead to inequality and oppression. To remedy this, radical therapists need to move past just analyzing how injustice impairs wellness at the personal level and include the interpersonal and structural levels. They should work collaboratively not merely with clients, but also with community members and policy makers to make changes on a larger scale.

2 Compassion and Justice: Integrating the Two Roles of Radical

Taking on the prophetic role and integrating discursive thought into their work enables radical therapists to not only recognize the experience of disillusionment that occurs when individuals awaken to how injustice has caused their suffering. It also enables them to foster and maintain the feelings of disappointment, frustration, fear, and anger that accompany this disillusionment in order to promote change. As an example, a common trigger for disillusionment occurs when individuals encounter contradictions and inconsistencies inherent to a toxic ideology (Langman, 2015). An example of this is critical psychology's critique of the destructive impact of capitalism on individuals' understanding of agency. It asserts that capitalism advances an extreme form of individualism and freedom that, in turn, creates a fragile sense of narcissism combined with a contradictory feeling that individuals must passively adapt to the demands made on them by prevailing social conditions. This leads to *restrictive agency* that compels people to adapt to existing power relations and forces them to exercise freedom only within limits imposed on them by society. Individuals believe that exercising their agency will lead them to come into conflict with others due to capitalism's promotion of competition and that they must accept their own oppression in order to garner some measure of advantage. This realization leads them to feel complicity with the status quo and deepens their sense of dependency, a significant source of their suffering.

Restricted agency leads to *guilt discourse* in which individuals feel an exaggerated degree of responsibility for this extreme individualism and competition, while diverting attention away from the role played by capitalist ideology. Due to its internalization, hegemony is mistakenly assumed to be a natural state of affairs that is universal, fixed, and inescapable. At the same time, individuals are placed in a damned if you do-damned if you don't situation that confuses and confounds them. Nonetheless, radical therapists can use this paradoxical situation to call the status quo into question. In order to do this, they need to first shift individuals from their passive, non-judgmental stance and encourage them to step back and ask themselves how this situation impacts them and their relationships with others. Next they encourage them to consider whether there are alternative ways in which to view and act upon these circumstances. It becomes a teachable moment.

Critical Psychology expands agency and subjectivity beyond the narrow confines of the individual to include other human beings. As social beings, it is possible for human beings to be able to jointly and cooperatively determine the life conditions to which they are subject. Moreover, by means of dialogue they are able to engage with others in mutual and collaborative critical reflection. This can begin in their relationship with a radical therapist and then expand to include others. The human capacity for self-reflection enables them to transcend their immediate situation and come to terms with the contradictions they have encountered by conceiving of ways that things can be different.

Such engagement in dialogue with others to achieve a collective transcendence of the status quo is called *reason discourse*. Individuals come to see how they sometimes unwittingly violate others' subjectivity and agency without judging themselves for this. This deeper social awareness helps them to put their responsibility into perspective, while at the same time seeing how coming to terms with the conditions under which they live can only be achieved together with others by coming to a shared understanding. By means of metasubjectivity, persons see their situation from the broadest possible perspective, recognizing that every individual has his or her own perspective and one's own is not privileged. Restrictive conditions can only be removed through collective action.

Being "uprooted" or having a "wake up" experience is the prelude to any meaningful change. In some instances this experience follows from a significant loss or trauma. This may be personal, but may also be a significant crisis that has widespread impacts. Naomi Klein (2007) describes these events as a *state of shock*, a sudden and unprecedented event that defies the ability of individuals to make meaning based on existing narratives (e.g., the COVID-19 pandemic). Klein's work provides extensive evidence of how the current neoliberal hegemony is responsible for triggering such crises, often with large-scale destructive consequences. Initially such experiences are typically accompanied by fear and a sense of disorientation that individuals seek to resist or avoid. When this occurs, the adverse consequences not only continue, but actually tend to grow worse. However, many destructive beliefs and values are exposed, offering the opportunity for transformation and growth (Gruba-McCallister, 2019, 2025). Frank and Frank (1991) correctly state that the experience of having one's worldview shattered, accompanied by feelings of insecurity, alienation, fear, and demoralization, is the prelude to seeking healing.

There is an Alternative: Socialism as Economic Democracy

Dissatisfaction with where one is requires clarity regarding where one wishes to be instead. For radical therapy to fulfill any promise of liberation on both an individual and collective level, it must have clarity regarding what is needed to replace capitalism (Gruba-McCallister, 2025). This question must be addressed by taking into careful consideration values necessary to truly promote well-being for all members of society. This raises the question, "What does it mean to be anti-capitalist in terms of an alternate ideology?" Different alternatives have been proposed, but the one advanced here is socialism in the form of an economic democracy. The work of the radical Marxist sociologist, Eric Olin Wright (2019), provides the rationale for and specifics of this alternative.

He writes that a critique of capitalism can be made most persuasively based on moral values. He puts forward three core values in his critique: equality/fairness, democracy/freedom, and community/solidarity. These essentially align with compassion and justice. He asserts that these values are necessary for a society to achieve the goal of human flourishing which he defines as a life "…in which a person's capacities and talents have developed in ways that enable them to pursue their life goals, so that in some general sense they have been able to realize their potentials and purposes" (p. 11). He outlines how the basic principles of capitalism interfere with the realization of these values. Capitalism violates egalitarian principles by virtue of creating massive inequalities in access to material and social conditions that foster flourishing by means of exploitation and extreme competition. Next capitalism is opposed to freedom and democracy in a variety of ways. These include: the distinction between public and private excludes a large number of people from decision-making; wealthy individuals having greater access to political power; the creation of dictatorships in the workplace; and inequalities hampering the disadvantaged from being able to act positively on realizing their life plans. Finally, capitalism is detrimental to values of community and solidarity based on its promotion of extreme individualism and competition rooted in fear and greed. It is meaningless for anyone with a sincere commitment to fostering human well-being and putting an end to unnecessary suffering to turn a blind eye to an ideology whose values run contrary to these goals.

Contrary to Margaret Thatcher's assertion that, "There is no alternative," socialism rests firmly on the three values needed to promote well-being. It does so by organizing economic and social structures in order to reallocate power and access to resources. Power is the capacity to do things in the world and must be exercised on both a personal and collective level and takes three forms. The first is control of economic resources. The second is state power which is control of rulemaking and enforcement over a territory. The third is democracy or rule by the people collectively organized into various voluntary associations. Wright (2019) specifies a range of specific policies for an economic democracy and strategies for achieving it.

Summary

Radical therapists must "root" their work firmly in advancing the values of compassion and justice to promote human flourishing. Acting in accord with these values requires transformation to begin with radical therapists themselves. They must compassionately but resolutely identify the harmful fictions and illusions of capitalist hegemony and then critique them. This better enables them to facilitate the development of critical consciousness in others, wherein they become aware of the causes of their oppression and the suffering it inflicts on them. They then engage in reflection that allows them to translate this understanding into actions aimed at opposing capitalist hegemony and conceive of a more just alternative. Often engaging in such reflection and critique is preceded by the experience of disillusionment in which one's world-view is threatened, leading to feelings of confusion, uncertainty, and fear. In accord with the value of compassion, radical therapists must convey acceptance and understanding to those experiencing such distress. However, compassion alone will not bring about real change. Compassion must be wed with justice. Radical therapists must assume a prophetic role in which the injustices of capitalism are forthrightly identified and condemned and there is a call for reform. These efforts must be aimed at liberation on both an individual and collective level. A viable alternative to capitalism to guide radical therapy is socialism as economic democracy. Radical therapists should heed the call of liberation psychology (Martin-Baró, 1996), "Comfort the afflicted and afflict the comfortable." In doing so, they embrace the roles of contemplative and prophet and act in accordance with compassion and justice.

References

Augoustinos, M. (1999). Ideology, false consciousness and psychology. *Theory & Psychology, 9*(3), 295–312.
Coles, S., & Mannion, A. (2017). Critical clinical psychology. In B. Gough (Ed.), *The Palgrave handbook of critical social psychology* (pp. 557–578). Palgrave Macmillan.
David, E. J. R. (Ed.). (2014). *Internalized oppression: The psychology of marginalized groups*. Springer Publishing Company.
Eagleton, T. (2003). *After theory*. Basic Books.
Fox, M. (1972). *On becoming a musical, mystical bear: Spirituality American style*. Paulist Press.
Frank, J. D., & Frank, J. B. (1991). *Persuasion and healing: A comparative study of psychotherapy* (3rd ed.). The Johns Hopkins University Press.
Friere, P. (1970). *Pedagogy of the oppressed*. Herder and Herder.
Fromm, E. (1941). *Escape from freedom*. Henry Holt.
Fromm, E. (1955). *The sane society*. Fawcett Publications, Inc.
Fromm, E. (1968). *The revolution of hope: Toward a humanized technology*. Bantam.
Goleman, D. (1985). *Vital lies, simple truths: The psychology of self-deception*. Simon and Schuster.
Gramsci, A. (1971). *Selections from the prison notebooks* (Q. Hoare & G. Nowell Smith, Trans.). International Publishers.
Gruba-McCallister, F. P. (1993). The imp of the reverse: A phenomenology of the unconscious. *Journal of Religion and Health, 32*(2), 107–120.

Gruba-McCallister, F. P. (2019). *Embracing disillusionment: Achieving liberation through the demystification of suffering*. University Professors Press.
Gruba-McCallister, F. P. (2025). *Radical healing: No wellness without justice*. University Professors Press.
Harvey, D. (2005). *A brief history of neoliberalism*. Oxford University Press.
Ihde, D. (1986). *Experimental phenomenology: An introduction*. State University of New York.
Klein, N. (2007). *The shock doctrine: The rise of disaster capitalism*. Picador.
Laing, R. D. (1967). *The politics of experience*. Pantheon Books.
Lakoff, G. (2002). *Moral politics: How liberals and conservatives think* (2nd ed.). The University of Chicago Press.
Langman, L. (2015). Why is assent willing? Culture, character and consciousness. *Critical Sociology, 41*(3), 463–481.
Martin-Baró, I. (1996). *Writings for a liberation psychology* (A. Aron & S. Corne, Eds.). Harvard University Press.
Nieman, S. (2002). *Evil in modern thought*. Princeton University Press.
Nouwen, H. J. M. (1972). *The wounded healer: Ministry in contemporary society*. Image Books.
Nussbaum, M. C. (2006). *Frontiers of justice: Disability, nationality, species membership*. The Belknap Press of Harvard University Press.
Palmer, P. J. (1993). *To know as we are known: Education as a spiritual journey*. HarperSanFrancisco.
Prilleltensky, I. (2008). The role of power in wellness, oppression, and liberation: The promise of psychopolitical validity. *Journal of Community Psychology, 36*(2), 116–136.
Schraube, E., & Osterkamp, U. (2013). *Psychology from the standpoint of the subject: Selected writings of Klaus Holzkamp*. Palgrave Macmillan.
Soelle, D. (2001). *The silent cry: Mysticism and resistance* (B. & M. Rumscheidt, Trans.). Fortress Press.
Underhill, E. (1915). *Practical mysticism*. E. P. Dutton.
Watts, A. W. (1966). *The book: On the taboo against knowing who you are*. Collier Books.
Williams, C. R. (2008). Compassion, suffering and the self: A moral psychology of social justice. *Current Sociology, 56*(5), 5–24.
Wright, E. O. (2019). *How to be an anti-capitalist in the 21st century*. Verso.

3

(Anti)Capitalist Therapeutics: Analyzing Psychotherapy's Role within Capitalism and Proposing a Critical-Liberation Psychotherapy (CLP) Alternative

Micah Ingle and Zenobia Morrill

Introduction

Though enticing, "radical therapy" can appear to some as an oxymoron. What role can individuals and relationships play when it comes to radical change, particularly when "radical" implies some overhaul of social and collective systems? Some may struggle to envision the compatibility between such transformative change and psychotherapy, an institution entrenched within these very systems and that focuses on individual-level change. In this chapter, however, we argue that precisely because psychotherapy already is political, it plays a role—whether or not we realize it—in shaping the stories we use to understand ourselves and the ways we go about enacting these selfhoods in our daily lives. Without recognizing

---

M. Ingle (✉)
Department of Psychology, Point Park University, Pittsburgh, PA, USA

Z. Morrill
Clinical Psychology Department, William James College, Boston, MA, USA
e-mail: Zenobia_Morrill@williamjames.edu

how psychology and psychotherapy influence us, we risk losing sight not only of what has been normalized about ourselves and the current status quo workings of the world, but also of what could be different—of what we may wish to resist or transform.

There is an internet meme currently making its way around newsfeeds with a bloated frog on a white background, captioned "everything is a social construct." The idea of something being a *social construct* entered popular consciousness following the so-called postmodern takeover of university humanities departments (especially English) in the latter half of the twentieth century (Pant, 2018). A social construct can be understood through the classic example of gender. Some people believe that the set of norms and behaviors we associate with masculinity is biologically determined. If someone has male genitalia and maybe the right hormonal makeup, they will behave in such and such way. A social constructionist account of gender instead emphasizes that masculinity is a "social practice" engendered by repeated performances within cultural and historical context (Connell, 2005, p. 71). Social constructionists argue that people are not bound to a narrow window of behaviors because of their sex characteristics. The 1990s debate between postmodern "social constructionists" who allegedly believe that everything is socially constructed and then scientific "realists" on the other side has been dubbed the "science wars" (Kofman, 2018).[1]

If you are familiar with this debate, you likely recognize the names of postmodern philosophers Michel Foucault and Jacques Derrida, as well as later figures influenced by these thinkers, such as Judith Butler—perhaps the most notable person to popularize the notion that gender, and even sex itself, is socially constructed. On the so-called scientific realist side of the debate, perhaps you know of the 1996 "Sokal affair." A physics professor submitted a nonsensical postmodern-style paper in a prominent cultural studies journal. This paper's acceptance and publication following peer review illustrated to some that postmodern scholarship relies upon mystifying jargon and irrefutable claims that bedevil gatekeeping

---

[1] We say "allegedly" because there is far more diversity of perspectives within the broadly "social constructionist" camp than is commonly represented in public debate. See Hacking (1999) to learn more.

standards and, in turn, makes its way into prominence despite lacking coherence (Hacking, 1999, p. 3).

Why bring up the science wars in a book on anticapitalism and psychotherapy? Well, we believe that some of the players in this debate still have something to say, especially the philosopher Michel Foucault. We expand on this line of thought in the main part of the paper, but before we move on, a word of caution. Philosopher Bruno Latour notes in his interview with *Science* that it is a mistake to use postmodernism to crudely assert that everything is relative or socially constructed (Vrieze, 2018). For instance, it would be disastrous for people to ignore the threat of climate change out of a naïve belief that scientific facts are *not real* because they involve processes of social construction. Of course, one could say that the scientific side of the debate won. A cursory glance at psychology and popular culture's dominant emphasis on neurobiology as the best way to understand all types of humans and experiences indicates this so-called victory.

There are aspects of how scientific ideas and methods are deployed in a field like psychology that are, in our view, extremely problematic and ripe for continued critique. Psychology also presents things as somewhat fixed and determined—often but not always grounded in biology. When we look out at the field of psychology right now, we worry that there are a lot of taken for granted assumptions and implicit understandings about what it is to be a person that exclude other approaches, practices, and ways of understanding people, sickness, health, and experiences. Excluding these methods and practices makes it difficult to understand or approach what it would mean to meaningfully incorporate radical politics into psychology and psychotherapy. This chapter will explore those implicit assumptions that stand in the way. Then, we offer some remarks on a possible alternative, the Critical-Liberation Psychotherapy (CLP) model (Morrill & Comas-Díaz, in press).

The Socially Constructed Self

Many things in the universe are *not* socially constructed, such as mitochondria.[2] However, the central thesis of this chapter is that there is a good argument to be made that *selfhood* is, to a significant degree, socially constructed.[3] What is selfhood? What is the self? We approach selfhood in this paper from a broadly historicist and hermeneutic perspective.[4] Philosophers such as Taylor (1989/2001) understand the self as intertwined with history and culturally available modes of self-interpretation. Selfhood is not just a biological achievement, although biology undoubtedly plays a part. In a very concrete sense, we develop out of sociohistorical and ecological contexts. The very *form* of our selfhood is fashioned in relation to the needs of the communities and social structures to which we belong. We expand on this insight in the *Practices of the Self* section of the chapter.

In the next section, we discuss the relationship between capitalism and the self, including what it means for selfhood to be socially constructed within a capitalist context. We argue that psychotherapy is one means of constructing selfhood in the western world. This argument works against an assumption in mainstream psychology that the self is relatively fixed—handed down by a combination of nature and nurture, genes and environment. We believe that mainstream psychology and many forms of psychotherapy implicitly work from the assumption that the self is relatively fixed, static, and universal. In this way, psychology generally excludes how culture, location, history, language, time, and other aspects play a role in dynamically shaping selfhood.

---

[2] Even this is complicated, because although we do not believe that mitochondria are socially constructed, it is undoubtedly the case that we as human beings—grounded in biology, history, language, et cetera—*understand* mitochondria from a particular vantage point that is *biased* or *perspectival*. There is no "view from nowhere" as philosopher Thomas Nagel (1986) says, despite scientists sometimes presuming this kind of all-knowing stance toward the universe.

[3] We do not claim biology has no impact on selfhood, just that historical and cross-cultural study shows a significant amount of variability, such that biology does not seem to determine selfhood nearly to the extent that some believe.

[4] In truth, social constructionism and hermeneutics are not the same, but they do share some commonalities. We chose to talk about social constructionism because we assume readers more likely to have some pre-existing familiarity with it than hermeneutic perspectives. For an explanation of their similarities and differences, see Schwandt (2003).

We argue instead that the self is a historical, social, and political construction. We also argue that psychotherapy plays a political function when it contributes to the social construction of the western self, emphasizing adaptation and normality. Finally, we hope to show that not only does psychotherapy function to shape selfhood, but that because psychotherapy is situated in a capitalist sociopolitical context, understanding how it does so grants insight into how the self could be *constructed differently*. In other words, we can glean how anti-capitalist forms of selfhood, for instance, may be constructed, as well as different alternatives beyond the confines of status quo selves.

The Person(al) Is Political

First it may be helpful to describe implicit assumptions about the self that psychology, psychotherapy, and western cultures more generally taken for granted and uncritically forwarded in theory, pedagogy, and practice.[5] This is not an easy task, because even though we argue that these disciplines and institutions *do* imply a particular understanding of the self, there is also a great deal of heterogeneity in how the self is understood in different psychological theories and practices. However, we take the position that there is a particular understanding of the self at the heart of these disciplines and institutions and it is important to demystify that. When these assumptions remain concealed, it is more difficult to imagine a relationship between radical politics and psychotherapy.

To illustrate the heterogeneity that does exist in psychology, we recently learned about an ongoing debate in psychology between Internal Family Systems (IFS) therapists and others who argue for a *plural identities* understanding of the self. An operative assumption in IFS is that the self is made up of several constituent parts—i.e., each person has multiple

---

[5] The relationship between psychology and western culture is complicated, but for the sake of argument in this paper we assume that psychology has a strong though necessarily reciprocal influence on how western culture comes to understand the self. We agree with Sass (2022), who says that "the psy professions are perhaps the major source of human self-interpretation in the modern Western world, having largely replaced the religious conceptions that dominated the majority of lives up until the beginning of the 20th century" (p. 17).

different *parts* that make up their psyche. The work of IFS therapy is therefore to put these parts into dialogue, with the assumption that a lot of emotional suffering emerges out of estranged relations between parts. Note that assumptions about the self quickly lead into key assumptions about the nature of suffering and implications for how to address it. In addition to working toward *integrating* these multiple self-parts, or self-states,[6] IFS therapists also tend to emphasize a core "Self"[7] which does the integrating. Conversely, some therapists who advocate a "plural identities" approach do not believe that integration is necessarily positive for everyone, preferring a "working relationship" between parts that is more boundaried, to respect the autonomy of each. This is just one debate within psychology about the nature of selfhood. There are *many* others, corresponding to the theoretical diversity of psychology as a field, ranging from psychoanalysis (of which there are also several distinct schools) to cognitive-behavioral psychology to existential-phenomenological/humanistic psychology—each with their own approach to clinical work proceeding from how they understand the self.

We will not attempt a deep dive into all of these theories and how their notions of selfhood emphasize different implications for clinical practice. Instead, we argue that there seems to be a fundamental underlying assumption about the self that links these diverse perspectives, and further that this underlying assumption is grounded in the history of the Western world.[8] Despite the many debates in psychology, in a global sense mainstream psychology still privileges an atomistic, "bounded" (Gergen, 2009), "buffered" (Taylor, 2007), and individualistic self (Parker, 2007). This socially constructed self is marked by principles, expectations, and behaviors associated with "autonomy, individual

---

[6] The psychoanalyst Philip Bromberg's (1996) work on dissociation and self-states may interest people as well.

[7] Recalling in some ways the work of Carl Jung, who posited a central Self. That said, some Jungians do argue against this centralizing notion of the Self. James Hillman, for example, centered multiplicity and a polytheistic psychology that need not lay down at the foot of a monotheistic notion of selfhood.

[8] For an informative take on the history of the western self, see historian Larry Siedentop's (2014) book *Inventing the Individual: The Origins of Western Liberalism*, as well as the Marxist Ellen Meiksins Wood's (2008) book *Citizens to Lords: A Social History of Western Political Thought from Antiquity to the late Middle Ages*.

reason, personal conscience, liberty, free competition, and self-knowledge" (Gergen, 2009, p. 5). This self is also marked by a focus on psychological interiority or individualized "inner depth" (Taylor, 1989/2001, p. x). As far as psychotherapy is concerned, Cushman notes (1992) that despite a plethora of therapeutic modalities available in Western culture, there is a common underlying thread in that therapists can be understood as "doctors of the interior" (p. 58). Likewise, despite accounting for differences between therapeutic modalities and acknowledging that some of them seek to reduce power differentials and issues of coercive control, Hook (2003) states that "psychotherapy does appear to elicit, with impressive regularity, a powerful gravity toward normative self-evaluations on the part of its patients" (p. 614).

Not all societies throughout history have understood or constructed the self in this way.[9] We do not contend that everyone who lives in a western country necessarily understands themselves this way, but rather that this is a predominant and institutionalized form of personhood inscribed into western law ("individual rights") and the practices of psychiatry/psychology. It is one of the main ways in which people are *able* to understand themselves. The raw materials for the construction of selfhood are in some sense *provided* to us by available cultural discourses and practices. This is a point to which we will return, but first, we will discuss the relationship between individualism and capitalism.

The Necessity of Individualism

For the Marxist historian Wood (1972, 2008), this type of individualism emerged in the West as the ideology of capitalism, associated with legal notions of private property. For the philosopher Foucault as well, individualism—as a mode of self-understanding—takes shape with the rise

---

[9] Taylor (2007) talks about how before the modern era, for example, people had a more "porous self," such that people understood themselves to be in closer immediate connection with the world around them, including phenomena like "spirits, demons, cosmic forces" (p. 38). Nowadays, rather than being possessed by and in constant taut relationship with outside forces, we might talk about people having mental health issues located in their minds or brains. This is the case even if we wave our hands toward acknowledging, as psychologists do, that these mental health issues can be caused by external factors like trauma or poverty.

of capitalism and the nation-state (with precursors in ancient Greek and Christian societies—see Foucault [2001/2005]). Foucault is useful for this chapter because he shows that this understanding of individualism was a *necessary* invention for capitalism. Foucault also articulates *how* people are constructed as individuals—a point to which we will return.

To oversimplify a long and complicated story, in order to flourish, capitalism *needs* individuals. It needs selves fashioned as individualistic in the unique ways described above. Capitalism cannot operate without marshaling and, crucially, *creating* its own brand of individualized subjectivity, or mode of being, that fits with capitalist kinds of labor and social organization. This creation or molding of subjectivity is sometimes referred to by Foucault as *objectification*—making an object of people which then comes to influence their subjective self-understanding. The most well-known example of objectification likely comes from feminism. Feminist critiques of objectification come from the recognition that, in some sense, when people are objectified, they are changed by that gaze—the male gaze for example. The male gaze, when it objectifies women, aids in *constructing* women as sexual objects, which has psychological, interpersonal, and societal repercussions. An illustration of objectification within capitalism comes from Foucault's point that in order to manage criminality during the transition from feudal to early capitalist economies in Europe, burgeoning nation-states needed to construct people as specific kinds of deviant objects requiring intervention. As Hook (2014) explains, in order "for proper intervention to be made, the object (be it criminal or crime) needed to be fixed as an individual entity and known in great detail. The criminal became a species to be known" (p. 214). This *objectification* of people constructs them specifically *as individuals* to function within the daily life and structures of capitalism.

Similar to the male gaze, Foucault describes the clinical gaze of psychiatry and psychology. The most comprehensive way to manage a population of people—to control crime, to regulate deviancy (mental health problems being defined as deviations from an established norm), to organize a productive labor force—is to map them out. That is, to give them increasing definition so that you can intervene on people's minds and behaviors at a granular level, and eventually to make it so that they *are responsible for themselves, as individuals.* For example, this process might allow individuals to understand *their depression* as a personal problem that should be addressed at the level of personal change, be that therapeutic techniques for cognitive restructuring or pharmaceutical interventions. Depression exists under this framework as a problem at the level of the person's mind or brain (each with its own personal, clinical, and sociopolitical implications). This is in contrast to an understanding of depression as primarily caused by sociopolitical or economic factors.

Another useful way to think about this individualizing process comes from the idea of the "panopticon",[10] an architectural design invented by nineteenth century social theorist Jeremy Bentham and later taken up by Foucault (1975/1995). Foucault's analysis of the panopticon is an attempt to illustrate how institutions like prisons (as well as schools and psychiatric facilities) coerce people into taking responsibility for themselves—internalizing forms of power that emphasize self-regulation—which is an extremely efficient way to organize capitalist societies. What does this "increasing (self)-definition" and consequent "intervention" look like in practice? Hook (2014) explains that in psychotherapy, there is often an emphasis on "self-attending" or "self-focus," with the goal of promoting greater self-understanding such that a person is more able to reflexively analyze and change their own psychology (p. 221). Of course, from Foucault's perspective, people are not *uncovering* or *discovering* themselves as much as they are *creating*, or *shaping and reshaping*, themselves. This is done to the benefit of capitalist social structures, because again, personal self-regulation takes the pressure of management away from the capitalist nation-state. The more people view themselves as individuals who must self-regulate their thoughts, emotions, and behaviors, the less top-down coercive control a society needs to exert to keep its citizenry in line and contributing to the total functioning of the sociopolitical system. This does not require us to forfeit the possible benefits of self-understanding for improving human existence, but only to look critically at how

---

[10] Hook (2014) describes the panopticon: "Foucault used the figure of the panopticon to exemplify the self-observing and self-policing quality of disciplinary power. The panopticon was a watchtower structure within the prison into which the prisoner could not see, and that therefore ensured that prisoners knew at all times that they might well be under surveillance. Prisoners, or 'souls' more generally, thus come to operate as if under constant surveillance, taking the role of controlling observer upon themselves. In this way power-relations are reproduced and implemented from within the internal position of the subject" (p. 225).

psychological self-understanding functions within capitalism. As we discuss later, the roots of the individualized self actually precede capitalism.

Foucault (1975/1995) calls this broad form of coercion, in which people are constructed as individuals that must become responsible for themselves, *disciplinary power*. Capitalism works because the people living under capitalism each assume their share of responsibility for behaving in ways that support capitalism. The instantiation of disciplinary power is typically not done at a conscious level but is baked into normative demands for selfhood and what it means to live a particular kind of life under capitalism. It is no coincidence that psychology has a huge emphasis on functionality in the workplace—from the focus in clinical psychology on helping people become functional and productive members of society, to industrial-organizational psychology which deploys psychological knowledge and practices to ensure more efficient workplaces.

This leads to the question of *how* people are constructed as individuals—or constructed as anything at all. To our mind, this question is anything but resolved. Foucault does, however, provide a useful starting point when he talks about *practices of the self*. Understanding something of the process for how normative social demands are internalized by individual people can help us in thinking through alternative possibilities—the selves *we might become*, and in fact that this is a possible horizon of action for us.

Practices of the Self—The Process of Individualization

Foucault's *practices of the self* is grounded in the notion that we as individual human beings do not arrive on earth pre-formed, nor is the process by which we develop through life simply one of a core self being conditioned by external factors. To take a critical approach to psychology and psychotherapy, we must understand that we are *constituted* as individual subjects by different kinds of practices. A certain kind of relationship to ourselves is established through behaviors we engage in, both externally and internally. An external example could be when I (Micah) worked as a behavioral technician at a community mental health clinic. The clinic was set up as a quasi-panopticon, with a central observatory space where clinicians and administrators could keep a watchful eye on patients. I was also tasked with checking in on each patient every fifteen minutes and taking written notes on their behavior. These spatial configurations and techniques of observation, as Foucault illustrates, encourage people to be watchful over their *own* behavior, because they never know when they are being observed. These external, material practices have a psychic effect on patients: the clinical gaze can become internalized.[11]

An example of an internal practice in psychology could be learning to interpret ourselves, to adopt a specific psychologically-inflected story about ourselves. For example, I might come to understand myself, through encounters with the psy disciplines, as problematic in some way. I might say that I am *codependent*, or that I engage in *black and white thinking*, or that I have problems with *emotional regulation*, or that I *have an illness called depression*. These are specific ideas—we could say cultural discourses or narrative fragments—handed down by the psy disciplines as raw materials for our own self-understanding. These are in fact new ways to "be a person" which did not exist before the ascendence of the psy disciplines, in the words of Hacking (2006, para 5).[12] These external and internal practices frequently work in conjunction, but it is useful to delineate them. Psychotherapy certainly works at the level of external, material relations—we are called forth as a certain kind of person when we enter a therapist's office, lie down on a psychoanalyst's couch, or hand our counselor money at the session's end. The internal practices are more germane to the therapeutic project, however, because in many ways the

---

[11] Of course, people can have a variety of different responses to these pressures. Straightforward compliance is not always assured. "Oppositional" or "antagonistic" behaviors are another kind of response, which may be for some a last resort assertion of agency against overbearing institutional settings.

[12] Hacking (2006) also talks about something called the *looping effect* which describes the positive feedback loops between psychological categories—like those found in the Diagnostic and Statistical Manual of Mental Disorders—and how we come to exist as new kinds of people.

substance of psychotherapy is an internal surgical operation we conduct on ourselves with the help of an expert.

Internal practices are most relevant to analyzing psychotherapy, but it is important to emphasize two things: (1) we are not *only* transformed into certain kinds of people by internal practices, but also by very concrete relations like the above-mentioned spatial configuration of a mental health clinic;[13] (2) these internal practices and their consequences—coming to think of yourself and relate to yourself and others as a specific kind of person—are always situated in a sociopolitical context. Someone or some*thing* benefits from us establishing a particular kind of relationship to ourselves, like being psychologically healthy enough to perform as a good student, worker, sibling, romantic partner, parent, and other social and relational roles.

To give a further example of these internal practices, in Foucault's later work, he describes early Greco-Roman and Christian relationships to the self. Foucault (2004/2009) describes the emergence of what he calls *pastoral power* corresponding to the early Christian shift in viewing the construction of the self as analogous to a shepherd leading his flock. Foucault views pastoral power as an "individualizing power," stating that although the shepherd is concerned with the safekeeping of the flock as a whole, he performs this task through attention directed toward the wellbeing of each individual sheep, even at the risk of abandoning the flock (Foucault, 2004/2009, p. 128). This practice of the self operates through mental activities such as rites of purification around confession. You might sit with a priest, and he might encourage you to think about every sinful thought or urge you had throughout the day. In this way, you might come to be "on guard" against these sinful temptations. You might begin to interpret yourself as a sinful being, but hopefully (within the Christian context) one that can exercise some degree of self-control, purifying yourself through prayer and confession. An important aspect of care of the self is that you are *transformed* by the practices you engage in, and this transformation simultaneously allows you to access new kinds of truth (for

---

[13] Some of Foucault's genealogical work focuses on these external relations. See his popular book *Discipline and Punish* for example, which talks about how the distribution of people in physical spaces like military barracks and factories helps to create certain kinds of persons (e.g., Foucault, 1975/1995, p. 141).

example, only through a process of *conversion* or in modern terms *letting Jesus into your heart* can you experience the love of God and know the truth and empowerment of that love).

Foucault describes these ancient practices of the self because he sees in them an ancestor to many current practices in the world, such as those practices developed, advanced, and encouraged by psychotherapy. Psychotherapy is also a set of practices meant to train and, in some cases, transform the self. It is also an individualizing technology like Christian pastoral power. Foucault stated that his work aimed to be a *history of the present*, with the goal of exploring where we come from, how things were different in the past, and how they could be different now. Foucault's work helps us to see that rather than a rigid biological necessity, the psychological self is a sociopolitical and historical construction. This has clear implications for thinking through anti-capitalist alternatives to psychotherapeutic practices. In the words of Fisher (2009): "emancipatory politics must always destroy the appearance of a 'natural order', must reveal what is presented as necessary and inevitable to be a mere contingency, just as it must make what was previously deemed to be impossible seem attainable" (p. 17).

Taking Foucault's ideas seriously, we must conclude that psychotherapy emerged in order to solve a certain sociopolitical problem: shaping the self so that it more easily fits with, or is more easily rehabilitated in relation to, the needs of capitalism. Generally, this means a kind of selfhood that is self-sufficient/individualistic, self-interested/competitive, and in keeping with neoliberal trends, entrepreneurial and flexible (Sugarman, 2015). We must also conclude that the self is much more malleable at a fundamental level than psychotherapeutic theories typically acknowledge. Many approaches to psychotherapy aim to tinker with and rehabilitate the western self, as in cognitive-behavioral therapies that emphasize using rational self-practices—like reality-testing "cognitive distortions" and tracking every time we feel anxious—to change "core beliefs" or "schemas" about ourselves and situations we find distressing (Dalal, 2018, pp. 105, 111). They rarely include awareness or interventions aimed at co-constructing the self in a way that would more fundamentally, at the very least, not align so closely with capitalist ideals.

Mainstream therapies are profoundly *adaptive*, emphasizing individual (interior) change.

If it is true that psychotherapy is in many ways a capitalist invention meant to solve capitalist problems, where does that leave those of us on the left who are trained and interested in psychotherapy? Should we quit our jobs *en masse* and become political organizers instead? We do not believe that this is the only solution available. We believe that psychological suffering is real, and although many of the causes of suffering are not exclusively localizable to individual minds and bodies, there is still a place for psychotherapy. If psychotherapy is a tool for shaping and reshaping forms of personhood, then how might we envision a psychotherapy that works against the grain of capitalist demands? We believe that it is possible to address the needs of those suffering from the deleterious effects of living under a capitalist system without merely shoring up existing forms of personhood that serve the sociopolitical needs of capitalism. In the next section, we discuss one potential alternative to existing approaches: a Critical-Liberation Psychotherapy (CLP) model for therapeutic work, developed by Morrill & Comas-Díaz (in press).

Introducing the Critical-Liberation Psychotherapy Model

When much of mainstream psychology is based on the notion that the self is highly individual, therapy clients' problems become contained and categorized as disorders of the self. Maladaptive thoughts, problem behaviors, traumatic symptoms, and interior sickness come into focus as the labels used to treat self problems. Implicitly, however, these external and internal self practices function to construct the sort of status quo selves we have described here. The diagnose-and-treat logic of mainstream psychotherapy measures individuals against a social norm and then, if deviation is present, works on changing individuals to adapt to and function within that norm. As we have argued, these norms are highly shaped by capitalist values and the commodification of everyday life.

Capitalist values also are inextricably linked to other social dynamics of power, such as coloniality, ableism, sanism, sexism, cisgenderism, and various self practices that sustain a social status quo. To be clear, it is not that other options, or exceptions to this type of status quo personhood, do not exist. Rather, social norms empower particular ways of understanding ourselves that dominate and become more readily available to take up, while other possibilities for ourselves are marginalized. For instance, in contrast to the entrepreneurial "self-made man" encouraged by practices of productivity and profit maximization, material consumption, and zero-sum competition, feminist and marginalized ethnoracial perspectives stress our relationality. While individualization risks exploiting others as objects for self-gain, feminism maintains that these dynamics of subjugation actually are incompatible with individuals' health *because* selfhood is bound up in relational and social collective wellbeing.

Another example includes how queer or social disability perspectives offer up selves that are dynamic, fluid, and expansive—so individuals' problems are not viewed primarily as interior as much as they signify how social structures, policies, and categories fail to accommodate, and sometimes pathologize, the diverse possible range of selves, relationships, and experiences. Finally, to offer just one more example, capitalist values collude with imperialist ones when selves are extricated from ecological context. Nature, land, and what might be considered the natural range of human experiences (e.g., grief, feelings, disorders deemed biogenetic phenomena) also are objectified—something to be commodified, managed, or controlled. In other words, mainstream versions of psychotherapy sustain capitalism and status quo power relations in part by evaluating health, sickness, and normality in terms of what is good for the market economy. These marginalized perspectives remind us that there are other values and models that can be recentered which provide pathways into different self practices, research methods, and psychotherapy approaches.

Critical-Liberation Psychotherapy (CLP; Morrill, 2021; Morrill & Comas-Díaz, in press) is a therapy model that works against dominant taken-for-granted assumptions to understand selves and problems in context. Rather than constructing the kinds of selves necessary for capitalism, CLP centers individuals' health as mutually dependent with collective liberation. At the heart of the CLP model is the assumption that individuals—and their health and wellbeing—can be understood within the variegated relational, linguistic, historical, political, structural, sociocultural, and ideological contexts in which they live and make-meaning of their lives. This assumption counters the status quo self of mainstream psychotherapies. Therapy is not to reduce, manage, or avoid our wounds, and find ways to adjust to painful contexts. Rather, CLP is fundamentally about exploring new ways of understanding selves and selfhood in relation to the many people and structures to which we are bound.

Many approaches and practices have taken a similar stance, or some variation of resistance to mainstream theory, so CLP is not "new" in that regard. What CLP does is bring several radical perspectives to bear on how psychotherapy broadly can approach re-conceptualizing distress, supporting liberation, and applying in-session practices toward constructing different kinds of selves, not just the status quo adaptation of selves to an unjust social order. We describe aspects of each part of CLP in the next section. However, we first articulate some of its main concepts. Any practitioner may draw upon CLP as a tool to radically rethink the taken-for-granted assumptions that permeate and constrain mainstream therapies. CLP itself was a project of recentering marginalized knowledge and practices from within *and outside* of psychology. It was developed out of research that applied critical-liberation theory to analyzing power dynamics in humanistic-existential and feminist-multicultural psychotherapies (Morrill, 2021; Morrill & Levitt, 2025). The aim of CLP is to serve as a comprehensive framework that empowers and recenters liberatory forms of selfhood. The CLP process prioritizes exploration of clients' lived experiences, as the therapist listens for patterns, contexts, and connections that tend to be decentered and unspoken. Moreover, it is within the client-therapist relationship itself, and through these radical dynamics of authentic relating and critical reclamation of narratives that CLP *enacts*, within the psychotherapy process, liberatory modes of being. Liberation psychologies (Comas-Díaz & Torres Rivera, 2020; Martín-Baró, 1996; Watkins & Shulman, 2010) provide opportunities to tailor in-session practices to support liberation and the liberatory construction of selves.

Altogether, CLP was designed to make space for a decolonial praxis in psychotherapy, to include what has been excluded as well as to integrate novel burgeoning approaches. It is not designed to be prescriptive nor amenable to a manual format. CLP stands in contrast to social justice approaches that take mainstream psychotherapy and simply apply or slightly modify its core assumptions and scale-up its universal delivery. CLP represents the inverse of that—psychotherapy's core assumptions are fundamentally refashioned to flexibly support a wide variety of methods and approaches conducive to critical exploration and liberatory self-practices. Though the scope of this chapter is limited, the basic components of CLP will be described briefly in terms of (1) clinical formulation, (2) the in-session processes and practices that can be used toward CLP's liberatory aims, and (3) the overall function of psychotherapy according to this model.

Elements of the CLP Model

Practitioners using a CLP model understand clients' experiences as interconnected, not just to others and the shared struggles of humans, but to social structures, policies, and ideologies. In other words, CLP **formulation** challenges the objectification of clients, experiences, and relationships. It recontextualizes them. Understanding individuals' experiences—and the inscribed dominant practices that sustain status quo selves—gives CLP practitioners the opportunity to rethink mainstream psychotherapy goals, such as symptom reduction. Alternatively, the function of CLP is to support *liberation* from the social, political, and economic structures that oppress and exploit individuals, and how these wider dynamics get patterned into individuals' self practices. Therefore, the aim of CLP is to construct different forms of selfhood—those that reclaim our interconnectedness and open up different possibilities for being in the world. If suffering is collective and entangled, then our healing processes must address these collective components as they arise in clients' bodies, relational life, fantasies, conflicts, and narratives. From such processes, the stranglehold of hegemony on personhood can be dislodged, undone, and done differently.

What types of psychotherapy **in-session practices** support liberation? And how could a client-therapist relationship nurture self-construction practices that provide novel opportunities for liberatory subjectivities? CLP argues that how we understand problems shapes what we do about them. First, this means that in order to *do* psychotherapy differently, therapists have to reconfigure their understanding of suffering, their relationship to the client, and their role in therapeutic processes. Rather than being an expert who teaches, intervenes, or prescribes in a top-down-fashion, CLP therapists approach a relationship of *mutual accompaniment* with clients. This means that their role is not to explain capitalism or dynamics of oppression, nor prescribe methods for resistance, because this approach simply recreates a dynamic of authority and subjugation with a different topic of focus. This way, the practitioner falls into the trap of attempting to teach or prescribe liberation from a place of authority. CLP practitioners endeavor to enter an authentic relationship to explore *with* the client using humility, exploration, skillful attunement, curiosity, and an understanding that they will be experiencing and reconfiguring liberatory possibilities and processes together.

In so doing, the therapist-client relationship itself resists dynamics of subjugation and objectification that reenact capitalism and oppression. The critical-liberation therapy relationship is at the heart of practicing, rather than simply discussing or individualizing, novel possibilities. The therapist and client grapple with understanding, and putting into motion interdependence as it exists and takes shape between them. For example, relational psychoanalysis, humanistic existential psychotherapies, and feminist therapies each offer specific practices and techniques designed to explore and assess what is happening here-and-now in the relationship, giving therapists the language to consider and navigate rupture and repair, metacommunications, genuineness, self-disclosures, relational (rather than individual) assessments, and scales that measure felt experiences. CLP draws from these approaches, as they all can be ways to practice mutual accompaniment as the foundational ingredient to liberatory change. Relationships are necessary to liberation movements and reworking self practices.

It takes a therapist who is thinking in this contextual way—with a type of *critical consciousness*—to hear, reflect, and be curious about the contextual patterns in clients' experiences. Such interactions disrupt the silences that maintain disconnection—critical consciousness makes implicit processes explicit. The CLP therapist uses their expert position and power by applying their skillful acumen to facilitate clients' exploration and *foster critical consciousness* (Freire, 1970) as the **function of therapy**. Critical consciousness refers to awareness and deep understanding of injustices and structural inequalities that impact individuals and communities. In session CLP practices focus on radical exploration to promote critical consciousness through narrative *testimonio* (Cervantes, 2020). It is by rethinking selves, relationships, and structures that we may reconfigure alternative possibilities for liberatory subjectivities. The skills, methods, and techniques that can be used in CLP include a vast range of practices from within (e.g., chair dialogues, cognitive restricting, interpretation) traditional psychology, outside of it (Ayurveda, sweat lodges, activism), and everything in between (e.g., *testimonio*, border thinking). Whether or not they fit within a CLP process is determined based upon whether they open up or constrain liberatory or status quo construction of selves. Rather than attempting to review all existing methods and psychotherapy practices, we have focused on advancing some particularly noteworthy ones within CLP, introduced and italicized throughout this section.

Conclusion

In this chapter, we discussed the social construction of individualized Western selfhood and its relationship to capitalist historical contexts. Following the work of Michel Foucault, we also analyzed the way that psychotherapy functions socio-politically. We concluded the chapter by introducing the CLP model of psychotherapy, which we view as an alternative to many existing forms of psychotherapy, assuming the goal of radical therapy is co-constructing selfhood in a direction less aligned with capitalist ideology. We hope that this chapter offers to radical therapists both a theoretically useful *deconstructive* analysis—aimed at an "emancipatory politics" which can "destroy the appearance of a 'natural order'" in psychology (Fisher, 2009, p. 17)—as well as *constructive* contribution in our proposal of the CLP model. The relationship between psychotherapy and capitalism is fraught with political dangers, but we hope this chapter inspires further thinking about the possibility for a different, radical psychotherapy, as well as for new modes of being human that resist adaptation to an unjust world.

References

Bromberg, P. M. (1996). Standing in the spaces: The multiplicity of self and the psychoanalytic relationship. *Contemporary Psychoanalysis, 32*(4), 509–535. https://doi.org/10.1080/00107530.1996.10746334

Cervantes, A. (2020). Testimonios. In L. Comas-Díaz & E. Torres Rivera (Eds.), *Liberation psychology: Theory, method, practice, and social justice* (pp. 133–147). American Psychological Association. https://doi.org/10.1037/0000198-008

Comas-Díaz, L., & Torres Rivera, E. (2020). *Liberation psychology*. American Psychological Association.

Connell, R. (2005). In 2nd ed. (Ed.), *Masculinities*. Polity.

Cushman, P. (1992). Psychotherapy to 1992: A historically situated interpretation. In D. K. Freidheim (Ed.), *History of psychotherapy: A century of change* (pp. 21–63). American Psychological Association.

Dalal, F. (2018). *CBT: The cognitive behavioural tsunami: Managerialism, politics and the corruptions of science*. Routledge.

Fisher, M. (2009). *Capitalist realism: Is there no alternative?* Zero Books.

Foucault, M. (1995). *Discipline and punish: The birth of the prison*. Vintage Books. (Original work published 1975)

Foucault, M. (2005). *The hermeneutics of the subject: Lectures at the Collège de France 1981–1982* (F. Gros, Ed., G. Burchell, Trans.). Palgrave Macmillan. (Original work published 2001)

Foucault, M. (2009). *Security, territory, population: Lectures at the Collège de France 1977–1978* (M. Senellart, Ed., G. Burchell, Trans.). Palgrave Macmillan. (Original work published 2004)

Freire, P. (1970). *Cultural action for freedom* (pp. 476–521). Harvard Educational Review.

Gergen, K. J. (2009). *Relational being: Beyond self and community*. Oxford University Press.

Hacking, I. (1999). *The social construction of what?* Harvard University Press.

Hacking, I. (2006). Making up people. London Review of Books. https://www.lrb.co.uk/the-paper/v28/n16/ian-hacking/making-up-people

Hook, D. (2003). Analogues of power: Reading psychotherapy through the sovereignty–discipline–government complex. *Theory & Psychology, 13*(5), 605–628. https://doi.org/10.1177/09593543030135006

Hook, D. (2014). *Critical psychology*. UCT Press.

Kofman, A. (2018). Bruno Latour, the post-truth philosopher, mounts a defense of science. *The New York Times Magazine.* https://www.nytimes.com/2018/10/25/magazine/bruno-latour-post-truth-philosopher-science.html

Martín-Baró, I. (1996). *Writings for a liberation psychology.* Harvard University Press.

Morrill, Z., & Comas-Díaz, L. (in press). Critical-liberation psychotherapy: Unsettling hegemonic power toward liberatory practice. *The American Psychologist.*

Morrill, Z. (2021). Power dynamics in psychotherapy: Eminent therapists' experiences navigating power from Humanistic-Existential and Feminist-Multicultural perspectives (Publication No. 28645574) [Doctoral dissertation, University of Massachusetts Boston]. Proquest Dissertations Publishing.

Morrill, Z., & Levitt, H. M. (2025). Power dynamics in psychotherapy: Navigating power from humanistic-existential and feminist-multicultural perspectives. [Unpublished manuscript]. Department of Counseling and School Psychology, University of Massachusetts Boston.

Nagel, T. (1986). *The view from nowhere.* Oxford University Press.

Pant, B. (2018). Postmodernism and the ideological corruption of the humanities. *Daily Collegian.* https://dailycollegian.com/2018/10/postmodernism-and-the-ideological-corruption-of-the-humanities/

Parker, I. (2007). *Revolution in psychology: Alienation to emancipation.* Pluto Press.

Sass, L. (2022). "A flaw in the great diamond of the world": Reflections on subjectivity and the enterprise of psychology (A diptych). *The Humanistic Psychologist, 50*(1), 3–32. https://doi.org/10.1037/hum0000186

Schwandt, T. A. (2003). Three epistemological stances for qualitative inquiry: Interpretivism, hermeneutics, and social constructionism. In N. K. Denzin & Y. S. Lincoln (Eds.), *The landscape of qualitative research* (2nd ed., pp. 292–331). Sage.

Siedentop, L. (2014). *Inventing the individual: The origins of Western liberalism.* Harvard University Press.

Sugarman, J. (2015). Neoliberalism and psychological ethics. *Journal of Theoretical and Philosophical Psychology, 35*(2), 103–116. https://doi.org/10.1037/a0038960

Taylor, C. (2001). *Sources of the self: The making of the modern identity* (10th printing). Harvard University Press. (Original work published 1989)

Taylor, C. (2007). *A secular age.* Harvard University Press.

Vrieze, J. D. (2018). *Bruno Latour, a veteran of the 'science wars,' has a new mission*. Science. https://www.science.org/content/article/bruno-latour-veteran-science-wars-has-new-mission

Watkins, M., & Shulman, H. (2010). *Toward psychologies of liberation*. Palgrave Macmillan.

Wood, E. M. (1972). *Mind and politics: An approach to the meaning of liberal and socialist individualism*. University of California Press.

Wood, E. M. (2008). *Citizens to lords: A social history of Western political thought from antiquity to the late middle ages*. Verso.

4

Radical Epistemologies for Radical Psychologists

Oliver Yimeng Xu and Laura Smith

Introduction

Throughout our training and licensure as psychologists, we are taught a common "language": all of us gained (or are gaining) an expert understanding of a broad range of topics that include subject matter immediately pertinent to practice, but also to other areas of research, such as developmental, educational, and occupational psychology. The aspects of this common language—the information, the vocabulary, the phrases, the verbal and nonverbal mannerism expected of practitioners—were taught by subject matter experts across the discipline. Changes to the vernacular occur constantly, often in the form of new research findings that enter the professional canon. Research therefore informs theory, which informs training and ultimately practice. Despite the continued

---

O. Y. Xu (✉) • L. Smith
Teacher's College, Columbia University, Counseling Psychology Program, New York, NY, USA
e-mail: yx2344@tc.columbia.edu; ls2396@tc.columbia.edu

development of psychological practice in the interest of client well-being, critics of conventional mental health pose the need for radical therapies—practices that advance practitioners beyond what is delineated by the common professional language (French et al., 2019; Prilleltensky & Prilleltensky, 2021; Smith & Romero, 2010).

This chapter contributes to the establishment of radical practices by providing a view of psychology through the lens of its *epistemology*—the study of how knowledge within a discipline is gathered and defined (Falmagne, 2014). We will explore the mechanisms underlying psychological knowledge production—paying particular attention to social and historical contexts—to show how our disciplinary language values certain types of knowledge while excluding others. This perspective will allow us to better see how dominant psychological paradigms tacitly continue to uphold status quo power structures to the detriment of marginalized groups. In essence, this examination of these paradigms' underpinnings will illustrate "how the sausage gets made"—how neoliberal, White, capitalistic assumptions and the associated interests of power have embedded themselves within the discipline's stock of knowledge and then are manifested as practices that align with those same assumptions and interests.

The logic of the chapter is rooted in philosopher Michel Foucault's conception of the relationship between power and knowledge—that power is always implicated in the production of knowledge (Foucault, 1980). We address his theories on *discourse* as a mechanism by which power is asserted in the form of knowledge that constitutes "truths" regarding the world, which in turn highlights the universality of power and implicates the role of psychology within this framework. Building on this foundation, we follow the historical and theoretical evidence that critical psychologist Thomas Teo (2020) presented in his critique of psychology as a "hyper-science," or a discipline that "uses ideal and material techniques to elide the fact that it is not a natural science" (p. 761). Teo's characterization will serve to elucidate the origins and current justification for dominant psychological epistemologies. The problems associated with these epistemologies are illustrated to invite alternative routes to knowledge production that may avoid the traps of contemporary paradigms.

We approach this exploration from a critical psychology framework and a psychology-of-the-humanities perspective (Held, 2020), incorporating knowledge from beyond the psychological silo with an emphasis on uncovering and problematizing status quo structures within the field. The work that will be highlighted often speaks most directly to research—work undertaken for the express purpose of knowledge production—but given that research informs theory and ultimately, training and practice, the relevance of epistemology for practitioners cannot be understated. If radical psychological practices are to align with the dismantling of systems of oppression, those practices must emerge from an understanding of how these structures were built and maintained. In other words, we contend that there is an inextricable link between radical practice and radical research.

The Sociopolitical Situatedness of Psychological Discourse

As mentioned, our examination begins with Michel Foucault's theorizing about the interconnected nature of discourse and status quo power agendas, with the result that investigation of the former can illuminate the operations of the latter. A prolific thinker whose work has profound transdisciplinary impact, Foucault analyzed the capacity of knowledge, power, and subjectivity to intersect with and shape human experience. Foucault, who had a degree in psychology, often directly addressed elements of mental life and produced numerous critiques of psychology and psychiatry (e.g., Foucault, 1970, 1972; Hook, 2007). Nevertheless (or perhaps more accurately, therefore), his scholarship exists largely outside the mainstream psychological canon. To comprehensively address Foucault's core ideas and their implications for psychology is beyond the scope of this chapter; other scholars have, however, written extensively regarding his analysis of psychology's role as "an indispensable vector of modern power" (Hook, 2007, p. 2). Below, we highlight relevant aspects of his theories regarding knowledge production as a means by which hierarchies of power are reflected, reinforced, and perpetuated.

Discourse, Episteme, and Power

In his work *The Archaeology of Knowledge* (*L'Archéologie du Savoir*), Foucault (1972) argued that conventional knowledge formations—or what most of us have received as the facts and "truths" of the world—are both fluid and transient, shaped by the social forces of a specific time and place. An active mechanism in the interplay of knowledge and power is *discourse*—the act and product of communicating about topics via speech or writing. Foucault expanded on this definition to encompass the complex networks of language, practices, and institutions that *produce and regulate knowledge within a given society*. A key attribute of Foucault's notion of discourse is its attention to specificity. We exist within a particular cultural *episteme*, or "the total set of relations that unite, at a given period, the discursive practices that give rise to epistemological figures, sciences, and possibly formalized systems" (Foucault, 1972, p. 191). Foucault argued that the episteme of each historical period is shaped by power, which he understood to be the ability to exert some form of change upon something else. According to this conceptualization, power does not solely reside within governments or other authoritative entities, but occurs in interactions across all of society (1970). Furthermore, discourse produces and legitimizes certain forms of knowledge as fundamental "truths" while marginalizing or silencing others. Spoken and written communications serve as enforcers that delimit both *what* we know and what we *are permitted* to know.

A "General Politics" of Truth

Foucault further contended that discourses are produced by power, and power, in turn, defines the criteria for determining the truth of discourse. It is through this cyclical process that discourse masks its own contexts of creation and presents itself as a set of objective and stable truths. Practically speaking, discourse—inflected and shaped by power—therefore determines what is societally deemed true or false, rational or irrational, healthy or pathological. While power is diffuse and exists across all aspects of society, certain actors are given greater degrees of status and privilege in the legitimization and promulgation of truth. Foucault has called this holistic system of truthmaking the "general politics" of truth:

> Truth is a thing of this world: it is produced only by virtue of multiple forms of constraint. And it induces regular effects of power. Each society has its regime of truth, its "general politics" of truth—that is, the types of discourse it accepts and makes function as true; the mechanisms and instances that enable one to distinguish true and false statements; the means by which each is sanctioned; the techniques and procedures accorded value in the acquisition of truth; the status of those who are charged with saying what counts as true. (Foucault, 1980, p. 131)

Psychological Epistemologies

Foucault, then, has prepared us to understand that social discourse is inextricably interwoven with power relations in a society, and that this knowledge is circulated as immutable truths about the world. How can we apply this analysis to psychology to shed light on the operations of its disciplinary "politics of truth"? As mentioned, Teo (2020) is among the critical psychologists whose work directly addresses the discursive characteristics and historical roots of the current hyper-scientific epistemologies and speaks to practical implications for psychology.

Reconstructing Psychological Science

Critical psychologists often begin their critiques of psychology with a *historical reconstruction*, a method used to understand the impacts of power, society, and culture in the formation of contemporary psychology's theories and methods (Teo, 1999). While we only skim the surface of these reconstructive analyses of psychology, readers are encouraged to explore these in greater depth (Danziger, 1997; Walsh et al. 2014; Teo, 2018). Moreover, critical to understanding dominant psychological epistemology is an understanding of the preeminence of particular approaches to scientific methodology in psychology. Critical psychologists have explicated the role that capitalistic and neoliberal ideologies—forces of power, prestige, and disciplinary legitimacy backed by tangible economic and financial interests—have had in the formation of contemporary psychology (e.g., Jovanović, 2010; Parker, 2014; Walsh et al., 2014). These forces were active in the construction of psychology as a scientific discipline from the time of its inception.

Wilhelm Wundt's establishment of the first experimental psychology laboratory in 1897 is widely regarded as the birth of the field of psychology (Gao, 2014). Despite his own philosophy of a dual approach to the study of psychology—one that was aligned with the natural sciences as well as the humanities—Wundt's experimental laboratory drew global recognition, funding, and power that ultimately pulled psychology into alignment with the natural sciences (Jovanović, 2010). Necessary to this shift was the active distancing of the discipline from philosophy, spirituality, religion, politics, and other domains of the humanities that also addressed mental life, but which typically relied on theoretical and speculative approaches (Teo, 2020). The advent of metrics for personality and intelligence in the post-World War II United States is credited with the further legitimization of psychology's scientific status, and the discipline benefitted from this status as funding for STEM disciplines grew (Gao, 2014; Walsh et al., 2014). This historical and sociopolitical context illustrates how the ascent of psychological science can be interpreted in the context of its funding sources, and therefore to capitalism, neoliberalism, and associated ideologies.

Methodologism and Positivism

The most evident result of psychology's historic turn towards the sciences is its privileging of scientific methodologies over qualitative and theoretical modes of study. Over time, what was originally construed by Wundt and others as one of many ways that psychologists could study the mind became the only valid method within mainstream psychology (Teo, 2015). Methodology therefore became the primary (and almost sole) criteria for determining a study to be psychological in nature. Other methods, including those used to address topics and questions beyond what can be quantifiably observed and analyzed via statistical means, were pushed to the margins of the field due to their "unscientific" and therefore presumably un-psychological nature. This overemphasis on methods at the expense of all other considerations has been referenced by various scholars as *methodologism*, methodolatry, or the methodological imperative (Gao, 2014). The major characteristics of methodologism include the "inflation of complex designs and statistical–analytic procedures that demand highly trained technical expertise, the rhetoric of objectivity, the implementation of operationism with no connection to reality, a lack of theorizing, and the repetitive reference to 'doing science'" (Teo, 2020, p. 761).

Mainstream psychology's methodologism has been justified by *positivistic* assumptions regarding the nature of what it studies. *Positivism* refers to the assumption that all phenomena that constitute knowledge must be provable via logic or science. Psychological research under positivist assumptions thereby seeks to discover laws of nature that undergird the phenomena or construct of interest, akin to how physicists might conduct experiments to uncover fundamental forces of nature (Teo, 2015). Positivism and methodologism are interconnected ideologies: psychology's fixation on scientific methodology is justified if all knowledge is construed to be scientific in nature, and if psychological knowledge is scientific in nature, the only method of study that can be considered valid and rigorous is the scientific method (Nelson, 2014).

Positivist assumptions imply that the psychological phenomena that can be studied must exist outside of social, cultural, and historical contexts, thereby possessing the same "ontic qualities" (Teo, 2018, p. 716) as most phenomena studied in the natural sciences, such as physical objects, chemical reactions, or living things. These phenomena moreover are assumed to have an observable existence in the external world independent of human perception. Danziger (1997) differentiated between the phenomena studied in the natural sciences and psychology by their ontic qualities. He posits that psychological phenomena are by nature less tangible: they typically do not have the same kind of independent, visible reality, and are often operationalized as constructs that have been developed by psychologists within particular historical and cultural contexts.

These constructs are deeply intertwined with language, meaning, and human experience, thereby having a different ontic quality that makes them less amenable to the same kind of objective measurement and experimentation found in the natural sciences (Danziger, 1997; Teo, 2018).

Psychology as a Hyper-Science

As mentioned earlier, the intersections of these ideologies and epistemologies gives credence to Teo's (2020) conceptualization of psychology as a *hyper-science*: a discipline driven by an agenda for scientific legitimacy, value, and status, and that uncritically emulates the methods and techniques of the natural sciences while lacking a natural-scientific basis. A hyper-science operates as if its phenomena possess the same ontic qualities as phenomena of the natural sciences. Teo suggested that psychology therefore "inflates and complicates its methodological activities in order to conceal the temporality and contextuality of psychological phenomena" (2020, p. 761) in an attempt to "pass" as a natural science. The prevalence of statistical terminology is an example of how psychological discourse reifies the discipline's identity as a "science" via words like sample, population, validity, and reliability. This a practice that has itself been a matter of mounting scrutiny for more than a decade (Wiggins & Christopherson, 2019). Teo did not reject the concept of scientific psychology, but he critiqued the overgeneralization and inflation of its utility for answering the wide array of questions that can be posed by psychologists. An alternative approach—as Wundt assumed more than a century ago—is that psychology can be studied through the lens of the humanities as much as the sciences.

How Epistemologies Manifest in Psychological Research and Practice

Psychological discourse has, therefore, evolved in the direction of what Jovanović (2010) described as being "built on the model of natural science, driven by method and obliged to quantitative imperative, committed to control as knowledge interest, inclined to withdraw from the complexities of intentionality, meaning, culture, society, and history" (p. 312). This epistemological position has broad consequences for practice, research, and institutional support for psychology. Various scholars (including other authors in this book) have developed extensive critiques of how context and power have shaped models of health and wellness (Prilleltensky, 2011) and how conventional psychotherapies often promote "wellness" as a return to productivity (i.e., exploitability by the wealthy) within a neoliberal, capitalistic society (Parker, 2014; Moncrieff, 2022). The social impact of psychological paradigms for knowledge production can be observed in characteristic knowledge stances that recur throughout psychological scholarship. As will be profiled below, these include assumptions of naïve empiricism and intrinsic value as well as the capacity for psychological approaches to inherently recreate and perpetuate racist assumptions.

Naïve Empiricism and an Assumption of Intrinsic Value

Because epistemology concerns the valuation and production of knowledge, its most direct implications pertain to research. At the same time, methodologism and positivism are theoretical concepts that may not fully represent the actual views held by psychological researchers. Teo (2018) suggested that a more accurate way of describing such views is *naïve empiricism*: the assumption that empirical research (i.e., the use of the scientific method) can directly capture phenomena in a capacity that corresponds exactly to their existence outside the research context. This belief requires the additional assumption that studies and their methods have minimal bias and are value-neutral.

Returning to Foucault, we can interpret naïve empiricism as a largely accepted force in dominant discourse—a "truth" regarding the nature of psychological research. Discourse perpetuates itself as truth and continually reifies its own existence and importance. Psychological discourse therefore perpetuates methodologism and the positivistic assumption that research using scientific methods is intrinsically valuable and productive because it uncovers truths of the natural world. The result of this discourse is that methodology and the pursuit of scientific inquiry becomes of primary importance for psychological research, with any meaningful practical implications that it might have outside of the research sphere considered to be a positive byproduct.

This discourse is immediately observable in the rhetorical elements common to empirical psychological research publications. In recent years, all American Psychological Association (APA) journals have required authors to submit a "Public Significance Statement" that allows even lay audiences to "[discern a] study's importance, practical implications, and conclusions for their own lives" (American Psychological Association, 2018). A frequent consumer of psychological research may observe the near universality of phrases such as "contributes to our understanding of" and "fills a gap in literature" as blanket statements used to justify the significance of a particular study (Smith et al., 2023). Within the discussions and implications sections of the same articles, the phrase "more research is needed" is typically used to divert any responsibility for a study to contribute practically to societally relevant needs (Smith et al., 2023). Teo (2018) described research that is conducted with little relevance to or regard for practical contribution as a "psychology based in the logic of variables" (p. 107) and considered it to be indicative of a discipline that perpetuates itself through the creation of an infinitude of future research through the reshuffling of various permutations of statistical variables.

Epistemological Violence and White Epistemology

The capacity of conventional psychology to self-perpetuate its importance speaks to the level of discursive power that the discipline holds. Shaped by social forces and the interests of power structures, conventional psychology is granted a degree of privilege and power via its ability to uphold the status quo. This power is most visible in the public sphere when psychological research is actively used to shape societal decision-making via governmental policies. Less visible, yet at least as powerful, is the effect that psychological discourse has on larger discourse. Researchers and their publications therefore continue to perpetuate certain forms of discourse and knowledge through their research that, if not critically examined, can cause harm for disenfranchised and marginalized groups. According to Teo (2011), the primary way in which a psychological study can cause harm is via *epistemological violence*. He describes this as the practice of interpreting empirical data in ways that "implicitly or explicitly construct the Other as inferior or problematic, despite the fact that alternative interpretations, equally viable, based on the data, are available" (Teo, 2014, p. 594).

One of the most prominent examples of such harm concerns the impact of conventional psychology upon the well-being of communities of color. In 2021, the APA published a resolution entitled "Apology to People of Color for APA's Role in Promoting, Perpetuating, and Failing to Challenge Racism, Racial Discrimination, and Human Hierarchy in U.S." This resolution highlighted the historical harm that the field has done and presented resolutions for the explicit promotion of antiracist work. Despite this and numerous other commitments to anti-discriminatory agendas, the field has yet to accomplish sustained field-encompassing change. Recent scholarly works highlight the ways that conventional psychological discourse frequently reifies racial difference and thereby upholds racial hierarchies (Teo, 2022; Smith et al., 2023). Critical race scholars therefore argue for further scrutiny and awareness of research epistemologies, which commit epistemological violence on people of color in service of what Teo (2022) calls *white epistemology*, or approaches to knowledge-creation that serve the interests of whiteness.

Radical Practice Through Radical Research

Without a critical perspective on the epistemological foundations of psychology, the work of psychologists will inadvertently tend to serve status quo power structures (Prilleltensky, 1989). These power structures, in return, provide psychologists with institutional funding, government grants, the creation of academic positions, and other forms of tangible and intangible societal privileges, resulting in a hierarchy that exists in both research and practice. Positivism and methodologism privilege research that utilizes empirical quantitative methods and that emphasizes the value of psychotherapeutic practices that undergo "rigorous" scientific scrutiny in the form of randomly controlled trials (i.e., evidence-based treatments). Positivistic biases towards more "observable" phenomena are therefore directly implicated in the increasing popularity and proliferation of behavioral practices, and the continued marginalization of "nontraditional" practices that involve metaphysical and unquantifiable qualities (Jovanović, 2022). By tracing the logical extensions from Foucauldian philosophy through Teo's epistemological analysis and towards implications for applied psychology, we see the potential for many aspects of psychological work—research, practice, and all other activities—to break out of dominant discursive paradigms.

Reflexivity and Psychopolitical Validity

To engage in work beyond dominant paradigms, radical psychologists must engage in *reflexivity*, the constant process of examining one's assumptions, beliefs, and judgement systems to understand how they influence their actions (Finlay & Gough, 2003). In the context of research, reflexivity works differently from positivist assumptions through an explicit acknowledgement of researcher positionalities—the influence of social identities on the process and outcome of research (Teo, 2017).

While practitioners typically engage in introspective processes that resemble reflexivity (e.g., understanding how certain identities inflect upon the therapeutic relationship), it is limited to specific applications. Radical psychologists, on the other hand, privilege reflexivity as a baseline, constantly interrogating the mechanisms by which individual, community, and system-level assumptions and biases inflect upon their practice.

Wielding this reflexive capacity, radical psychologists are called to contend with the *psychopolitical validity* of their research and practice. Critical psychologist Issac Prilleltensky defined psychopolitical validity as a set of criteria for psychology that account for the "role of power in wellness, oppression, and liberation at the personal, relational, and collective domains" (2008, p. 129). He specified two dimensions of psychopolitical validity: epistemic and transformative. Epistemic validity calls for the direct incorporation of contexts into all understanding of psychological phenomena, in direct opposition to the conventional discursive practices that obscure power relations. Transformative validity calls for the practical applicability of psychological knowledge to bring about social justice and equity. Radical psychologists should therefore consider whether their research and practice answers the following question in the affirmative: Does the work account for the influence of power, and does it *actually* help people?

Liberation Psychology

A prime example of a radical philosophy of psychology that merges research and practice is *liberation psychology*. Developed by Salvadoran psychologist Ignacio Martín-Baró (1994), liberation psychology is a framework for the "exercise of psychology in a participatory manner for the purposes of undertaking transformative action and advancing social justice" (Moane, 2014, p. 1079). In addition to its overlap with many of the aforementioned concepts, liberation psychology promotes the idea of community-based, participatory action research to center the voices of the oppressed communities and directly involve them in the psychological work. Drawing inspiration from Paulo Freire's (1970) conception of a critical pedagogy based in dialogue—the co-creation of knowledge between teacher and student based in mutual respect and equality—radical psychologists seek to engage in community-based research and healing practices that runs counter to the expert-driven model of psychology and psychotherapy.

Radical Practice via the Humanities

Critical psychologists often apply ideas from philosophy, sociology, legal studies, and the humanities into psychology. The establishment of the *psychological humanities* is essential to the development of psychology beyond its neoliberal, positivist, and methodological biases. According to Teo (2017), the psychological humanities can serve both constructive and reconstructive functions for the discipline; that is, it can generate new knowledge (constructive) on mental life that cannot be captured with the use of scientific methods, and it can study the practice, theory, and history of psychology itself (reconstructive). In recognizing that conventional scientific epistemology cannot capture all aspects of psychology (and that its unfettered use often causes harm), radical psychologists must go beyond the disciplinary silo to seek other approaches. Researchers might begin to actively incorporate transdisciplinary works to serve as both inspiration and justification for a nonconventional approach to their studies. Practitioners might find that knowledge deemed unscientific, "non-academic," and lacking in value for conventional psychology may be the exact sources of knowledge to seek for radical practices.

Conclusion

This chapter has addressed how psychological discourse and its underlying ideologies and assumptions perpetuate a certain language that maintain the value and identity of psychology within society. Every action we take as psychologists matters because, as credentialed professionals, psychologists tend to be afforded a relatively high degree of influence as arbiters of "truth." Such professionals have worldmaking power—the

4 Radical Epistemologies for Radical Psychologists   67

power to create what the public deems to be the truths of the world. For radical psychologists to work against conventional psychological paradigms, they must develop a critical understanding of the individual, community, and system-level forces that created these paradigms. Essential to this process is an understanding of how neoliberal capitalism has contributed to the molding of psychological epistemology into the positivist, naïve empiricist approach that we often see today.

The radical theories, concepts, and practices that we have highlighted are not only relevant with regard to the immediate impact that they can have on psychology, but because of their potential to redress *epistemic oppression*, which philosopher Kristie Dotson described as the "persistent epistemic exclusion that hinders one's contribution to knowledge production" (2014, p. 115). Dotson identified three orders of epistemic oppression, alongside a commensurate order of change required to redress them. In this concluding section, these conceptions of oppression and change are applied to psychology as a way of charting a path towards epistemic liberation as a part of the work of radical psychologists.

According to Dotson (2014), first-order epistemic oppression describes the "inefficiencies" (p. 123) within the dominant epistemologies that hinder equal participation by marginalized groups. In psychology, these hindrances are represented by the most overt (i.e., identifiable) types of inequities—racial inequities in grant funding (e.g., Chen et al., 2022) or the culturally oppressive nature of Western psychotherapies (e.g., Sue, 2015). These issues require accepted levels of change that can accomplished through different approaches to the utilization of existing resources and tools, such as calls for diversity in academic funding or the use of evidence-based psychotherapies in a way that is more applicable across cultures (e.g., Castro et al., 2010).

Because first-order change entails working within existing paradigms, the work of radical psychologists is especially necessary with regard to the higher orders of epistemic oppression. Second-order epistemic oppression describes structural issues pertaining to the system of knowledge production that leads to exclusion for marginalized knowers (Dotson, 2014). The overcoming of these barriers requires that entirely new approaches and tools be developed within the existing conceptual landscape. Such barriers are manifested in psychology by the marginalization of non-scientific epistemologies and non-Western healing practices, as is described by this chapter. Radical psychologists could therefore enact second-order change via the incorporation of new transdisciplinary frameworks (e.g., Teo, 2017; Held, 2020) for the practice of radical forms of healing (e.g., French et al., 2019).

While radical psychology inherently offers redress at the level of second-order epistemic oppression, third-order epistemic oppression requires psychologists to imagine what exists beyond the confines of *what we are permitted to know*. The overcoming of third-order epistemic oppression seeks to curtail the rejection of certain knowledge and epistemologies as "unknowable" (Dotson, 2014). In psychology, a third-order epistemic change would involve changes to the entire conceptual landscape regarding what psychologists know about the tools they use and the problems they address. It requires multilayered, reflexive, and transformational thinking (or radical imagination; Kelley, 2002) that targets the very foundations upon which existing epistemological systems are built, such as addressing capitalism and whiteness directly. Despite its paradoxical nature (to "know" what is "unknowable"), third-order change is something that radical psychologists are uniquely positioned to attempt. Through the application of nonconformist practices and a nuanced understanding of history, discourse, and epistemology, radical psychologists can imagine radical futures beyond third-order epistemic oppression.

References

American Psychological Association. (2018). *Guidance for translational abstracts and public significance statements*. https://www.apa.org/pubs/journals/resources/translational-messages

American Psychological Association. (2021). *Apology to people of color for APA's role in promoting, perpetuating, and failing to challenge racism, racial discrimination, and human hierarchy in the U.S.* https://www.apa.org/about/policy/racism-apology

Castro, F. G., Barrera, M., & Holleran Steiker, L. K. (2010). Issues and challenges in the design of culturally adapted evidence-based interventions.

Annual Review of Clinical Psychology, 6(1), 213–239. https://doi.org/10.1146/annurev-clinpsy-033109-132032

Chen, C. Y., Kahanamoku, S. S., Tripati, A., Alegado, R. A., Morris, V. R., Andrade, K., & Hosbey, J. (2022). Systemic racial disparities in funding rates at the national science Foundation. *eLife, 11*. https://doi.org/10.7554/elife.83071

Danziger, K. (1997). *Naming the mind: How psychology found its language*. Sage Publications.

Dotson, K. (2014). Conceptualizing epistemic oppression. *Social Epistemology, 28*(2), 115–138. https://doi.org/10.1080/02691728.2013.782585

Falmagne, R. J. (2014). Epistemology. In T. Teo (Ed.), *Encyclopedia of critical psychology* (pp. 596–599). Springer. https://doi.org/10.1007/978-1-4614-5583-7_95

Finlay, L., & Gough, B. (2003). *Reflexivity: A practical guide for researchers in health and social sciences*. Blackwell Science.

Foucault, M. (1970). *The order of things*. Tavistock.

Foucault, M. (1972). *The archeology of knowledge*. Tavistock.

Foucault, M. (1980). *Selected interviews and other writings* (C. Gordon, Ed.). Pantheon.

Freire, P. (1970). *Pedagogy of the oppressed*. Herder and Herder.

French, B. H., Lewis, J. A., Mosley, D. V., Adames, H. Y., Chavez-Dueñas, N. Y., Chen, G. A., & Neville, H. A. (2019). Toward a psychological framework of radical healing in communities of color. *The Counseling Psychologist, 48*(1), 14–46. https://doi.org/10.1177/0011000019843506

Gao, Z. (2014). Methodologism/methodological imperative. In T. Teo (Ed.), *Encyclopedia of critical psychology* (pp. 1176–1179). Springer. https://doi.org/10.1007/978-1-4614-5583-7_614

Held, B. S. (2020). Taking the humanities seriously. *Review of General Psychology, 25*(2), 119–133. https://doi.org/10.1177/1089268020975024

Hook, D. (2007). *Foucault, psychology and the analytics of power*. Palgrave Macmillan. https://doi.org/10.1057/9780230592322

Jovanović, G. (2010). Historizing epistemology in psychology. *Integrative Psychological and Behavioral Science, 44*(4), 310–328. https://doi.org/10.1007/s12124-010-9132-9

Jovanović, G. (2022). Epistemology of psychology. In J. Zumbach, D. A, Bernstein, S. Narciss, & G. Marsico (Eds.), *International handbook of psychology learning and teaching* (pp. 1–25). Springer. https://doi.org/10.1007/978-3-030-26248-8_54-2

Kelley, R. D. (2002). *Freedom dreams: The Black radical imagination.* Beacon Press.
Martín-Baró, I. (1994). *Writings for a liberation psychology.* Harvard University Press.
Moane, G. (2014). Liberation psychology. In T. Teo (Ed.), *Encyclopedia of critical psychology* (pp. 1079–1084). Springer. https://doi.org/10.1007/978-1-4614-5583-7_173
Moncrieff, J. (2022). The political economy of the mental health system: A Marxist analysis. *Frontiers in Sociology, 6.* https://doi.org/10.3389/fsoc.2021.771875
Nelson, J. (2014). Positivism. In T. Teo (Ed.), *Encyclopedia of critical psychology* (pp. 1437–1444). Springer. https://doi.org/10.1007/978-1-4614-5583-7_468
Parker, I. (2014). Psychotherapy under capitalism: The production, circulation and management of value and subjectivity. *Psychotherapy and Politics International, 12*(3), 166–175. https://doi.org/10.1002/ppi.1333
Prilleltensky, I. (1989). Psychology and the status quo. *American Psychologist, 44*(5), 795–802. https://doi.org/10.1037/0003-066X.44.5.795
Prilleltensky, I. (2008). The role of power in wellness, oppression, and liberation: The promise of psychopolitical validity. *Journal of Community Psychology, 36*(2), 116–136. https://doi.org/10.1002/jcop.20225
Prilleltensky, I. (2011). Wellness as fairness. *American Journal of Community Psychology, 49*(1–2), 1–21. https://doi.org/10.1007/s10464-011-9448-8
Prilleltensky, I., & Prilleltensky, O. (2021). *How people matter: Why it affects health, happiness, love, work, and society.* Cambridge University Press.
Smith, L., Madon, N., Gordon, T., Asencio, C., Xu, O. Y., & Sheffey, M. (2023). Psychology, race, and "the politics of truth." *Journal of Theoretical and Philosophical Psychology.* Advance online publication. https://doi.org/10.1037/teo0000249
Smith, L., & Romero, L. (2010). Psychological interventions in the context of poverty: Participatory action research as practice. *American Journal of Orthopsychiatry, 80*(1), 12–25. https://doi.org/10.1111/j.1939-0025.2010.01003.x
Sue, D. W. (2015). Therapeutic harm and cultural oppression. *The Counseling Psychologist, 43*(3), 359–369. https://doi.org/10.1177/0011000014565713
Teo, T. (1999). Methodologies of critical psychology: Illustrations from the field of racism. *Annual Review of Critical Psychology, 1,* 119–134.
Teo, T. (2011). Empirical race psychology and the hermeneutics of epistemological violence. *Human Studies, 34*(3), 237–255. https://doi.org/10.1007/s10746-011-9179-8

Teo, T. (2014). Epistemological violence. In *Encyclopedia of critical psychology* (pp. 593–596). Springer. https://doi.org/10.1007/978-1-4614-5583-7_441

Teo, T. (2015). Historical thinking as a tool for theoretical psychology. In *The Wiley handbook of theoretical and philosophical psychology* (pp. 133–150). Wiley. https://doi.org/10.1002/9781118748213.ch9

Teo, T. (2017). From psychological science to the psychological humanities: Building a general theory of subjectivity. *Review of General Psychology, 21*(4), 281–291. https://doi.org/10.1037/gpr0000132

Teo, T. (2018). *Outline of theoretical psychology.* Springer. https://doi.org/10.1057/978-1-137-59651-2

Teo, T. (2020). Theorizing in psychology: From the critique of a hyper-science to conceptualizing subjectivity. *Theory & Psychology, 30*(6), 759–767. https://doi.org/10.1177/0959354320930271

Teo, T. (2022). What is a white epistemology in psychological science? A critical race-theoretical analysis. *Frontiers in Psychology, 13.* https://doi.org/10.3389/fpsyg.2022.861584

Walsh, R. T., Teo, T., & Baydala, A. (2014). *A critical history and philosophy of psychology: Diversity of context, thought, and practice.* Cambridge University Press.

Wiggins, B. J., & Christopherson, C. D. (2019). The replication crisis in psychology: An overview for theoretical and philosophical psychology. *Journal of Theoretical and Philosophical Psychology, 39*(4), 202–217. https://doi.org/10.1037/teo0000137

Part III

Practice

5

The Radical Circle: Toward a Psychological Counter-Hegemony

Jon Hook

> *Despair is typical of those who do not understand the causes of evil, see no way out, and are incapable of struggle.*
> Vladimir Lenin

Introduction

Psychotherapy and its related fields aim to alleviate and, where possible, prevent psychological suffering. The commitment to prevention is core to the missions of all applied psychologies under the American Psychological Association (APA), including clinical psychology, social work, and counseling psychology (American Psychological Association, 2014). In recent decades, mental health prevention has been identified as both a method and a goal of social justice itself (Kenny & Hage, 2009). Economic exploitation and oppression are correlated with psychological distress (Belle & Doucet, 2003) and rather than treating the symptoms alone,

---

J. Hook (✉)
Counter-Psych, Chicago, IL, USA

psychologists are increasingly called to address the root causes of this suffering (Kenny & Hage, 2009; Vera, et al., 2009). The connection between social justice and prevention is explicit in the mission statement of the professional division of my own field, Counseling Psychology (Society of Counseling Psychology, 2024).

The prevention section of Division 17 Society of Counseling Psychology's mission statement emphasizes the importance of preventing anti-Black racism and addressing interlocking systems of oppression (Society of Counseling Psychology, 2024). Under the heading of Liberation, it calls for collective action toward freedom from oppression for all people, highlighting the need for advocacy and social justice to realize a better world. This emphasis on liberation draws directly from liberation psychology, founded by the socialist Ignacio Martín-Baró (Ratner, 2009). Anti-capitalism is central to Martín-Baró's work, yet there is not even a passing mention of capitalism in counseling psychology's liberation-infused mission statement. According to Carl Ratner, this omission is part of a broader trend where "new liberation psychologists never mention Marx or socialism or class struggle or false consciousness," all foundational elements of liberation psychology (Ratner, 2009, p. 36). Ratner argues that these psychologists "compound abstractions and vagaries with omissions and silences about concrete problems and alternatives" (Ratner, 2009, p. 36). Pointing out this omission is not to insist that psychologists adopt a Marxist stance on capitalism, but rather to emphasize that if they discuss systemic oppression, they should at least acknowledge the dominant global economic system that underpins their profession. Avoiding capitalism is not merely a theoretical oversight, but an immediate practical concern.

In 2019, under the guidance of its counseling psychologist president, the APA launched the Deep Poverty Initiative, which aimed to "put deep poverty on everyone's radar and give you the tools to address deep poverty in your community and beyond" (American Psychological Association, 2019a, para. 2). Here one would expect that the economic system that creates poverty would be a matter of discussion, but this again is not so. In the online 5-week learning challenge provided to psychologists and other workers by the Deep Poverty Initiative (American Psychological Association, 2019b), I could find no mention of

5 The Radical Circle: Toward a Psychological Counter-Hegemony

capitalism. Furthermore, the goals of the Deep Poverty Initiative treat public policy as a tertiary consideration. It is common sense that the elimination of poverty should, without question, be seen as a primary, not secondary or tertiary, political matter. On this point, thinkers as different as Ronald Reagan and Ho Chi Minh would agree.

To be fair, the limitations of the psychologization of material suffering have long been criticized by radical counseling psychologists themselves (DeBlaere et al., 2019). In their 2003 paper, Vera and Speight plainly state that, "Any multicultural movement that underemphasizes social justice is likely to do little to eradicate oppression and will maintain the status quo to the detriment of historically marginalized people" (pp. 254–255). From a Marxist perspective, this analysis is spot on. Marxism maintains that the oppressive practices and hierarchies within Western industrial society—from racism and sexism (Chapman, 2021) to imperialism (Lenin, 2015)—have their roots in the capitalist system. Capitalism is not only the historical progenitor of many of these oppressions, but its present material foundation (Lenin, 2015). Specifically speaking, private ownership of the economy is the legal foundation that ultimately maintains the tyranny of the few (capitalists) over the many (workers). The capitalist class relies on and benefits from racism, sexism, imperialist violence, and all other forms of oppression to maintain class division and position themselves on top. The Marxist theorist Antonio Gramsci would heartily agree with Vera and Speights' take on the dangers of passivity.

Gramsci believed the ruling capitalist class retains control not merely by force, but through coercion wherein "organic intellectuals" produce pro-capitalist ideology to justify the rule of capital thus obscuring true sources of oppression (Gramsci, 2000, p. 306). The role of organic intellectuals in maintaining the status quo explains counseling psychology's omission of capitalism from its mission statement as well as the absence of serious material considerations from the APA's initiative to address poverty. Neoliberal ideology (Adam et al., 2019) is so embedded in the practices and policies of mainstream psychology that even its social justice vanguards cannot escape capitalist ideology. The result is a profession that alleviates individual suffering at the expense of preventing it. The result is oppression.

If counseling and the other applied psychologies are going to fulfil their mission of addressing and preventing suffering, then they are going to have to take a radical political turn. And clearly, those radical therapists who are ahead of the curve on this matter cannot afford to wait for their professional leaders or organizations to get on board with true liberation. Radical therapists are going to have to develop their own anti-capitalist and socialistic formations here and now. Before doing so, radical therapists should acquaint themselves with the psychological authorities whose jobs depend on stopping them. Psyauthorities are typically members of the professional managerial class (PMC), whose role is to reproduce and uphold the capitalist system by administering, supervising, and disseminating its ideologies (Graeber, 2014). This function serves to maintain social order and restrict the lower classes from accessing the power of the upper classes. While the PMC may not constitute a formal class in the Marxist sense, it remains a highly useful heuristic for analysis. Within this framework, psyauthorities occupy a uniquely prominent standing, even among the PMC.

Not only do psyauthorities determine what personalities or moods are unhealthy, but in doing so they also tell us what kinds of people are unhealthy. Whether they are writing op-eds on cultural moments, testifying on the capacity of a defendant to stand trial, or therapizing a couple in a domestic violence situation, psyauthorities are imbued with the power to tacitly decide right from wrong. In deciding what behaviors are acceptable to our culture, psyauthorities are much more directly involved in the production of capitalist ideology than many other members of the PMC who may only coordinate resources or manage labor. In training settings, psyauthorities inculcate future psyworkers into their role as pro-capitalist agents and constrain would-be radical therapists by predetermining the acceptable ways of conceptualizing and treating psychological distress. The psyauthorities also carry in themselves a degree of reputational purity that comes when one's job is to help people. No doubt many psyauthorities do help people. To call into question the legitimacy of an authority is at the heart of any radical tradition, not because one wonders *whether* authorities ever help people, but because one questions *how* they do so.

Like so many culture workers, psyauthorities exert their power through their cultural capital, a concept developed by sociologist Pierre Bourdieu, which refers to the non-financial social assets that confer social power and mobility (1986). In the context of psychology, cultural capital includes credentials, professional titles, institutional affiliations, and other bona fides that carry legitimacy in the eyes of society. Most of the time cultural capital is a useful heuristic. Cultural capital helps us distinguish between real medical doctors and snake oil hucksters or between genuine scholars and conspiracy theorists. Unfortunately, in the field of psychology and psychotherapy the value of these heuristics is quite limited. Independent of any political considerations, the social capital conferred to psyauthorities relies on the assumption that education, training, and experience produces an expertise in healing which the psyauthorities can then confer onto their trainees and clinical employees. This presumption cuts to the heart of the matter because it is presumed to rest on a scientific foundation. It is the basis for expensive years of schooling, costly continuing education credits, and for the wage theft that takes place in many clinics. Not only is there strong evidence against the assumption that education, training, and experience confers outcomes, but astonishingly, there never existed much evidence to support this conclusion in the first place.

Several studies show that clinical training, continuing education, and even years of experience contribute little to improving outcomes (Neimeyer et al., 2009; Rousmaniere et al., 2017). Furthermore, instead of improving with time, therapists' effectiveness often plateaus early in their careers and may even decline, as evidenced by research documenting steady reductions in performance over the years (Miller & Hubble, 2011; Goldberg et al., 2016). In a study of client outcomes among trainees and staff members at a university training clinic, Beyebach et al. (2000) found no significant differences between expert and trainee therapists in terms of successful cases at both termination and follow-up. A separate study that analyzed 892 cases over seven years extended this finding by showing that trainees often achieved better outcomes than experienced staff members (Minami et al., 2008). These final two findings represent an inversion of the assumption that clinical training is based on; that more experienced therapists train and supervise lesser experienced therapists to help them improve.

Traditional clinical supervision, wherein a more experienced clinician provides guidance on cases to a less experienced clinician at a high cost (about $150 an hour/ week), is similarly bereft of any evidence for its efficacy. Research spanning decades has shown no significant link between supervision and better client results (Watkins, 2011). A five-year study involving over 6,500 clients and 175 trainee therapists found that supervision only contributed to 1% of the variance in client outcomes, with supervisor experience and qualifications playing no identifiable role (Rousmaniere 2016). If clinical training were based on a legitimate scientific approach, then these findings and the many others like them would have brought the field to a standstill while the psyauthorities figured out how to deliver on their promised outcomes. Indeed, so vast is the disconnect between perceived and actual competence of psyauthorities that it is not so much an unexamined claim as it is a total myth. Dismaying though these findings are, they do not negate the value of therapy.

Findings from the same body of research have shown that psychotherapy has consistently proven to be effective, achieving outcomes comparable to major medical interventions like coronary artery bypass surgery. Decades of research (Duncan et al., 2010; Hubble et al., 1999) reinforce these findings. What's more, therapists in actual practice where variables are hard to control, obtain outcomes similar to those found in clinical trials where variables are tightly controlled (Minami et al., 2008; Saxon et al., 2017; Stiles et al., 2008; Wampold & Brown, 2005) Furthermore, there is such a thing as therapeutic skill. Okiishi et al. (2003) found that certain therapists, termed "supershrinks", had clients improve at rates 10 times faster than average. Furthermore, research on deliberate practice has shown it is possible to obtain superior therapeutic results over time (Chow et al., 2015).

Taken together, the scientific findings do indicate that there is such a thing as therapeutic skill, that it can be developed, and that very skilled healers exist. What they do not indicate is that a more experienced, better trained, more highly educated, or highly paid psyauthority should be imbued with the assumption of greater legitimacy. Like a member of any profession, their authority should be questioned and supported only when the evidence warrants it. This knowledge is of particular importance to the radical therapist who should be aware of the obstacles that stand in the way of their progressive views and who may feel reticence in transgressing the wisdom of the psyauthorities. Radical therapists can be assured that when lacking solid empirical and ethical justification for their pronouncements, psyauthorities are often little more than the therapeutic *Men in Black*.

Therapeutic Neuralzyer

Men in Black (Sonnenfeld, 1997) is a sci-fi buddy cop movie about two G-Men who hunt down aliens and perform psychological damage control on the fragile human minds they encounter along the way. At the heart of this damage control is a nifty device called a neuralyzer. With the flash of white light, the neuralyzer allows the G-Men to erase the memory of any humans who have definitely just seen an alien. After their memories dissolve into nothing, the G-Men can then replace said memory with a more terrestrial explanation. In one scene, Agent K (played by Tommy Lee Jones) erases the memory of a farmer woman who had a bizarre interaction with an insectoid alien wearing her husband's skin. After he flashes away her memory Agent K says, "What you saw in the sky was not a UFO. Swamp gas from a weather balloon was trapped in a thermal pocket and refracted the light from Venus." Presumably, this is enough to convince the woman that aliens aren't real for the rest of her life. After all, a man from the government is saying it.

Isn't this just like what the psyauthorities are doing today with ideology? "You're not suffering from capitalist alienation, you have a complex mind problem that only I, an outsider to your psyche, am capable of seeing. Forget that you've seen the true face of your oppression. Ignore what you suspect is an open conspiracy to exploit you. Take a look within."

The metaphor of the neuralyzer illustrates how ideology works to not merely hide reality, but to warp it entirely. While we believe we understand the reasons behind our thoughts and actions, we are often unaware of the real conditions shaping them. This leads many well-meaning individuals and even entire well-meaning professions to focus on surface-level explanations at the expense of the deeper forces at play. Perhaps more revealing than the neuralyzation of the general public is the neuralyzation the Men in Black perform on themselves. At both the beginning and end of the film, agents who have reached the end of their careers use the neuralyzer on themselves, erasing the memory of their years of service and the countless lies that came with it. This is the final role of ideology; to blind us to what we are doing to ourselves.

The blinding white light of the therapeutic neuralyzer is all around us. It fills the white spaces of academic journals and pours out of televisions and smart phones. It blinds and spreads at the speed of thought until it comes from the mouths of regular people who describe their distress in officially sanctioned psychological terms becoming psychiatric discourse (Cohen, 2016). The radical therapist is neither the compliant citizen who looks into the light nor the cynic who looks away, but the one who looks beyond it to the hand that holds it up.

The Path of Subversion

The psyauthorities do not make anti-capitalist therapy easy. Clinicians in training are often under scrutiny in everything they say, write, and do by their evaluators and employers. Early career therapists can feel a similar pressure as they remain under direct supervision and may remain so for many decades. It is important to not understate these pressures. Dissent to capitalist norms can be swiftly punished and the expression of rebellious thinking may cost one their career. Until radical therapists are free from the scrutiny of the psyauthorities, their only option will be subversion. The word "subversion" can have dark connotations, such as the subversion of democracy, but here subversion is taken to mean quite the opposite. To subvert illegitimate authority does not mean to leave suffering humanity in chaos nor to lie to people about your intentions, but rather to uplift and if possible to establish a scientifically legitimate and prosocial authority in its place. It means advocating alongside working humanity and agitating for effective care and systemic change. It means to advocate for socialism even if, at present, socialism is a distant goal. It bears repeating that the purpose of radicalism is not to write books and articles complaining of how far away this hope is, but to do something about it here and now. By far the fastest way to materialize liberation from capitalism is to form a circle of radicals oneself.

The Radical Circle

A radical circle (RC) is a small, organized, and mobile group of radicals committed to materializing socialist practices immediately in their therapy work and gradually in the wider world. RCs are a fundamental unit toward the formation of a genuine counter-hegemony (Gramsci, 2000) within psychology. Gramsci's concept of counterhegemony aims to dismantle bourgeois cultural hegemony by building a war of position in order for working-class values and ideologies to gain influence within civil society before political power shifts toward socialism (2000). While capitalist organic intellectuals work to reinforce and rationalize the ruling class's control through consent-based institutions and ideology, counter-hegemonic intellectuals, like radical therapists, strive to create an alternative historical bloc that aligns subordinate groups with a socialist vision. This approach contrasts with a direct assault on capitalist power (war of movement) by gradually preparing the proletariat and allies to establish a broader societal consciousness and organization that can ultimately replace capitalist hegemony (Gramsci, 2000). RCs operate like a political vanguard (Lenin, 2014) in that they work with an advanced understanding, but agitate for change effectively and functionally.

RCs are not the end of political struggle nor a replacement for mass line party politics. However, given the almost total absence of real socialist movements in the United States (and many industrialized nations), they are an acceptable starting point. Furthermore, RCs have several advantages over large groups. Foremost of its strengths, an RC can be formed immediately. Even today, the radical therapist can text or call a few friends and get one going. RCs are also discrete and may allow like-minded students to question the status quo without running into the problems that visibility creates. They are also flexible, able to grow, shift, and adapt as old challenges are overcome or new needs are discovered. Finally, they are combinable not only with other RCs, but with political parties and activist movements more broadly. RCs are not an abstract idea or consideration, but an imminently useful social construction here and now. Indeed, it was an RC that brought the present book you are reading into existence. In the following section, I provide guidelines toward the formation of an RC using the formation of this text as a direct example of this may be done. Finally, I offer a few guidelines for avoiding pitfalls that might be encountered on the way.

Step 1: Connect with Comrades

Feelings of isolation are common for those who question the status quo, and this isolation serves the interests of capitalists. The odds that you will just so happen to be around committed anti-capitalists is possibly quite low. In all my educational training, I only ever met two or three people with radical politics and in every case, they weren't terribly interested in doing anything about their beliefs. Most of the connections I have made came instead from emailing people whose work I admired or whose work I wanted to learn from. In 2021, I began reading voraciously about the intersection of psychotherapy and Marxism. I simply couldn't stand not doing something about this issue, so I began very simply searching for scholars' and activists' contact information. Through my reading on a variety of topics, I encountered a Philadelphia-based non-profit called Incite Seminars, which focuses on critical, leftwing alternative education (2024).

Step 2: Establish Clearly Stated, Obtainable, and Measurable Goals

A cold email can feel intimidating, but in my experience people with devotion to a cause will be delighted to speak to almost anyone about it, so long as you make it easy and attractive to them. When I previously reached out to the founder of Incite Seminars, I hadn't gotten much traction. Undoubtedly this is because I was merely talking about the issue of psychotherapy, not intending to do anything about it. This time, I made sure my proposal was more focused and actionable. Instead of just wanting to chat, I came with a clear project idea that connected with the work they were already doing. I decided to reach out to them with an idea for a reading group I wanted to start, provocatively titled *Anti-Therapy*. Not

5 The Radical Circle: Toward a Psychological Counter-Hegemony

long after I sent my email, the head of their curriculum responded enthusiastically, and from there, I started drafting a plan for how the group would be organized.

All great undertakings begin with the end in mind. I recommend writing this end goal down in clear plain language. When you have an end in mind, you can determine if you're succeeding at it and iterate on this goal when you're not. Every therapist knows that goals need to be measurable, but this is as much a political strategy as it is a therapeutic one. One of the best ways to identify a goal is to identify a gap or need. What is it that you and your comrades, your clients, or other groups are missing, needing, or asking for?

When I formed *Anti-therapy*, the goal was to create a reading and discussion group that could explore vital questions at the intersection of therapy and radicalism. I formed this group because of the concrete and constantly expressed need to form a leftwing approach to social justice within psychotherapy. At the heart of all of these was the question of "How to move forward without giving in or giving up" (2022, para. 2). *Anti-therapy* very quickly became Incite Seminar's most popular offering and it became clear to me that my skepticism with the field was shared widely. Our members had many productive discussions in *Anti-therapy* with former and current therapy clients, other clinicians and professionals in various fields. Gradually I felt I had a better understanding of how psychotherapy worked ideologically and, more importantly, I had learned from people who had used therapy themselves. Stepping outside of our professional bubbles and connecting with regular working people is a critical component of developing an actionable political movement. Moreover, I became convinced that giving up therapy was not a good idea. The bulk of the attendees were former or current users of therapy and, while they were critical of mainstream psychotherapy, most if not all were adamant that what was needed was improvement, not abolition. After over a year of meetings, I had gathered enough ideas about what might be done about psychotherapy. Personal and workplace time commitments made the group untenable for me, and so I closed shop. A few months passed and just as I began to question my next steps, I received an email from a former guest speaker with a book offer.

Step 3: Remain Flexible, but Committed

The focus of your RC will change with time as your old goals are met and new horizons are identified. You must remain flexible in these goals and attainments, but focused and determined to continue on the path you have set out on. The important thing is that you start on this path and do not stop. Your movements may be too slow for some or too fast for others, but steadiness is all that matters in the end. While your goals shift, be mindful that you are moving toward a positive material change, rather than away from it in spite of how you might initially react. When Marxist sociologist, Bruce Cohen, emailed me about writing a book in the Critical Mental Health series, he indicated the book could be about literally anything. You would think I'd be excited, but at the time I was so fed up with the impossible bureaucracy of the academia and faux radicalism of my field that I almost declined his offer. Other priorities, like going outside and touching grass, were becoming much more appealing to me than writing a book for what I presumed were very few readers who would really take interest. Fortunately, good sense prevailed, and I began drafting the proposal for the present book. With a book proposal now in the works, my goals and commitments had shifted, but my commitment remained.

One thing that kept cynicism at bay was the people I encountered on this path. In my day-to-day work, conversations with clients and with clinicians would almost invariably confirm the need for new radical ideas about psychotherapy as both a system and a practice. Moreover, each time I reached out to a potential chapter author, the response was incredibly enthusiastic. People almost invariably stated some version of the sentiment that, "It's about time someone made this book!" Similarly, you may find that staying in tune with the needs of your immediate circles and the broader world is one powerful way to maintain a long-term commitment to your RC.

More powerful than any personal commitment I had was meeting people with a shared commitment to socialism. My co-editor, Frank Gruba-McCallister, entered this project as a chapter author, but his enthusiasm, knowledge, and reach carried far beyond what I could have ever done alone, and so I invited him to co-edit with me. The neoliberal approach to scholarly work is to bear the burden as a singular entity and to take credit for everything. Individual achievement is laudable and sometimes the only path ahead, but cooperation takes us all much further. The ultimate aim of an RC is to extend our cooperation until it reaches the highest levels of politics.

Step 4. Connect with a Political Party

To be truly effective, RCs must connect with larger political movements and parties. Historically, left-wing political parties have proven to be the most effective method for advancing socialism by educating the masses, unifying diverse struggles, and fostering genuine political change. The radical therapist and their RC is invited to connect their RC to whatever leftwing movement speaks to them. They should avoid throwing in their lot with bourgeois party structures. Mainstream political parties are capitalist and imperialist in nature and have no interest in socialism. It is possible that voting in elections for bourgeois parties may be a useful tool if they are part of a broader strategy. Even for Lenin, provisional support for liberal parties had its place on occasion "to isolate reaction" as part of "alliances but not unity" (Nimtz, 2014, p. 98). Nonetheless, there is a light year of distance between provisional support for a party in a single election and making that one's sole political identity. The pull of capitalist politics is just one liability you will encounter in forming and maintaining a RC. As you navigate this path, certain general guidelines will help your RC avoid common pitfalls and stay focused on meaningful, material change.

Guidance on Pitfalls

Catharsis Versus Action

RCs are not intended to produce momentary catharsis alone. Often when people get together to complain about an issue, from casual conversations to formal meetings, I have found that many people complain simply to feel better so that they can go back to complying with authority. This is reminiscent of popular political movements that capture popular sentiment against the status quo, but then do nothing when they gain power. To capture radical energy only for emotional release is worse than expressing blind outrage and a reactionary (conservative) tendency. RCs should absolutely lead to emotional release and catharsis, but should do so in order to change the social environment around them, not because you are simply coping better.

Interminable Book Clubs

RCs must avoid becoming nothing more than book clubs. Revolutionary education is paramount and careful study of practical Marxism or other radical theories must be ongoing, but the point of an RC is, as Marx said, to change the world, not interpret it (1978). Keep your RCs goals related to something obtainable and material and constantly monitor against the ultimately useless cycle of endless education.

Guilt and Shame

Radicals tend to be people with a strong sense of right and wrong and a powerful moral duty. Because radicalism involves disobeying authority, feelings of guilt and shame are common whether it is the feeling that one is not doing enough or the fears that come with disobeying psyauthorities. Under capitalism, morality is subordinated to the interests of the ruling class. It's not generally seen as immoral to force someone into an unpaid internship, nor is it considered justifiable to steal from your boss. This moral framework is so deeply embedded in our consciousness that we rarely question it. Historically, this logic has been used to uphold even the most brutal systems. During America's era of slavery, many conceded that slavery was morally wrong—but still argued it was unethical to use "illegitimate" means to oppose or dismantle it. The system itself was horrific, yet resistance was framed as the true moral transgression. But what if we flipped the script? What if, instead, we understood all morality through the lens of class struggle? Then acts of resistance against our oppressors would feel no more ethically troubling than protecting an abused animal from its tormentor. After all, such resistance would simply be an assertion of our inherent human dignity. Whatever you do to overcome or subvert psyauthority you should do so with integrity and compassion. But on this matter we must be clear: the capitalists and the bosses are not your allies. They may be good people, they may be more moral than you, but in their position and with their authority they exploit your labor by stealing your wages as profits. Even when they are not doing this, they are actively maintaining a problematic and oppressive status quo. Of course, there may be positive class traitors in your midst; bosses who are serious in their commitments to radicalism. In such a case, solidarity is warranted. Friedrich Engels was himself a class traitor against the bourgeoisie as he owned a paper mill in England and his income funded Marx's work.

Divide and Conquer

In many liberal social justice spaces, the conversation often fixates on social interactions that reflect bias or privilege. While these are undeniably important and must be addressed—particularly by those who hold social privilege—there is a danger in letting the analysis stop there. When we reduce systemic oppression to questions of individual bias or interpersonal dynamics, we risk reproducing the very structures of inequality we claim to resist. Oppression is not born from prejudice alone. Social hierarchies persist because they serve material interests. White Europeans did not enslave Africans and colonize the Global South because they harbored bad feelings—they did so in pursuit of land, labor, wealth, and control. Capitalism's dominance hierarchies remain intact today for the same reasons: they are profitable.

To meaningfully confront injustice, those with relative social power—white radicals, heterosexual radicals, citizens—must take responsibility for naming and dismantling racism, queerphobia, and xenophobia. But this cannot stop at personal reflection or performative allyship. Without organized and collective action aimed at disrupting material exploitation endless discussions of social power become hollow rituals. This is the precise mechanism through which radical politics become office politics.

If you have spent time in an APA approved practicum or internship, you have likely noticed how salaried professionals urge unpaid interns (a fancy word for servants) to "reflect on their privilege." This isn't justice. It's control. It weaponizes moral language in service to liberalism in order to suppress class consciousness, turning potential organizers into self-monitoring subjects. Liberalism without class struggle doesn't challenge power—it camouflages it, dressing up settler capitalism in progressive language while keeping the machinery intact. The moralizing stance of liberalism is so effective at preserving the status quo that many professionals don't even realize they're complicit in it. I recall sitting through yet another social justice training, this time led by a widely cited and influential head of a counseling psychology department. During the session, one of my exhausted and marginalized colleagues asked a sincere question: What can leaders in our field actually do to make internships and training experiences less oppressive? To this very reasonable question, the department head responded that he and his colleagues had started changing the pictures on the walls. Yes—changing the pictures. But it didn't stop there. He added that they had also begun removing some of these photos due to the anti-DEI policies of the current federal administration. It was as my colleagues and I left the meeting—our eyes locked, jaws completely agape—that I finally understood the true meaning of gobsmacked.

When workers from marginalized identities see the source of injustice but are steered into fighting each other instead of their employers, capital wins. This is no accident—it's strategy. Divide, distract, defuse. Don't fall for it. Name it. Reject it. A radical circle that won't confront material exploitation is not radical at all. It's a holding cell. Draw the line. Justice without class struggle is just window dressing for empire.

The socialist answer is unity through shared material struggle. Start with what binds you—exhaustion, underpayment, and your certainty there is a better way. This is not colorblindness; it is solidarity. Ask: Who is unpaid? Who is afraid to speak out? These are your comrades. This ethic of mutual aid is ancient. Pre-colonial hunter-gatherer societies survived through reciprocity and care—not competition. No one starved while others hoarded. This isn't utopian nostalgia—it is your nature.

Anti-Science Rhetoric

The historic rift between some forms of progressive politics and scientific endeavors is entirely unacceptable and unnecessary. The gradual formation of counter-hegemony within psychology should not only be ethically radical but scientifically radical. Although not all questions can be answered by empiricism, the world is knowable and amenable to change and it cannot be changed without high quality science. Radical clinicians should critique flawed science to improve it, not to dismiss the study of human behavior as somehow unknowable as some postmodernist or post-structural perspectives might. These anti-scientific perspectives are historically the result of left-wing retreats and in the past 40 years, they have done nothing whatsoever to challenge the supremacy of capital except in the imaginations of their thinkers. Radical therapists should study their own processes and outcomes scientifically whether with individual clients or on a global scale.

Socialism as the Ultimate Psychotherapy

If the purpose of psychotherapy is to alleviate and prevent psychological suffering, then the only possible way for it to realize this ambition is to become socialist. Socialism is the sole system, yet devised, that creates a true political and economic democracy wherein regular people are given the power to address their suffering in creative ways. Socialism is the fulfilment of the humanistic aims of self-actualization presented by Maslow and Rogers (Lethbridge, 1992), but it is not merely an idea, aspiration, or dream. In these matters, any radical should be wary of those in the academia whose actions and research programs subtly enforce the golden rule of the liberal order that the best thing to do, is nothing at all. Radical therapists must study history as well as current politics to avoid the morass of the Western Marxist tradition that merely studies political issues rather than working toward political change (Losurdo, 2024). You who are reading this are not fundamentally different than any author in the present text. You are an agent of history and catalyst for a society in which, "Our productions would be as many mirror from which our natures would shine forth" (Marx, 1947, p. 278).

References

Adams, G., Estrada-Villalta, S., Sullivan, D., & Markus, H. R. (2019). The psychology of neoliberalism and the neoliberalism of psychology. *Journal of Social Issues, 75*(1), 189–216.
American Psychological Association. (2014). Guidelines for prevention in psychology. *The American Psychologist, 69*(3), 285–296.
American Psychological Association. (2019a). *Deep poverty initiative.* https://www.apa.org/about/governance/president/deep-poverty-initiative
American Psychological Association. (2019b). *Deep poverty challenge.* https://www.apa.org/about/governance/president/deep-poverty-challenge
Belle, D., & Doucet, J. (2003). Poverty, inequality, and discrimination as sources of depression among US women. *Psychology of Women Quarterly, 27*(2), 101–113.
Beyebach, M., Rodríguez-Sánchez, M. S., Arribas de Miguel, J., Herrero de Vega, M., Hernandez, C., & Rodríguez-Morejón, A. (2000). Outcome of solution-focused therapy at a university family therapy center. *Journal of Systemic Therapies, 19*(1), 116–128. https://doi.org/10.1521/jsyt.2000.19.1.116
Bourdieu, P. (1986). The forms of capital. In J. G. Richardson (Ed.), *Handbook of theory and research for the sociology of education* (pp. 241–258). Greenwood.
Chapman, F. (2021). *Marxist-Leninist perspectives on black liberation and socialism.* Freedom Road Socialist Organization.
Chow, D. L., Miller, S. D., Seidel, J. A., Kane, R. T., Thornton, J. A., & Andrews, W. P. (2015). The role of deliberate practice in the development of highly effective psychotherapists. *Psychotherapy, 52*(3), 337–346.
Cohen, B. M. (2016). *Psychiatric hegemony: A Marxist theory of mental illness.* Palgrave Macmillan.
DeBlaere, C., Singh, A. A., Wilcox, M. M., Cokley, K. O., Delgado-Romero, E. A., Scalise, D. A., & Shawahin, L. (2019). Social justice in counseling

psychology: Then, now, and looking forward. *The Counseling Psychologist, 47*(6), 938–962.

Duncan, B. L., Miller, S. D., Wampold, B. E., & Hubble, M. A. (2010). *The heart and soul of change: Delivering what works in therapy* (pp. xxix–455). American Psychological Association.

Goldberg, S. B., Babins-Wagner, R., Rousmaniere, T., Berzins, S., Hoyt, W. T., Whipple, J. L., et al. (2016). Creating a climate for therapist improvement: A case study of an agency focused on outcomes and deliberate practice. *Psychotherapy, 53*(3), 367.

Graeber, D. (2014). Anthropology and the rise of the professional-managerial class. *HAU: Journal of Ethnographic Theory, 4*(3), 73–88.

Gramsci, A. (2000). Intellectuals and education. In D. Forgacs (Ed.), *The Gramsci reader: Selected writings, 1916–1935* (pp. 300–322). New York University Press.

Hubble, M. A., Duncan, B. L., & Miller, S. D. (1999). *The heart and soul of change: What works in therapy* (pp. xxiv–462). American Psychological Association.

Incite Seminars. (2022). *Anti-therapy group.* https://inciteseminars.com/anti-therapy-group/

Incite Seminars. (2024). *About Incite Seminars.* https://inciteseminars.com/about-2/

Kenny, M. E., & Hage, S. M. (2009). The next frontier: Prevention as an instrument of social justice. *The Journal of Primary Prevention, 30*(1), 10–19.

Lenin, V. I. (2014). *What is to be done?* (Reprint of 1973 edition). Red Star Publishers. (Original work published 1902)

Lenin, V. I. (2015). Imperialism, the highest stage of capitalism. In *Conflict after the Cold War* (pp. 319–326). Routledge. https://socialist-alliance.org/sites/default/files/imperialism_the_highest_stage_of_capitalism.pdf

Lethbridge, D. (1992). *Mind in the world: The Marxist psychology of self-actualization.* (Vol. 26). MEP Publications.

Losurdo, D. (2024). *Western Marxism: How it was born, how it died, how it can be reborn.* NYU Press.

Marx, K. (1947). *Economic and philosophic manuscripts of 1844.* (M. Milligan, Trans.). International Publishers. (Original work published 1844)

Marx, K. (1978). *Theses on Feuerbach.* In R. C. Tucker (Ed.), *The Marx-Engels reader* (2nd ed., pp. 143–145). W. W. Norton & Company. (Original work published 1845)

Miller, S. D., & Hubble, M. (2011). The road to mastery. *Psychotherapy Networker, 35*(3), 22–31.
Minami, T., Wampold, B. E., Serlin, R. C., Hamilton, E. G., Brown, G. S. J., & Kircher, J. C. (2008). Benchmarking the effectiveness of psychotherapy treatment for adult depression in a managed care environment: A preliminary study. *Journal of Consulting and Clinical Psychology, 76*(1), 116.
Neimeyer, G. J., Taylor, J. M., & Wear, D. M. (2009). Continuing education in psychology: Outcomes, evaluations, and mandates. *Professional Psychology: Research and Practice, 40*(6), 617.
Nimtz, A. H. (2014). *Lenin's electoral strategy from Marx and Engels through the revolution of 1905*. Palgrave Macmillan.
Okiishi, J., Lambert, M. J., Nielsen, S. L., & Ogles, B. M. (2003). Waiting for supershrink: An empirical analysis of therapist effects. *Clinical Psychology & Psychotherapy: An International Journal of Theory & Practice, 10*(6), 361–373.
Ratner, C. (2009). *Recovering and advancing Martin-Baro's ideas about psychology, culture, and social transformation*. Retrieved November 6, 2024, from http://www.sonic.net/~cr2/Montero%20review.pdf
Rousmaniere, T. (2016). *Deliberate practice for psychotherapists: A guide to improving clinical effectiveness*. Routledge.
Rousmaniere, T., Goodyear, R. K., Miller, S. D., & Wampold, B. E. (Eds.). (2017). *The cycle of excellence: Using deliberate practice to improve supervision and training*. John Wiley & Sons.
Saxon, D., Ashley, K., Bishop-Edwards, L., Connell, J., Harrison, P., Ohlsen, S., et al. (2017). A pragmatic randomised controlled trial assessing the non-inferiority of counselling for depression versus cognitive-behaviour therapy for patients in primary care meeting a diagnosis of moderate or severe depression (PRaCTICED): Study protocol for a randomised controlled trial. *Trials, 18*, 1–14.
Society of Counseling Psychology. (2024). *Mission & values*. Retrieved November 6, 2024, from https://www.div17.org/mission-values
Sonnenfeld, B. (Director). (1997). *Men in black* [Film]. Columbia Pictures.
Stiles, W. B., Barkham, M., Mellor-Clark, J., & Connell, J. (2008). Effectiveness of cognitive-behavioural, person-centred, and psychodynamic therapies in UK primary-care routine practice: Replication in a larger sample. *Psychological Medicine, 38*(5), 677–688.
Vera, E. M., Buhin, L., & Isacco, A. (2009). *The role of prevention in psychology's social justice agenda*. American Psychological Association.

Wampold, B. E., & Brown, G. S. J. (2005). Estimating variability in outcomes attributable to therapists: A naturalistic study of outcomes in managed care. *Journal of Consulting and Clinical Psychology, 73*(5), 914.

Watkins, C. E., Jr. (2011). Does psychotherapy supervision contribute to patient outcomes? Considering thirty years of research. *The Clinical Supervisor, 30*(2), 235–256.

6

Personal and Social Liberation: Necessary Foundations for Radical Therapy

Frank Gruba-McCallister

The Hazards of Individualism

The need for radical therapy to be holistic is particularly important based on the constricted and one-sided view of human beings that places an exaggerated emphasis on the individual advanced by capitalist hegemony (Davies, 2022; Gruba-McCallister, 2019, 2025). The person is portrayed as hedonistic, self-interested, and competitive. The healthy individual is one who is autonomous and self-reliant as well as motivated by mastery and acquisitiveness. Freedom is portrayed as liberty or being free of obstacles and prohibitions. Individualism is a moral virtue such that persons have sole responsibility for whether they succeed or fail.

This image of the person serves a number of harmful economic and political purposes that serve capitalism. Situating the causes of one's suffering solely within the person renders the more prominent social causes invisible. This is a form of mystification that depoliticizes discontent by

F. Gruba-McCallister (✉)
Counter-Psych, Chicago, IL, USA

blaming victims (Ryan, 1971) for their unfortunate state. Unjust systems are rendered blameless. Similarly, it legitimizes morally condemnable inequality using meritocracy (Sandel, 2021) that asserts differences are based on talent, effort, and achievement. This is the myth of the American Dream that persons who work hard and avail themselves of the opportunities provided to them will succeed and have a better life. Chetty et al. (2017) found that the rates of absolute mobility have fallen from 90% for children born in 1940 to 50% for children born in the 1980s. Individualized explanations for suffering serve economic interests as well. Davies (2022) illustrates the close relationship between neoliberalism and the dominance of the biomedical model. Individuals are indoctrinated to define their problems in medicalized terms. This restricts the focus to what is happening inside of them, while also boosting the profits of a commodified health care system (Boggs, 2015; Esposito & Perez, 2014). Also individualized well-being is defined in ways consistent with the goals of the economy and market (Davies, 2022). Behaviors and feelings that negatively affect competition and productivity need to be brought to medical attention. Finally, this ideology has resulted in a precipitous decline in community that has had detrimental effects (Putnam, 2000).

These destructive impacts of individualism have been adopted and advanced by mainstream psychology in ways contrary to advancing well-being. As Prilleltensky (1989) observes:

> At a structural level, a pervasive dichotomy between the individual and society is observed in psychology…The immediate ideological benefit derived from such a dichotomy is that the individual is studied as an asocial and ahistorical being whose life vicissitudes are artificially disconnected from the wider sociopolitical context. Consequently, solutions for human predicaments are to be found, almost exclusively, within the self, leaving the social order conveniently unaffected. (p. 796)

Nightingale and Cromby (2001) emphasize the need for mainstream psychology to adopt critical psychology's view of humans being inextricably related to social, material, and historical contexts. Otherwise, therapy—even if it may serve some palliative function—reinforces and replicates an ideological view that supports individualistic explanations for suffering and disguises its political and economic causes.

Small (2005) uses a materialistic framework to critique *psychologism*. This is the transformation of social processes and conflicts into internal factors such as impulses, intentions, and cognitions which then become the target of intervention. Thus, much psychotherapy engages in the mystification of the actual cause of suffering by diverting attention from the prominent role of inequality and oppression. An important contribution of his argument is the role he assigns to embodiment in understanding the impact of the environment. He writes:

> The person exists as an embodied being in a material environment that is structured both physically and (more important for our purposes) socially. The principal dynamic of social structure is *power*, which is transmitted through *interest*…The most powerful influences that end up impinging upon the individual tend to be those furthest from him/her, i.e., economic, political and cultural powers, etc. These are mediated by lesser powers closer to the individual, ultimately via other individuals encountered in families, social groups, workplaces, etc. (p. 26)

Psychology's failure to assign significance to lack of material means for survival leads to a neglect of the destructive impacts of capitalism.

The Essential Societal Nature of Human Beings

From this we can derive the first principle from critical psychology essential to radical therapy. Holzkamp (Schraube & Osterkamp, 2013) critiques capitalism's depiction of the "worldless" person as it denies the essential social nature of human beings. Contrary to seeing greed and competitiveness as natural and thus inevitable, the most distinguishing character of human beings is their societal nature. The evolution of the human species would have been impossible without their ability to cooperate with others and organize themselves into mutual relationships to ensure their survival. Radical therapy must reject fragmented and alienated conceptions of human beings by recognizing that wholeness and integrity are essential to well-being (Gruba-McCallister, 2025). All of the diverse aspects of human beings and the ways in which they are intricately interwoven must be accorded respect. This relational perspective can be described in terms of a number of fundamental dialectical polarities in which the two sides are seen as inseparable. Examples include individual-collective, wholeness-alienation, and mind-body. A rigid, one-sided approach to these polarities leads to heightened states of alienation and imbalance and thus dis-ease. An open and accepting stance based on tolerance for ambiguity is necessary for well-being.

Existential thought provides a description of four fundamental spheres of existence to be included in a holistic approach. There is an inseparable relationship between persons and the world as in Heidegger's (1962) concept of being-in-the-world. The first three, proposed by Heidegger, include individuals' relationship to themselves (capacity for self-reflection), to other human beings (the social), and to the natural world (which includes the embodied nature of human existence). A fourth sphere proposed by van Deurzen (1997) includes humans' relationship with a higher or transcendent order (spirituality). Transpersonal psychology provides important insights into the significance of spirituality. The image of the human person across spiritual traditions condemns extreme individualism as a form of hubris and self-idolatry. It denies the universal interconnectedness of all beings that forms the basis of compassion. These traditions have also provided a system of beliefs and practices valuable for understanding and giving meaning to suffering. Existential and transpersonal theory see the roots of suffering in inevitable losses that threaten one's sense of wholeness and control. Existential anxiety is related to awareness of one's mortality and triggers uncertainty, insecurity, and fear. It can encourage individuals to live more authentically or lead to greater suffering if resisted. This is similar to the Buddhist (Rahula, 1974) analysis of suffering being rooted in attachment and the inherent transience of existence. Negotiating loss in ways that promote a greater degree of wholeness is a central task of radical therapy.

The Role of Power: Oppression vs. Well-Being

The second principle that guides radical therapy is the inescapable role of power in all aspects of life (Foucault, 1999[1975]). Power is exercised through discourse or a set of ideas that has culturally important meaning and shapes how we interpret events and behave accordingly. Power is not merely a personal attribute, but also relational in that social structures exert influence over individuals. Small (2005) sees power as the means of obtaining security or advantage. It takes three forms: biological, coercive, and ideological. Understanding the role of power highlights the imperative that radical therapy address the significant role of oppression in inflicting suffering (Gruba-McCallister, 2019, 2025). Power can be used to oppress or to resist oppression. Deutsch (2006) observes, "Oppression is the experience of repeated, widespread, systemic injustice" (p. 10). Such injustices are based in material and social processes. Friere (1970) states that oppression is a form of violence that dehumanizes its victims as well as its perpetrators.

Prilleltensky and Gonick (1996) provide a more detailed definition:

> ...*oppression entails a state of asymmetric power relations characterized by domination, subordination, and resistance, where the dominating persons or groups exercise their power by restricting access to material resources and by implanting in the subordinated persons or groups fear or self-deprecating views about themselves.*" (italics in the original, p. 130)

Political oppression refers to barriers to persons' ability to fulfill self-determination, access resources and opportunities, and engage in democratic participation. Psychological oppression is the internalization of a negative self-image and feeling undeserving of resources or participation in social affairs. It is based in affective, behavioral, cognitive, linguistic, and cultural mechanisms used to enforce political domination. Classifying suffering inflicted by oppression into categories of personal pathology is intended to disguise their ideological roots. This suffering is actually natural and expected reactions to adversity, trauma, and unhealthy physical and social environments (Jacobs & Cowen, 2009). Cudd (2006) describes oppression's two harms. The first is material, including damage to one's physical being or violence and economic impacts or being deprived of the resources needed for a decent life, such as food, housing, income and health care. These basic needs are granted primacy because satisfaction of higher needs depend on them being met. The second harm is psychological including feeling worthless, helplessness, pessimism, humiliation, guilt, anger, and depression. Helping victims experiencing these impacts and unveiling their ideological roots are essential to radical therapy (Gruba-McCallister, 2025).

Development as the Promotion of Flourishing

Another related guiding principle of radical therapy is the necessity that suffering be understood within a developmental framework. Dependence on others and on the adequacy of the environment are inherent to the societal nature of humans. Critical psychology links suffering to depriving persons the opportunity to exert control over the resources necessary to satisfy their needs. Such deprivation is the essential criterion for the need for social change. It is not just deprivation that inflicts suffering, but also denial of agency which constitutes an assault on one's very humanity. Schraube and Osterkamp (2013) describe these negative consequences:

> Human suffering or, generally, any injury, including anxiety, has the quality of being exposed to and dependent upon other-directed circumstances, dissociated from possibilities of controlling essential, long-term conditions, i.e., constraints on possibilities to act. Correspondingly, overcoming suffering and anxiety, and the human quality of satisfaction is not obtainable merely by actual satisfaction and protection, but only by achieving control over the resources of satisfaction—that is, the conditions upon which one's possibilities of living and developing depend. (pp. 20–21)

Thus, both the material and psychological harms of oppression must be removed to achieve justice.

Wilber (2000) asserts that development is a central framework for understanding optimal function. He provides a comprehensive review of theories that specify how development can be described across multiple lines such as cognitive, moral, ego, and spiritual. Many theories propose that development occurs as a series of stages that represent growth moving toward increasing degrees of complexity, inclusiveness, and wholeness. This does not negate earlier stages because they are subsumed by later ones. The stage that individuals occupy exerts a considerable influence on their world-view and the rules they employ to negotiate life (Wilber et al. 1986). For example, early stages are based on a more constricted form of consciousness centered on the self; whereas, at later stages there is expanded self-understanding that enables individuals to appreciate an increasing diversity of perspectives. As Wilber (2000) argues promoting well-being first requires therapists to understand where individuals are developmentally and discern what their growing edge might be. Work is then devoted to enabling individuals, where possible, to progress developmentally.

Viewed from a developmental perspective, justice is the creation of conditions that promote flourishing or the optimal fulfillment of human potential (Williams, 2008). This corrects an overly individualistic view that sees individuals as solely responsible for their growth. As Jacobs (1994) argues, humans' biological immaturity as a percentage of the total life span is greater than any other species. This leads to an unprecedented vulnerability to failures in the nurturant social environment, making environmental failure/oppression the greatest cause of impaired well-being. Rawls (1971) provides a powerful argument that inequity in the distribution of advantages and disadvantages, resources and opportunities, constitutes a profound form of injustice. He explains:

> The basic structure [of society] is the primary subject of justice because its effects are so profound and present from the start. The intuitive notion here is that this structure contains various social positions and that men born into different positions have different expectations of life determined, in part, by the political system as well as by economic and social circumstances. In this way the institutions of society favor certain starting places over others. These are especially deep inequalities. Not only are they pervasive, but they affect men's initial chances in life; yet they cannot possibly be justified by an appeal to merit or desert. It is these inequalities, presumably

inevitable in the basic structure of any society, to which principles of social justice must in the first instance apply. (p. 7)

What Rawls makes clear is the gross injustice of the mere accident of one's birth—something that no one has any control over—dictating an individual's life chances.

This has been described as *cumulative deprivation or disadvantage* related to a distributive view of justice that focuses on the detrimental consequences of inequity. This pertains to resources which are material and non-material things that can be used by people to achieve their goals or better enable them to. It also refers to opportunities or the range of options available to individuals to realistically exercise choice or achieve their goals. Access to resources and opportunities is disproportionately or unfairly distributed due to capitalism based on group membership, as illustrated in the problem of poverty. What this means is that inequality exerts a profound impact on individuals' development. As Barry (2005) states,

> Children start with, and grow up with, an enormous variety of different resources. On the basis of just a few facts about a child, such as its social class and its race or ethnicity, we can make a good prediction of where it will finish in the distribution of earnings, the likelihood that it will spend time in jail, and many other outcomes, good and bad. (p. 41)

He rightly concludes it is morally indefensible to believe a child is responsible for this gross injustice.

Radical therapy must remove the burden of blame and stigma from the victims of injustice by expanding their awareness of the deleterious impact of their life circumstances on their development (Gruba-McCallister, 2025). This is not to negate their agency, but to situate it within a broader context that elucidates the ways in which inequities have limited both their resources and opportunities. This work is supported by research on the social determinants of health (Marmot & Wilkinson, 2006) and the impacts of inequality (Wilkinson & Pickett, 2009, 2018). Social determinants are the conditions in which people are born, grow, live, work, and age. There is extensive evidence that factors such as neighborhood, availability of healthy food, education, employment, exposure to environmental toxins, and access to health care influence morbidity and mortality. Moreover, in their Whitehall studies Marmot and Wilkinson found what they described as the *social gradient of health*. The risk of illness and disease increases as occupational status decreases.

This led to an inquiry into how human beings biologically incorporate their lived experiences over the course of their lives. This relates again to the embodied nature of human beings. In *ecosocial theory* Krieger (2005) uses the concept of embodiment to explain the complex interaction between the biological and social. The concept of stress has been used to explain how inequality "gets under the skin." For Marmot and Wilkinson (2006), individuals occupying lower occupational status experience more demands placed on them combined with lower degrees of control. This disparity causes them greater stress. Additionally, lower occupational status is associated with having a poorer opinion of oneself. These findings were expanded on by Wilkinson and Pickett (2009, 2018) who examined the relationship between inequality across developed nations with multiple indicators of well-being. They found that inequality was associated with life expectancy, teenage pregnancy, drug use, imprisonment, obesity, educational attainment, and social mobility. Their later work focused more on the relationship between inequality and mental health. Confirming the importance of the social nature of human beings, inequality fosters competition and thus tears at the social fabric that binds individuals. Wilkinson and Pickett (2018) propose the idea of *status anxiety* in which individuals experience fear, shame, and low self-esteem based on seeing themselves as inferior to others. This then damages relationships with significant others, fosters greater consumption in an attempt to boost self-esteem, and increases the risk for depression. Given the long-term effects of the material and social environment, radical therapy cannot restrict its efforts to trying to remediate the damage inflicted on individuals. In some instances the damage cannot be undone. Instead, radical therapists strive to create conditions for the optimal development of all individuals by working actively with others to ameliorate or remove obstacles to development. The goal is establishing a more just society.

Fostering a Critical Stance

A fourth principle forming a foundation for radical therapy is the need to adopt a skeptical stance by interrogating and rigorously examining all assumptions and statements of authority and truth in order to elucidate their ideological underpinnings. As described in my previous chapter, the dominant ideology or hegemony (Gramsci, 1971) of capitalism infuses all levels of society and saturates the consciousness of its members. The powerful pose it as "commonsense" and thus as objective, irrefutable, universal, and unchangeable. It is internalized as a form of what Fromm (1941) called social character. This consists of prevailing beliefs, norms, and motivations that are for the most part unconscious but exert considerable influence over behavior. This is the means employed by the ruling class to ensure that subordinate classes conform and police their own actions. Social character can also be described as a form of internalized oppression. Various strategies are employed by the powerful (i.e., mystification) to legitimize and disguise hegemony by barring it from awareness and normalizing its negative consequences (Gruba-McCallister, 2019, 2025).

As Teo (2015) observes, human subjectivity is interwoven with social, cultural, and historical contexts. This understanding is lost when human beings are viewed solely at the individual level. Radical therapy utilizes an expanded perspective in order to ensure understanding of the role of context in those they work with to liberate. This is in keeping with the necessity of a truly holistic approach. Therapists must focus on the concrete and everyday circumstances of lives of those who experience injustice to uncover mutually with them how these conditions affect their thoughts and actions. This requires taking a reflective and critical stance that submits what is ordinarily taken for granted to rigorous examination and questioning. Those things about which questioning and doubt has been forbidden particularly need to be challenged and resisted. This means a radical reorientation that no longer asks, "What is wrong with me?' but instead "What is wrong with the world I live in?" Teo (2015) writes:

Critical psychologists intend to challenge society structures of injustice, ideologies, psychological control, and the adjustment of the individual. Instead of making individuals and groups into problems, CP attempts to work on problems that individuals and group encounter in a given society. (p. 246)

By focusing on the political and economic contexts they share, therapists and clients are able to identify what is asserted to be health and success under capitalism, deconstruct these notions, and expose the fallacies they contain.

As described above, the surest indication of how individuals are harmed by the dominant ideology is in the suffering it inflicts on them. Part of that suffering is a direct effect of the material and psychological harms it causes. However, another and more important source of suffering follows from the realization of individuals that the "bill of goods" sold to them by capitalism is false when its lies are exposed. They have become disillusioned and disappointed. That second suffering often is accompanied by fear rooted in a sense of having lost one's most cherished beliefs. This is accompanied by feeling deeply unsettled due to a loss of a sense of security and control. Existential and transpersonal theory provide valuable guidance to radical therapists in how to negotiate this second form of suffering. It has been described as the boundary experience (Jaspers, 1984), a time when one's world is abruptly turned upside down. A less extreme form of this is existential anxiety (Yalom, 1980) triggered by encounters with loss that remind us of our imminent mortality, accompanied by feelings of dissatisfaction, emptiness, alienation, and dread. Because of the threat posed by these unsettling experiences, individuals often try to avoid them and meet them with resistance. However, this proves to be self-defeating as individuals end up suffering because they are suffering, what I describe as self-created suffering (Gruba-McCallister & Levington, 1995). This is based on the illusion that one should be free of any suffering. This illusion is deeply tied to capitalist ideology which valorizes happiness as the goal of life (Ahmed, 2010; Davies, 2022). It is an instrumental part of what has been described as the *materialistic value orientation* (Kasser et al., 2004) that fuels over-consumption. Thus, when it is exposed as false, the opportunity is opened for critique and reflection.

This self-defeating pattern is described in spiritual literature as the *problem of the ego* (Huxley, 1944; Watts, 1966). It bears similarities to existential thought. The ego grows out of the powerful need for order and control. This is explained by Buddhism (Rahula, 1974) which attributes suffering to desire or the tendency for human beings to form attachments to things or persons seen as vital to their well-being. It is seen as a way of exercising control over the impermanence of life and so serves as a buffer against pain and death. However, this leads to a vicious cycle due to the inherently transient nature of life. That is, all attachments are eventually subject to loss leading to disappointment and suffering. The more tightly we hang on to our attachments and more vigorously oppose their loss, the more we suffer. The ego itself can be seen as the sum total of one's attachments or identifications. Similar to Fromm's (1941) notion of social character, Watts (1966) observes that the ego is largely a social creation and evidence of how vulnerable human beings are to the power of the social environment. The illusions that make up the ego are the product of social conditioning and support the status quo. An excellent example is how advertising is used to create a sense of emptiness and insecurity to fuel over-consumption and greed (Cushman, 1990).

Another adverse consequence of capitalism has been a rise in narcissism (Gruba-McCallister, 2007, 2025; Lasch, 1979). Fromm (1964) describes this as a malignant form of narcissism focused on having, selfishness, and greed. Such individuals possess an irrational and excessive degree of self-love and egocentricity, accompanied by a lack of empathy for others. The most powerful attachment of the ego is itself. The ego becomes an idol or a false god. Fromm (1964) writes, "The fight against idolatry…is at the same time a fight against narcissism. In idolatry one partial faculty of man is absolutized and made into an idol. Man then worships himself in alienated form" (p. 89). What this means is that loss of the ego represents a threat to one's very being.

This has been correctly seen as a spiritual problem by writers like Tillich (1957). For example, Tillich asserts that human beings have a deep spiritual need for an *ultimate concern* the object of which is sacred or holy. An ultimate concern demands total surrender and sacrifice of all other concerns and in response integrates and unifies all facets of human beings and thus provides wholeness or healing. However, the risk involved in committing all to an ultimate concern is always accompanied by doubt and fear. Thus, to answer their longing or fill their emptiness, many people instead pursue *preliminary concerns* for which they are willing to sacrifice everything, but are left disappointed. In other words, the very means they use to decrease their suffering actually increases it. Capitalism entices individuals with a dazzling array of such false promises to undermine resistance to its claims.

Existential and transpersonal psychology both enable radical therapy to employ a holistic approach essential to fully understanding how and why individuals suffer from capitalist ideology. In light of this, traditional methods of assessment that suffer from individualist bias must be abandoned. In place of it a truly integrative method must be employed that incorporates individual and collective factors that affect individuals at both an internal and external level (see Marquis, 2008, for an example) and that assesses personal, social, and spiritual sources of suffering (Gruba-McCallister, 2025). These theories make another valuable contribution. As described above, there are two forms of suffering that radical therapy must address. One is suffering inherent to the human condition and therefore unavoidable. The other is suffering that is attributable to human actions and thus is avoidable. These two forms of suffering, while distinct, are also inextricably linked because one of the greatest causes of avoidable suffering is human beings resisting and denying inevitable suffering (Gruba-McCallister, 2019). A central task of radical therapy is assisting clients in correctly distinguishing between these forms of suffering and adopting approaches to them that do not prove to be self-defeating. Suffering can be transformative and promote greater wholeness.

Summary: The Goal is Liberation

The final principle central to radical therapy is acknowledging that the status quo is not fixed and can be challenged. To be radical is to be committed to the emancipatory potential of knowledge wedded with action. Teo (1998) writes:

It is difficult to deny the existence of exploitation, humiliation, degradation and injustice in the world. Psychology can either ignore or address these facts. If psychology chooses to address itself to these problems, then it would seem necessary to develop a *psychological theory* of liberation whereby the term 'psychological' refers to the subject's conceptual-empirical liberating possibilities with regard to power, and whereby an emancipated subjectivity refers to a subjectivity that is conscious of these possibilities. (p. 536)

On an individual level, this means radical therapists collaborate mutually with clients to become increasingly politically aware and active. By working out political attitudes and engagements in order to come to terms with their suffering, individuals are better able to achieve healing through true liberation. Simultaneously, they see the need to be an activist and so join others to throw off the chains of injustice (Samuels, 2015). When the twin values of the radical therapist, compassion and justice, are adopted by others, the possibility of profound individual and collective transformation can be truly realized.

References

Ahmed, S. (2010). *The promise of happiness*. Duke University Press.
Barry, B. (2005). *Why social justice matters*. Polity Press.
Boggs, C. (2015). The medicalized society. *Critical Sociology, 4*(3), 517–535.
Chetty, R., Grusky, D., Hell, M., Hendren, N., Manduka, R., & Narang, J. (2017). The fading American dream: Trends in absolute income mobility since 1940. *Science, 356*, 398–406.
Cudd, A. (2006). *Analyzing oppression*. Oxford University Press.
Cushman, P. (1990). Why the self is empty: Toward a historically situated psychology. *American Psychologist, 45*(5), 599–611.
Davies, J. (2022). *Sedated: How modern capitalism created our mental health crisis*. Atlantic Books.
Deutsch, M. (2006). A framework for thinking about oppression and its change. *Social Justice Research, 19*(1), 7–41.
Esposito, L., & Perez, F. M. (2014). Neoliberalism and the commodification of mental health. *Humanity & Society, 38*(4), 414–442.

Foucault, M. (1999 [1975]). *Discipline and punishment: The birth of the prison* (A. Sheridan, Trans.). Vintage/Random House.
Friere, P. (1970). *Pedagogy of the oppressed*. Herder and Herder.
Fromm, E. (1941). *Escape from freedom*. Henry Holt.
Fromm, E. (1964). *The heart of man: Its genius for good and evil*. Harper & Row.
Gramsci, A. (1971). *Selections from the prison notebooks* (Q. Hoare & G. Nowell Smith, Trans.). International Publishers.
Gruba-McCallister, F. P. (2007). Narcissism and the empty self: To have or to be. *The Journal of Individual Psychology, 63*(2), 182–192.
Gruba-McCallister, F. P. (2019). *Embracing disillusionment: Achieving liberation through the demystification of suffering*. University Professors Press.
Gruba-McCallister, F. P. (2025). *Radical healing: No wellness without justice*. University Professors Press.
Gruba-McCallister, F. P., & Levington, C. (1995). Suffering and transcendence in human experience. *Review of Existential Psychology and Psychiatry, 22*, 99–115.
Heidegger, M. (1962). *Being and time* (J. Macquarrie & E. Robinson, Trans.). Harper & Row.
Huxley, A. (1944). *The perennial philosophy*. Harper.
Jacobs, D. H. (1994). Environmental failure-oppression is the only cause of psychopathology. *Journal of Mind and Behavior, 15*(1–2), 1–18.
Jacobs, D. H., & Cowen, D. (2009). Does "psychological dysfunction" mean anything? A critical essay on pathology versus agency. *Journal of Humanistic Psychology, 50*(3), 312–334.
Jaspers, K. (1984). *General psychopathology* (J. Hoenig & M. Hamilton, Trans.). University of Chicago Press.
Kasser, T., Ryan, R. M., Couchman, C. E., & Sheldon, K. M. (2004). Materialistic values: Their causes and consequences. In T. Kasser & A. D. Kanner (Eds.), *Psychology and consumer culture: The struggle for a good life in materialistic world* (pp. 11–28). American Psychological Association.
Krieger, N. (2005). *Ed (Embodying inequality: Epidemiologic perspectives)*. Baywood Publishing Company, Inc.
Lasch, C. (1979). *The culture of narcissism: American life in an age of diminishing expectations*. Warner Books Inc..
Marmot, M., & Wilkinson, R. G. (Eds.). (2006). *Social determinants of health* (2nd ed.). Oxford University Press.
Marquis, A. (2008). *The integral intake: A guide to comprehensive idiographic assessment in integral psychotherapy*. Routledge.

Nightingale, D. J., & Cromby, J. (2001). Critical psychology and the ideology of individualism. *Journal of critical psychology, Counseling and Psychotherapy, 1*(2), 117–128.
Prilleltensky, I. (1989). Psychology and the status quo. *American Psychologist, 44*, 795–802.
Prilleltensky, I., & Gonick, L. (1996). Politics change, oppression remains: On the psychology and politics of oppression. *Political Psychology, 17*, 127–147.
Putnam, R. (2000). *Bowling alone: The collapse and revival of American community*. Simon & Schuster.
Rahula, W. (1974). *What the Buddha taught*. Grove Press.
Rawls, J. (1971). *A theory of justice*. The Belknap Press of Harvard University Press.
Ryan, W. (1971). *Blaming the victim*. Pantheon Books.
Samuels, A. (2015). Everything you always wanted to know about therapy (but were afraid to ask): Fragments of a critical psychotherapy. In D. Loewenthal (Ed.), *Critical psychotherapy, psychoanalysis and counselling: Implications for Practice* (pp. 159–174). Palgrave Macmillan.
Sandel, M. J. (2021). *Tyranny of merit: Can we find the common good?* Picador Press.
Schraube, E., & Osterkamp, U. (2013). *Psychology from the standpoint of the subject: Selected writings of Klaus Holzkamp*. Palgrave Macmillan.
Small, D. (2005). *Power, interest and psychology: Elements of a social materialist understanding of distress*. PCCS Books.
Teo, T. (1998). Prolegomenon to a contemporary psychology of liberation. *Theory & Psychology, 8*(4), 527–547.
Teo, T. (2015). Critical psychology: A geography of intellectual engagement and resistance. *American Psychologist, 70*(3), 243–254.
Tillich, P. (1957). *The dynamics of faith*. Harper & Row.
van Deurzen, E. (1997). *Everyday mysteries: Existential dimensions of psychotherapy*. Routledge.
Watts, A. W. (1966). *The book: On the taboo against knowing who you are*. Collier Books.
Wilber, K. (2000). *Integral psychology: Consciousness, spirit, psychology, therapy*. Shambhala Press.
Wilber, K., Engler, J., & Brown, D. P. (1986). *Transformations of consciousness: Conventional and contemplative perspectives on development*. Shambala Press.
Wilkinson, R., & Pickett, K. (2009). *The spirit level: Why greater equality makes societies stronger*. Bloomsbury Press.

Wilkinson, R., & Pickett, K. (2018). *The inner level: How more equal societies reduce stress, restore sanity, and improve everyone's well-being.* Penguin Press.

Williams, C. R. (2008). Compassion, suffering and the self: A moral psychology of social justice. *Current Sociology, 56*(5), 5–24.

Yalom, I. D. (1980). *Existential psychotherapy.* Basic Books.

7

Transformative Therapies for Holistic Liberation

Sebastienne Grant

Introduction

One of the most fundamental aspects of humanity is our relationship with and responses to suffering. We all want to suffer less and have more joy and happiness. Understanding the conditions of suffering, including its sources, manifestations, and alleviations, is essential not only in reducing individual suffering but also in creating societies that support the flourishing of all.

Much human activity, including culture, belief systems, scientific inquiry, etc., has developed around attempts to address suffering in some capacity. Spiritual and religious traditions have historically been important go-to sources of wisdom and practices for dealing with suffering. Recognizing the impacts of societal injustice and oppression in human

S. Grant (✉)
Department of Research Psychology, California Institute of Integral Studies, San Francisco, CA, USA
e-mail: sgrant@ciis.edu

suffering, numerous spiritual and religious leaders have become deeply involved in social justice and liberation movements. In modern Western societies, however, psychology has increasingly become the go-to source for addressing much of our suffering (Loy, 2015). Unfortunately, psychology has been slow to recognize and address the role of societal factors in suffering, often supporting the status quo and contributing to unjust and oppressive conditions (Cushman, 1996; Loy, 2015; Morris et al., 2020; Prilleltensky, 1990; Sugarman, 2015).

Some causes of suffering, such as physical pain or loss of a loved one, are often unavoidable. However, much of the suffering we endure is human-caused and avoidable. Oppression, and its multitude of consequences, has been identified again and again as one of the greatest sources of avoidable suffering (Gruba-McCallister, 2019; Rosado, 2007; Watkins & Shulman, 2008). Relatedly, environmental degradation and climate change have become a major sources of material and psychological suffering globally (Clayton, 2020). Despite this, mainstream psychological theories and practices rarely give serious consideration to these factors in their analyses and treatment of suffering. Instead, psychology continues to concern itself almost exclusively with the individual, regarding societal and environmental issues as outside of its purview (Morris et al., 2020; Prilleltensky, 1990; Sugarman, 2015).

Rather than identifying patterns of struggle as symptoms of an unhealthy society, helping others understand these underlying conditions of their suffering, and advocating for societal change that would better support well-being, psychology has long embraced the approach of working to adjust the individual to existing social structures as a means of reducing tension and discomfort (Fromm, 1955; Sugarman, 2015). While this approach may provide short-term alleviation of symptoms for some, it fails to provide meaningful healing and ultimately enables and contributes to societal and environmental harms.

There are, of course, many disciplines and movements working to support social and environmental change. However, most of the focus is on the macro- and meso-level intervention—changing laws and policies, fighting for economic justice, organizing movements to pressure systemic action, etc. And while Pyles (2018) notes that many of these transformative social practices also seek transformation at the individual level, they take a top-down approach (change the systems to change the individuals). But intervention can equally occur at the micro-level, the level of individual. Psychology is well-positioned to put its otherwise often problematic focus on the individual to effective use supporting this kind of bottom-up transformative change. The present work is a call for psychologists, and therapists in particular, to commit to exclusively engaging in and utilizing practices that support *both individual and societal wellbeing* and to reject the use of any practices that fail to do so.

The Role of Psychology in Modern Dis-Ease: Oppression, Colonialism, and Capitalism

Systemic oppression is based on the "fundamental falsehood that people have a right to dominate others" (Pyles, 2018, p. 5). This falsehood not only shapes our systems and institutions, but is internalized to shape to our perceptions, beliefs, values, behaviors, identities, and relationships. Through this largely unconscious internalization, each of us participates in the continuation of oppressive systems, often taking on both roles of oppressor and oppressed in different areas of our lives, and suffering in the grips of both (Pyles, 2018; Rosado, 2007; Watkins & Shulman, 2008).

While many factors have contributed to oppressive ideologies and actions throughout history, current factors in Western societies, including the United States, are heavily entangled with histories of colonialism and the ensuing rise of global capitalism, neoliberalism, and consumer culture (Gruba-McCallister, 2019; Loy, 2015; Morris et al., 2020; Watkins & Shulman, 2008). This milieu has led to increasing individualism, competition, greed, internalized superiority/inferiority, (Morris et al., 2020; Watkins & Shulman, 2008), and decreasing connection, cooperation, care, and compassion (Loy, 2015; Morris et al., 2020; Trzeciak & Mazzarelli, 2019), resulting in both greater psychological and societal dis-ease.

Liberatory theories and practices stress the necessity of transformation at both systemic and individual levels. Without systemic change, access to the resources of surviving, healing, and thriving remain limited, and harm continues to compound. Without individual change and healing, however, we remain stuck in reproducing the harms of oppression (within ourselves and towards others) even when systems open space for new ways of being (Rosado, 2007).

As stated earlier, psychology is particularly well-situated to support liberation from the "bottom up," focusing on individual healing and transformation, while also using observed patterns of suffering to advocate for greater societal change. Unfortunately, psychology has historically failed to assume this role. Instead, it has contributed to oppressive systems by supporting and protecting the status quo through individualizing suffering and wellness, basing norms and ideals on those with the most power and privilege (and pathologizing deviations), fueling hyper-individualism and comparative/superiority based self-esteem, promoting self-deception and distraction as a means of coping, overly emphasizing hedonic and material approaches to happiness, and remaining silent on or pathologizing oppression-related suffering and resistance (Gruba-McCallister, 2019; Mullan, 2023; Rosado, 2007; Watkins & Shulman, 2008)

Individualism and Other Disconnections from the Whole

Colonialism and capitalism have both been bolstered by reductionistic and dualistic narratives that have served to obscure interconnectivity and disconnect parts from the whole. As Mullan (2023), states, "[c]olonialism thrives on isolation, denial, confusion, historical and interpersonal forgetfulness, and separation" (p. 40). Some of these disconnections include the individual and community/society, the mind and body/heart/spirit, the masculine and feminine, the "natural" and "unnatural," personal time and historical time, and the human and non-human.

Mainstream psychology, having absorbed hegemonic ideologies, has contributed to these false and harmful disconnections, often privileging those that serve the status quo. Psychology has ignored and obscured societal and environmental impacts on suffering and well-being; while also neglecting to consider or take responsibility for how its powerful theories and practices, and the subjectivities they help construct, further contribute to oppressive and unsustainable conditions (Morris et al., 2020). This fragmentation, echoed in other social sciences like sociology, political science, and economics, has led to a widening gap between fields that work to understand and improve societal functioning (including progressive aims like social justice and equity) and those that focus on individual health and well-being (Morris et al., 2020). These fields often then unwittingly work against one another, presenting one of our greatest obstacles to transformative change (Gruba-McCallister, 2019).

In order to truly promote equitable and holistic well-being, people working in all sectors dealing with human experience must acknowledge and understand the interconnectivity of the personal, societal, and environmental, and *commit to rejecting* any practice or approach that fails to facilitate well-being *at all levels* (Morris et al., 2020).

Neoliberal Subjectivities and the Empty Self

Many have argued that the modern "neoliberal subject"—characterized by excessive individualism, narcissism, and greed—is strongly antagonistic to individual well-being and incompatible with socially just societies (Cushman, 1996; Gruba-McCallister, 2007; Morris et al., 2020; Sugarman, 2015). This subjectivity construction contributes to the experience of the "empty self," a pervasive sense of lack or emptiness at the core of one's being. The empty self is associated with feelings of alienation, lack of identity and meaning, and a constant need for external validation and fulfillment, all of which contribute to psychological struggles, such as depression and anxiety, while also fueling excessive consumerism and social and environmental injustice.

While emptiness has long been identified as source of human struggle by theologians, philosophers, and psychologists (Loy, 2000), it seems particularly prevalent and problematic in modern capitalist societies, where the loss of community, cultural connections, and systems of meaning-making have led individuals to seek self-worth and meaning through consumerism, materialism, and superiority over others. These pursuits exacerbate feelings of emptiness by taking us further away from effective sources of meaning, connection, and value, creating a cycle of grasping that fails to provide genuine fulfillment (Cushman, 1990; Gruba-McCallister, 2007; Morris et al., 2020). At larger levels, neoliberal subjectivities and the empty self not only negatively impact societal systems, but also social justice movements, which are inevitably infused with ego-based approaches to action and change, including the harmful and often ineffective use of shame and blame tactics (Morris et al., 2020).

Through its absorption of capitalist and consumerist ideologies and its prominent cultural role as the go-to source of the alleviation of suffering, psychology has played a significant role in the creation and reproduction of neoliberal subjectivities and the empty self. While therapeutic practices promise to treat the symptoms of emptiness, they often do so by reinforcing the problematic individualistic and self-serving attitudes that give rise to the empty self in the first place. Instead, therapeutic approaches could focus on providing an antidote to the empty self through intentionally fostering more interconnected and compassionate identities (Morris et al., 2020).

Misidentification of Suffering

Pain and suffering are unpleasant, and it's only natural that we seek to avoid them when we can. Yet they are also inevitable aspects of the human experience and often serve as important indicators that something harmful is occurring. Capitalism and consumerism—and the scientific, technological, and cultural developments they produce—have specialized in catering to both our desires and aversions, offering an abundance of quick-fixes to anesthetize our pain and increase opportunities for hedonic pleasures (Grant, 2017). Between this and the pressures of insurance companies to treat people in as few sessions as possible, psychology has also produced a plethora of "therapeutic" approaches targeting the immediate experience of suffering without addressing its underlying conditions. This approach to suffering has led to the pathologization of valuable and potentially adaptive reactions—such as grief, depression, and anxiety—to societal and environmental harms (Clayton, 2020; Gruba-McCallister, 2019).

Additionally, psychological theories of struggle—and the diagnoses and treatment approaches they have produced—reflect "the social amnesia so characteristic of the individualistic paradigm common to capitalist societies" (Watkins & Shulman, 2008, p. 54). These theories, reflecting dominant cultural fixations such ego-based self-esteem and success, "development" (towards dominant ideals), individuation and independence, and unrealistic states of constant hedonic happiness, add to rates of misdiagnosis and ineffective therapy. Our instinctual reactions against harm are invalidated, misidentified, and pathologized, while oppression and injustice benefit from this misdirection away from the underlying problems (Gruba-McCallister, 2019; Watkins & Shulman, 2008).

To be fair, psychology is in a challenging position. People often seek out help when they are in crisis, when their suffering is so great that it is impairing their ability to function. This state is not only unpleasant—and at times unbearable—but also not conducive to effectively participating in societal change. Psychology has an important role to play in helping us manage distress, but has an equally important obligation to reject methods for doing so that contribute to ongoing systems of harm (Clayton, 2020).

Fortunately, there are many approaches to individual healing that fit this obligation, including numerous theories and practices emerging out liberation, decolonial, Indigenous, peace, somatic, transpersonal, eco, and (some) depth psychologies (Morris et al., 2020; Watkins & Shulman, 2008). I refer to these approaches here collectively as "transformative psychologies" to denote their shared commitments to going beyond the reduction of immediate discomfort and facilitate radical multi-level healing and transformation.

Transformative Psychologies: Aims and Approaches

In addition to their commitment to radical transformation and liberation from oppression, transformative psychologies share the awareness that transformation takes more than the mere recognition of a problem and desire to change. There is a need for deep knowledge and *understanding* of the conditions of suffering, authentic healing of generational harm at individual and community levels and the capacity to move from "reaction" to "response" (Rosado, 2007) in order to enable new ways of being. Below is a compilation of necessary elements in healing and transformation that could be incorporated into therapeutic approaches to reduce individual suffering, while simultaneously supporting conditions for social and environmental well-being. This list is in no way exhaustive, but meant as a starting point for considering what commitments to transformative practices might entail. They are categorized based on their aims.

Critical Consciousness and Action

One of the first tasks of transformative and liberatory therapeutic approaches should be to support the development of conscientization, or critical consciousness (Freire & Macedo, 2006; Prilleltensky, 1990; Rosado, 2007; Watkins & Shulman, 2008), "the process whereby people attain an insightful awareness of the socio-economic, political, and cultural circumstances which affect their lives, as well as their potential capacity to transform that social reality" (Prilleltensky, 1990, p. 311). This process involves challenging hegemonic beliefs and "the notion that this social order is the best possible one" (Prilleltensky, 1990, p. 313). Therapists can invite those they work with into explorations of their cultural and familial histories, making note of the potential influences of oppression and generational traumas that may have shaped their ancestors', and their ways of being in the world (Mullan, 2023). They may look for strengths that have emerged through these experiences, and challenges they'd like to heal from.

The process of conscientization can be hard for many who may encounter atrocities in their past and undergo a kind of ontological and existential trauma as they awaken to previously obscured systems of oppression and injustice. Therapists must be mindful to provide support in the form of compassionate witnessing, guidance in narrative framing, somatic and depth work, and more to prevent additional harm and effectively use critical consciousness as a tool for healing and transformation. One of the most crucial aspects of this work to avoid overwhelm and despair, according to Rosado (2007), is moving from consciousness alone to "consciousness-in-action." This process, related to the concept of healing justice (*What Is Healing Justice?*, n.d.), healing justice is intentionally engaged as people confront oppression for the purpose of moving toward integral well-being "[through which] internalized oppression—both superiority and inferiority—is gradually transformed, healing and regenerating the self-system while collectively co-creating a culture of liberation to uphold a new self" (Rosado, 2007, pp. 102–103).

Therapists can support this work through inviting exploration into how increasing critical consciousness can be put in service of healing and transformation, for the self and others. This might include getting involved in community work, advocacy, or activism, or it might focus more on developing one's skills in responding (rather than reacting) differently with their families. The point isn't to prescribe any particular action, but rather to open space for consideration of how individuals can contribute to change in their own realm of influence. Those already engaged in this work, as well as those just beginning, might also benefit from support and explorations around how to do so sustainably in order to avoid burnout. This is discussed further in the section on Transformative Service and Action.

Compassion, Interconnectivity, and Whole Selves

Contemplative traditions have long recognized a misunderstanding of the self as separate and bounded to be a major source of human suffering. This view of the self contributes to the empty self through feelings of vulnerability, isolation, alienation, greed, narcissism, and more as we seek to fill and bolster the false self. This fundamental misunderstanding of the self is implicated in what Buddhist theory calls the "three poisons": ignorance (of our true interconnected nature), desire/greed/attachment, and aversion/hate (Loy, 2015; Pyles, 2018). These three poisons are thought to be at the root of virtually all human-created suffering. If these poisons aren't addressed and transformed (primarily through a deep understanding of interconnectivity and the cultivation of compassion), hope of truly transformative change at either individual or social levels remains low (Loy, 2015). Emerging research on "quieting the ego," reducing attention on the separate self and shifting awareness towards our interconnected nature, and on the benefits of compassion practices to support this process, is adding empirical support to this ancient wisdom (Grant, 2018; Morris et al., 2020; Wayment & Bauer, 2008).

Compassion refers to "the emotional response to another's pain or suffering, involving an authentic desire to help" (Trzeciak & Mazzarelli, 2019, p. xii). Differing from empathy, which can cause distress, burnout, and avoidance, compassion—*feeling for* another—includes the recognition that my experience is distinct from yours and is associated with decreased burnout and distress, increased approach motivation, and heightened activity in pleasure and reward centers in the brain (Ricard, 2016; Trzeciak & Mazzarelli, 2019). The therapeutic benefits of practicing and developing compassion for the self and others are rapidly gaining recognition within psychology, with research showing significant decreases in anxiety and depression and increases in joy, meaning, and feelings of connection (Pinos-Pey, 2017; Ricard, 2016; Trzeciak & Mazzarelli, 2019). Compassion also attunes us to the suffering and well-being of others and motivates pro-social and pro-environmental action, making it a powerhouse for transformative psychologies.

Interconnectivity, a close companion of compassion, refers to the deep interconnectedness and interdependence of all things. Through the recognition of interconnectivity, we come to understand that our suffering and our well-being are inseparable from the suffering and well-being of others and the planet, and that the liberation of one is tied to the liberation of all (Dorje, 2017). This awareness can support both personal healing—through easing shame and guilt and increasing our understanding of our impact on others—as well as social and environmental action. Compassion and interconnectivity work together to reconstruct and transform the empty self by reducing our acquired hyper-focus on the individual self and focusing more of our attention outward. They help us feel more connected and less alone and vulnerable, give us a sense of purpose and meaning, and remind us that we (and others) are a valuable part of a larger whole.

Opening to Grief and Hope

> We need a psychology that breaks our hearts, because only that kind of psychology could awaken us to our entanglements in strategies of dissociations, to the despairs of trauma, to grief from mourning and to potential joy in restoration and healing. Only such a psychology could move us from fatalism that unconsciously yields to the status quo, to tentative hope for gradual transformation. (Watkins & Shulman, p. 31)

As discussed earlier, mainstream psychology often pathologizes adaptive and informative suffering and offers quick-fix solutions or inaccurate interpretations that enable the continuation of the underlying societal and environmental harms (Clayton, 2020; Gruba-McCallister, 2019). Obscuring or denying suffering is a mechanism of oppression, and "[t]his abolition of awareness is itself an act of violence committed against a person's experience" (Gruba-McCallister, 2019, p. 2). Acknowledging and validating oppression-related suffering, and expanding our capacity to sit with, listen to, and honor our grief are essential in the process of individual and societal healing. Through this work, we can learn to more accurately identify the underlying sources of our suffering and move towards reframing, integration, and healing. We can then envision and participate in truly transformative change to address the root causes of this suffering for ourselves and others.

Acknowledging our suffering and grief is also important for the equally crucial task of cultivating joy and hope for healing and change. While grief is a necessary and healthful response to harm and loss, despair shuts down healing and action. Therapists can play a role in supporting the attunement to and cultivation of love, gratitude, physical and emotional pleasure, and hopeful visions for the future. This must be done *alongside* grief-work, however, in order to avoid lapsing back into the tendency in mainstream therapeutic approaches to use these positive experiences as a kind of psychological-bypassing.

Transformative Approaches

When practiced within a commitment to transformative therapies, each of the approaches outlined below meet the criteria for providing effective individual healing while also supporting social and environmental healing and well-being. Again, this list is in no way exhaustive (either in approaches or descriptions), but is meant to provide examples for larger ongoing conversations and explorations. To use these approaches to the greatest benefit, therapists and healers should seek further education, understanding, and practice of techniques, and engage in their own healing and growth work to reduce the risk of inadvertently perpetuating harmful ideologies and practices.

Depth Psychologies

Depth psychologies, including psychoanalytic approaches, can provide valuable frameworks for supporting individual healing as well as social justice and liberation efforts (Watkins & Shulman, 2008). These approaches argue that particularly painful or challenging experiences are often repressed. These repressed experiences, along with things like biases and beliefs absorbed through culture and language, reside in the unconscious where they are difficult to access for understanding and healing. Depth psychologies work to decode content and communication from the unconscious, often in the form of "symptomatic" individual and collective behaviors. By exploring these symptoms in a therapeutic context, depth psychologies can help individuals and communities recognize how systemic oppression and unhealthy ideologies manifest in psychological and social structures (Watkins & Shulman, 2008). This work can support self-reflection, (self)compassion, and critical consciousness. It can also support the recognition of harm and trauma, decrease feelings of shame and personal failings, and allow opportunities for grief and healing.

Decolonial Trauma-Informed Work

Decolonial trauma-informed therapies are crucial for transformative healing (Mullan, 2023; Watkins & Shulman, 2008). These approaches recognize the historical and systemic roots of trauma and oppression and their roles in continued human suffering. While much of this work focuses on consciousness raising and healing within historically oppressed populations, decolonial approaches also recognize that everyone living within oppressive systems occupies roles of both oppressed and oppressor and that both cause harm and trauma within the individual and beyond (Mullan, 2023; Rosado, 2007; Watkins & Shulman, 2008). Echoing a depth psychology approach, "symptoms" are recognized as often being the result of generational trauma, containing both strengths that have supported survival as well as maladaptive elements that contribute to personal, interpersonal, and societal harm. Practices place importance on promoting safety, empowerment, and healing through culturally sensitive and inclusive approachs that validate experiences and support resilience. These approaches work to raise critical consciousness and address the need for taking suffering seriously, work with grief, and work towards more hopeful futures for all.

Mindfulness and Compassion

Mindfulness and compassion-based practices offer powerful tools in individual and societal healing and well-being. Mindfulness practices help individuals to develop a deep awareness of their thoughts, emotions, and behaviors and facilitate the recognition of personal biases and conditioning. This supports the important work of moving from reaction to response (Rosado, 2007) by creating a space of awareness that allows for more agency and intentionality in responding to internal and external stimuli. Compassion-based therapies harness the incredible power of compassion (discussed earlier) to ease experiences of depression and anxiety, while nurturing pro-social and pro-environmental action. Mindfulness and compassion practices have also been shown to re-wire the brain (through neuroplasticity), producing long-lasting positive changes relatively short amounts of time (Pyles, 2018; Trzeciak & Mazzarelli, 2019). Therapists can guide those they work with through practices such as meditation, mindful self-compassion, and loving-kindness, or encourage them to practice individually or in other group settings. Compassion practices also provide a powerful antidote to burnout (Trzeciak & Mazzarelli, 2019), making them a great tool for supporting therapists in the important work of supporting others.

Somatic Work

Johnson (2023) argues that the disconnection between mind and body so pervasive in Western societies is not just an outcome of colonial and oppressive systems, but a tool used by these systems to enable their continuation. This amounts to what Johnson calls "percepticide," "the mechanism through which oppressive social forces require us to deny the truth of our senses in the face of chronic or pervasive threat" (Johnson, 2023, p. 49). As we lose the ability to *feel*, this disconnection prevents the identification of harm within to self and others. Our bodies also communicate internalized biases and habits that we may not be aware of. Increasing somatic capacity and literacy can help us expand our ability to experience, hold, and work with difficult (as well as pleasurable) feelings and to recognize the ways that our own and other bodies reproduce and/or resist oppressive systems (Johnson, 2023). Therapists can use practices such as somatic awareness, mindful movement, breathwork, and touch, as well as explorations into the stories our bodies hold and tell, to cultivate greater somatic capacity and literacy.

Service and Social Action

Closely related to compassion, service and social action are powerful sources of individual and societal healing and well-being. Engaging in service and volunteer work is correlated with higher rates of multidimensional well-being, including eudaimonic and social wellbeing (Son & Wilson, 2012; Trzeciak & Mazzarelli, 2019). Likewise, participating in social action to address systemic injustices and support transformative change contributes to a sense of agency and empowerment crucial for healing from personal trauma and oppression (Mullan, 2023). Service can facilitate transcendent experiences (see below), which work to increase feelings of interconnectivity and meaning and reduce the symptoms and consequences of the empty self (Deikman, 2000). Therapists can encourage those they work with to get involved (or continue their involvement) with volunteering, advocacy, community organizing, and activism aimed at challenging and transforming oppressive structures in ways that feel sustainable and nourishing. Through service and social action, individuals can also build community and social support networks and develop greater feelings of self-efficacy which may reduce depression and anxiety (Clayton, 2020).

Transcendent Experiences

Transcendent experiences vary in nature and take on different meanings in diverse cultural and personal contexts. However, they typically involve moments of profound connection with something larger than oneself. These experiences may occur spontaneously, or be facilitated by intentional practices, referred to as "technologies of the sacred" by Stanislav Grof (2008). Techniques include prayer, contemplation, and meditation; participation in religious and spiritual practice; experiences involving awe and connections to nature; practices of compassion and altruism; use of entheogenic (psychedelic) substance; and more. By transcending the narrow confines of the individual ego, people often experience intense feelings of joy, meaning, and interconnectivity—all of which serve to heal the empty self (Grant, 2018; Loy, 2000; Morris et al., 2020). Such experiences also foster empathy, compassion, and a deeper understanding of and concern for social and environmental injustices. Through transcendent experiences, individuals can expand their perspectives and contribute meaningfully to creating a more compassionate and equitable world.

Community/Group/Peer Work

Transformative healing approaches incorporating community, peer, and group work provide valuable opportunities for individuals to share experiences, build solidarity, and receive support from others who can offer lived understanding. Sharing struggles in a group setting with peers can help individuals realize that these are part of shared patterns of struggle that affect others, aiding in the development of critical consciousness and easing feelings of personal shame and failure (Watkins & Shulman, 2008). People may feel safer and more empowered to explore and address personal and generational traumas in a group of peers than they would with a therapist alone (Mullan, 2023; Watkins & Shulman, 2008). When group work is done in a therapeutic context (with or without an official therapist present), this work can also support the development of relational and listening skills, compassion, perspective taking, allyship, and collaboration. Therapists wanting to support transformative change can offer group sessions incorporating some of the above suggestions, and/or can encourage those they work with to seek out external opportunities for collaborative healing.

Concluding Thoughts

As agents of transformation, we must ask ourselves "[does our work] lead all of society's members towards greater levels of well-being; does it foster the ongoing development of individuals, families, groups, communities, organizations, institutions, nations, and ultimately humanity?" (Rosado, 2007, p. 57).

Throughout this chapter I have argued that psychology has historically supported oppressive and unsustainable social and environmental systems, reinforcing the status quo and obscuring the systemic sources of suffering. I have further called for psychologists and therapeutic practitioners to commit to exclusively engaging in and utilizing theories and practices that support both individual and societal well-being and to reject any approaches that fail to do either. Finally, I provided some examples of aims and approaches characterizing a transformative psychology. I want to acknowledge that many others are already engaged in this kind of transformative work, contributing much needed research, theory, and practices, particularly within critical, liberation, Indigenous, decolonial, community, peace, transpersonal, and eco psychology traditions. I encourage readers to seek out as much of this work as they can, starting with some of the sources used here including Mullan's *Decolonizing Therapy* (2023), Watkins & Shulman's *Toward Psychologies of Liberation* (2008), Rosado's *Consciousness-in-Action* (2007), and Johnson's *Embodied Activism* (2023). And to keep the conversation going!

References

Clayton, S. (2020). Climate anxiety: Psychological responses to climate change. *Journal of Anxiety Disorders, 74*, 1–7. https://doi.org/10.1016/j.janxdis.2020.102263

Cushman, P. (1990). Why the self is empty. Toward a historically situated psychology. *The American Psychologist, 45*(5), 599–611.

Cushman, P. (1996). *Constructing the self, constructing America: A cultural history of psychotherapy*. Da Capo Press.

Deikman, A. J. (2000). Service as a way of knowing. In T. Hart, P. L. Nelson, & K. Puhakka (Eds.), *Transpersonal knowing: Exploring the horizon of consciousness* (pp. 303–318). State University of New York Press.

Dorje, O. T. (2017). *Interconnected: Embracing life in our global society* (2nd ed.). Wisdom Publications.

Freire, P., & Macedo, D. (2006). *Pedagogy of the oppressed*. Continuum.

Fromm, E. (1955). *The sane society*. Holt Paperbacks.

Grant, A. S. (2017). What exactly are we trying to accomplish? The role of desire in transhuman visions. In C. Mercer & T. J. Trothen (Eds.), *Religion and human enhancement: Death, values, and morality* (pp. 121–138). Palgrave Macmillan.

Grant, A. S. (2018). *Beyond buffering: An empirical investigation of the interconnective self-construal as a mediator in existential death anxiety* (2018-48576-011). ProQuest Information & Learning.

Grof, S. (2008). Brief history of transpersonal psychology. *International Journal of Transpersonal Studies, 27*, 46–54.

Gruba-McCallister, F. (2007). Narcissism and the empty self: To have or to be. *Journal of Individual Psychology, 63*(2), 182–192.
Gruba-McCallister, F. (2019). *Embracing disillusionment: Achieving liberation through the demystification of suffering*. University Professors Press.
Johnson, R. (2023). *Embodied activism: Engaging the body to cultivate liberation, justice, and authentic connection*. North Atlantic Books.
Loy, D. (2000). *Lack and transcendence: The problem of death and life in psychotherapy, existentialism, and Buddhism*. Humanity Books.
Loy, D. (2015). *A new Buddhist path: Enlightenment, evolution, and ethics in the modern world*. Wisdom Publications.
Morris, B., O'Gwin, C. K., Grant, S., & McDonald, S. (2020). *Subjectivity in psychology in the era of social justice* (1st ed.). Routledge.
Mullan, J. (2023). *Decolonizing therapy: Oppression, historical trauma, and politicizing your practice*. W. W. Norton & Company.
Pinos-Pey, K. (2017). The social psychology of compassion and altruism. In J. Loizzo, M. Neale, & E. J. Wolf (Eds.), *Advances in contemplative psychotherapy* (1st ed., pp. 89–101). Routledge.
Prilleltensky, I. (1990). Enhancing the social ethics of psychology: Toward a psychology at the service of social change. *Canadian Psychology/Psychologie Canadienne, 31*(4), 310–319. https://doi.org/10.1037/h0078954
Pyles, L. (2018). *Healing justice: Holistic self-care for change makers*. Oxford University Press.
Ricard, M. (2016). *Altruism: The power of compassion to change yourself and the world*. Little, Brown and Company.
Rosado, R. Q. (2007). *Consciousness-in-action: Toward an integral psychology of liberation & transformation*. ilé Publications.
Son, J., & Wilson, J. (2012). Volunteer work and hedonic, eudemonic, and social well-being. *Sociological Forum, 27*(3), 658–681. https://doi.org/10.1111/j.1573-7861.2012.01340.x
Sugarman, J. (2015). Neoliberalism and psychological ethics. *Journal of Theoretical and Philosophical Psychology, 35*(2), 103–116. https://doi.org/10.1037/a0038960
Trzeciak, S., & Mazzarelli, A. (2019). *Compassionomics: The revolutionary scientific evidence that caring makes a difference* (1st ed.). Studer Group.
Watkins, M., & Shulman, H. (2008). *Toward psychologies of liberation*. Palgrave Macmillan.

Wayment, H. A., & Bauer, J. J. (Eds.). (2008). *Transcending self-interest: Psychological explorations of the quiet ego.* American Psychological Association.

What is healing justice? (n.d.). Kindred Southern Healing Justice Collective. Retrieved July 1, 2024, from https://kindredsouthernhjcollective.org/what-is-healing-justice/

8

Psychoanalysis, Revolution, and the Red Clinic

Ian Parker

Psychoanalysis and Then Revolution, or Vice Versa, or Both

The way into the question of psychoanalysis, revolution and the Red Clinic is, first of all, through the co-authored book project 'Psychoanalysis and Revolution: Critical Psychology for Liberation Movements,' in which David Pavón-Cuéllar and I articulate psychoanalysis with the practice of left movements (Parker & Pavón-Cuéllar, 2021). We are addressing activists in a number of different movements, from explicitly anti-capitalist groups to ecological, indigenous, and feminist networks, and we are using the signifier 'critical psychology' strategically to speak about psychoanalysis. We are concerned with practice, here political practice, but we know that there is no direct unmediated practice as such. It must be mediated, explicitly or implicitly, by a theory of the world and a theory of the

I. Parker (✉)
Red Clinic, Manchester, UK

human subject. If it is not explicit, reflected upon, worked through, then that mediation is usually, by default, ideological.

Let us look at the question of psychoanalysis and revolution from two different perspectives: first from the perspective of psychoanalysis, and then revolution. Then we can attempt to knit them together, and that is what this book tries to do. So, the first perspective, from psychoanalysis, will look simplistic to those versed in psychoanalytic theory and practice, but bear with me, because really this is addressed to the revolutionaries. I speak as a psychoanalyst. I try to answer along the way the question as to why revolutionaries, including those working inside psychology, should take psychoanalysis seriously.

Psychoanalysis

Psychoanalysis is a theory and practice of our personal most intimate experience of subjectivity, of what it is to be a human subject. This experience is intimately bound up with language, of what it is to speak of our experience and what the effects of that are. The link between subjectivity and language is why, from the beginning, psychoanalysis was described, by one of the first patients, as a 'talking cure.' Our distress at living in unbearable conditions that is tied to what has happened to us, or what we think has happened, and is difficult to think about, is trapped inside us. The distress festers inside our minds, and we push it away. That is exhausting and it is pushed into our bodies. So that is how we live it and repress it and then, in distorted form, express it.

It was not always like this. Freud invented the theory and practice of psychoanalysis, and in the process, he had to invent this approach from the cultural-historical resources that were available to him. He gave a name to what we push away, what we repress, what we cannot think about; that is the unconscious. It is not, as some psychiatrists and psychologists would have it, that he 'discovered' the unconscious, but he invented it. That enabled Freud to key into the personal experience of alienation in this political-economic system we live under, one that was gathering power as the dominant set of social relations as he developed his theory. That also enabled him to key into abuse of power, particularly of women, and to home in on what had become so painful to speak about, that is sex.

In Freud's work at the end of the nineteenth century and in the first half of the twentieth century, and then in the writings of his followers, we have much puzzling and theorising about what this 'sex' that psychoanalysis talks about really is. Some will tie it to biological urges, a dead end, and some will tie it to the need for love and connection with others, a better bet. And psychoanalysis carries on working with images and metaphors that speaks of its time, of its own place in history. For example, Freud refers to women's sexuality as a 'dark continent' and he writes that phrase 'dark continent' in English. So, we have colonial metaphors, images of uncivilised barbaric 'natural' untamed desires, being used to talk about what the human being is.

But while Freud is describing and finding a way for us to think and talk about patriarchy, he is not prescribing it. This is crucial, and this is something that feminist psychoanalysts insisted. Freud is not saying this is how things should be. Sometimes he does, yes, and some psychoanalysts, conservative psychoanalysts, think that is the way things should be. But Freud is focusing on how things have come to be how they are, and how we live them. That is why many of the psychoanalysts in central Europe before the rise of fascism were on the left, supporters or members of the socialist parties or communist parties. And that is why Freud himself spoke during the Hungarian revolution in 1918 of the need for psychoanalysis being available in the early equivalent of a free national health service.

Psychoanalysis was radical and was linked to radical movements. It spoke of distress and opened a space for people to speak of distress. To put it into words, to make it, in some limited way in the contained space of the clinic, public. Did it become an elite treatment in conditions of exile after it was driven out by the fascists and condemned as a Jewish science? Yes, but what in this world has not been recuperated, neutralised, and absorbed, turned into a commodity for those who can afford it. What psychoanalysis spoke about then is still the case now, maybe even more so. The political-economic system it described, capitalism and patriarchy organised around the nuclear family, has spread around the world.

Now many of us speak about sex a lot, or try to avoid speaking about it, but it is the commodification of sex, and the intensification of its links with power, with humiliation and shame that makes it so touchy, sometimes impossible to speak about. Like psychoanalysis itself, sex is turned into something to be bought and sold. We repeat the self-destructive images of ourselves that we learnt, and those self-destructive images become linked to toxic images of sex and our bodies and the colour of our skin. That is why anti-colonial psychoanalysts like Frantz Fanon who worked in a psychiatric hospital and then joined the Algerian independence movement saw psychoanalysis as a way of accounting for what drives the racist oppressors as well as the oppressed into miserable exercises of power or subjugation and self-hatred.

When we speak to psychiatrists about our distress, their medical training makes them look for illness and search for drugs or physical treatments to cure us. When we speak to psychologists, they focus on the bad thoughts and try to put them right, usually in line with what they have been told is right. When we speak to psychotherapists, they too often so want to help us, and have a too clear idea of what would help. This is unless they are psychoanalytic psychotherapists. Remember that psychoanalytic work is not confined to psychoanalysts as such, but that approach, its radical elements, can be there in the practice of psychoanalytic psychotherapists and psychodynamic counsellors. Part of the problem radical practitioners today face is the status hierarchy that distorts psychoanalytic work.

So, there is an internal struggle in and against the professions that we psychoanalysts must engage in. Psychoanalysis is part of the psy professions, moulded by its collusion and turf wars with psychiatrists, psychologists, psychotherapists, and counsellors. And it needs to set itself against the psy professions to be able to reclaim its radical history, breaking from the idea that there is something fixed in human nature, or the supposed nature of gender and sexuality or race that it should organise its theory and practice around. If it breaks from its enclosure in private practice, reaching out again to politics so it can link personal change with social change, then it can be revolutionary.

Revolution

Let us look at this another way now, from the perspective of revolution. I will cover some of the same ground again. But now I speak as a revolutionary, as a revolutionary Marxist. So that limits what I say in some ways, but this is in order to speak across from revolutionary politics to psychoanalytic types, to those who might be too closely wedded to their psychoanalytic ideas. There are some parallels, and maybe more than that. The bet of this argument is that it is more than that. It can be more than that.

We rebel against racist hetero-patriarchal capitalism not only because this political-economic system is unfair and ruinous, with the drive for profit destroying the planet. Short-term gain exploits nature with no thought for the consequences for humankind—let alone the other species we share this earth with. It is not only that. The development and globalisation of capitalism requires colonial power and the power of the male heads of the household in the nuclear family. It is not only that, but it is that this capitalism systematically distorts who and what we are in our relations with nature and with each other. That distortion also fuels a desperate search for what we have lost and promotes equally self-destructive images of what our real nature is that are modelled on the commodified images of ourselves that are sold to us.

That at its core was what fired Marx to develop his critique of capitalist political economy as a critique that was designed not merely to interpret the world but to change it. It was designed to harness the consciousness of those who labour, those whose labour power is exploited. The alienation that Marx described was of a separation of our creative labour from what we produce when others control and sell the fruits of our labour, separation of us from each other in competition for jobs and resources, separation of ourselves from our own bodies that are turned into instruments of labour, and separation from nature as such which is viewed as something to be dominated, as a threat or something romanticised.

That critique of capitalism chimes with other critiques of exploitation and oppression, from feminism and anti-colonial politics. And they not only force Marxists to take sexism and racism seriously but provide their own autonomous leadership of liberation movements. It was anti-racist and feminist theorists who also showed how pernicious and insidious alienation is, how it leads people to blame themselves for distress that is a function of this political-economic system. And they reminded us Marxists that we experience that exploitation and oppression at depth, within us, and reproduce it in our relations with others. This is structural, systemic, beyond consciousness, and we need to tackle political and personal resistance to be able to think about what is happening to us and work through how we collude with it.

Here is reason enough to be suspicious of the psy professions who ask us to forget about changing the world and to just change ourselves to adapt better to this wretched existence. When socialist feminists argued inside and alongside and against Marxist organisations that the 'personal is political,' they already knew that it would be a mistake to dissolve politics into personal change. They did not need the Marxists who wanted to caricature their slogan to tell them that. And it means that they demand of any approach to personal change, any attempt to tackle the distress that paralyses people and stops them from struggling against oppression, that they also tackle the problem of individualisation, competitive individualism that is part and parcel of alienation.

For revolutionaries of all kinds, the psy professions who have crystallised a status hierarchy with psychoanalysts at the top, psychotherapists below them as an obedient second tier, and the many counsellors, most of whom are women at the bottom, sometimes reminds them of terrible betrayals and bureaucratisation in their own history of struggle. For Marxists, for example, this bureaucratisation reminds them of the awful betrayal of the hopes for real change in the early years of the Russian revolution, and the way that the Stalinist bureaucracy revived racist Russian chauvinism and antisemitism in the Soviet Union as it outlawed again homosexuality and reinforced the nuclear family and the power of men. Some Marxists will be dimly aware that psychoanalysis was prohibited in the Soviet Union in the 1930s as well as in Germany, and that opposition figures like Trotsky defended the psychoanalysts. Why would that be?

So many activists in the revolutionary anti-Stalinist tradition as well as those in feminist and anti-colonial movements were drawn to psychoanalysis. Our worry has always been that they could have been drawn too far in, to the point where they swapped one belief system for another. That they turned their faith in revolutionary theory into faith in psychoanalysis as a kind of all-encompassing worldview that would explain everything now and everything back to the dawn of time. There is a keen reminder that anyone who wants to tackle the distress we suffer needs to know and that is our revolutionary ideas do not function as a 'belief system' at all. They are tools of struggle, and those tools of struggle are themselves transformed when they engage with and change social reality.

So, the questions that revolutionaries might pose to psychoanalysts are questions that also point back to them. You could say that the questions are necessarily reflexive. That is, the questions have consequences for those who ask them as well as those they demand answers from. Are you going to listen to us without fitting what we say into your own theoretical grid, reducing us to it? Are you going to offer us a space to speak that enables us to transform ourselves without attempting to predict or pathologise what we might make of ourselves? Are you up to the task of transforming yourself as a result of listening to us? Can you make another world possible that does not need your kind in it, self-critical of the identity you have won for yourself in your training as psychoanalysts?

This manifesto makes a case that there is struggle at work inside the history of psychoanalysis and in its intersection with revolutionary struggle. It is a struggle between conservative bureaucratised psy professionals who want to adapt people to reality, and another tradition that has attempted to answer these questions, attempted, and sometimes failed. The attempts say something about the nature of psychoanalysis, though, which is that it can, it could be revolutionary.

Red Clinic: Putting Radical Theory into Practice

I now turn to the Red Clinic, a practical project that was set up entirely independently of my theoretical work on 'psychoanalysis and revolution,' but in which I have found a clinical home for the issues that I explored there (and described above). This initiative of the Red Clinic, our comrades said at the outset, would be informed by Marxist, anti-racist, queer feminist, and radical disability theories. It should be explicitly internationalist. It began with an outline of where we were up to so far and gave examples of the kind of work we had in mind. Now I think of my clinical-political activity as taking place through the Red Clinic.

The Red Clinic initiative is in its early days. It began in London following a Mental Health Workers Inquiry to explore clinical approaches that foreground anti-capitalism and anti-imperialism. We are dealing here with at least two issues. One is the nature of global capitalism which, intersecting with vicious racism and sexism, is driving spiralling rates of distress. Mental health suffering is a political matter. The other is access to mental health support, with privatisation of services replicating the isolation that people feel. Mental health provision is a political matter.

So, there was a decision by a small group of radical therapists, lawyers, and activists to set up something that would badge itself as run by communists. This term 'communist' is deliberately chosen to point to the need for collectively run services that increase people's capacity to engage in conscious activity together with others to change the world (Pospihalj, 2022). Solidarity in the practice of therapy, in its form as well as its content, is crucial here. Perhaps it would be possible for those committed to this project to bring in therapists to work face-to-face and online.

We began to advertise for therapists, thinking to employ therapists who would take on a high fee-paying client in order to subsidise work with a low or no-fee paying client. We started to think about how to manage this, and then we took a step back. It seemed too much of a stretch with the small group we had collaborating with us to do all of this. Now Red Clinic is taking another step forward, but on two tracks of work. One is to engage in political dialogue with practitioners, and to set up a political education programme to discuss how to connect therapy with radical theory and practice. The other track of work is to build bases for the Red Clinic and work out how to offer practical clinical support to those in distress, including to working with trades unions, grassroots organisations, and social movements (Titus, 2024).

There are in post-pandemic global capitalism, a host of issues that compound those that have beset red or radical therapy initiatives in the past. We know we are reinventing some of those past initiatives in new conditions, and we need help to do that, which is why a meeting in a context of a strike seemed a good place to begin again. We are asking

8 Psychoanalysis, Revolution, and the Red Clinic   143

whether we can do this, as well as how and whether different questions and answers can be developed if we are to have any success in the project. These twenty-two points briefly introduce and review questions of politics, therapy, psychologisation, organisation and practice.

Politics: Why We Are Communist

1. The Red Clinic project began with a 'mental health workers inquiry', and the link between mental health and labour is at the core of why we say we are communists. Mental distress that is brought into therapy is intimately bound up with the nature of work in capitalist society. Therapy itself can be turned into a form of alienated labour, and therapists are also workers. Questions for us include asking what work therapists do, and how they link with working-class struggle.
2. There is a history of 'free clinics' in psychoanalysis and of 'radical therapy' in general that is closely connected with socialist and communist politics. This history, which is obscured by the professionalization of therapy, and the attempt to adapt people to society to make them good productive citizens, is our history. We remember this history, learn from it, and take it forward as part of the broader communist project.
3. The link between psychotherapy and radical politics was closed down in capitalist societies and in those societies that claimed to speak for the working class. Remaking the link now means that we open communism again to the struggles of all of the exploited and oppressed. The mission statement on the website signals this as an open form of communism that is inclusive of difference, that is non-normative.
4. The communist link between what is 'red' and what is 'clinic' has been theorised before and needs to be theorised again. Our work is the product of individuals, but the work must also be collectivised, making multiple connections between history, theory, and practice. That means working with radical clinicians and with communist activists who are willing to engage with the question of personal change.
5. We insist on the 'red' of the Red Clinic. We are communists in the clinic, not because we want to turn the clinic into an arena for

propaganda, but because we want to make clear the necessary link between communism and care. Being communist here is more than simply providing free therapy. It is part of a political project to make communism visible again in culture and public debate, communism as something that has a good as well as a bad history, something that is worth reclaiming.

Therapy: Addressing Differences of Approach and Institutional Divisions

6. We insist on the 'clinic' of the Red Clinic. What we mean by 'clinic' is very different from the medical treatment that some mental health practitioners jealously guard for themselves as a professional speciality. Our clinic is an open space that includes those working in and against any of the 'psy' professions, and those who make use of those services, and anyone who want to engage with the question of how to link personal change with radical social change.
7. The collectivising of experience and collective activity of the Red Clinic has immediate implications for how we think about the privatising of distress under capitalism. The individualisation of experience is replicated in one-to-one 'individual' therapy, and we need to find a way to connect with forms of group therapy. We acknowledge and respect and work with the personal singular nature of distress and need to draw upon different approaches to tackle it.
8. Psychoanalytic ideas are useful, but not all of them are radical; quite the contrary. These ideas underpin the development of most other models of psychotherapy and counselling. We do not privilege psychoanalysis over other models and actively include practitioners who are not psychoanalytic. We are learning from what 'radical therapy' might look like that also refuses psychoanalysis as such.
9. We also question the hierarchical pyramid structure of psychotherapy in which psychoanalysis is assumed to be at the top, a larger number of psychotherapists underneath them, and a huge mass of mainly working-class women counsellors consigned to what is supposed by those at the top of the pyramid to be a lesser and less intense

level of provision. We cut across this division, against the bureaucratic professionalization and regulatory divide-and-rule structures.
10. We are not developing a new 'model' for psychotherapy, but harnessing the strength of different approaches, questioning each of them. We do not adhere only to therapy as such or to the 'clinic' as the only place for personal and social change. There is no one perfect model of therapy and therapy itself is not a cure for the ills of capitalism. Our engagement with the clinic is tactical and strategic.

Psychologisation: Resisting Therapeutic Discourse

11. The Red Clinic is critical of mainstream therapy that aims to adapt people to this society. It is critical of psychiatry that medicalises distress, connecting with radical critiques of mental health services and connecting with users of services. It is critical of psychology that wants to make people think more positively about their lives and of the role of 'psychologisation' in society, as well as the intensely ideological message that problems are individual and should be addressed at an individual level.
12. We also acknowledge and connect with existing communist practice, working with the contradictions between conservative institutions and well-meaning practitioners. There are many practitioners, whether self-consciously 'communist' or not, who attempt to do radical work and resist the lures of psychologisation. They already offer low-cost or, in some cases, free therapy. They attempt to take questions of class, 'race,' disability, gender, and sexuality seriously, and we want to help open up the contradictions these practices pose.
13. We need to find ways of addressing the connection between material oppression and felt experience, distress, which does not reduce politics to therapy. We do not evangelise about psychoanalysis or any other model of psychotherapy. We do not reframe political questions in line with therapeutic discourse, either in the application of therapeutic theory to understand political phenomena or in practical proposals for ameliorating distress.

14. The obverse is as important. We do not reduce the therapeutic process to politics, and do not inject our understanding of what it means to be communist, for example, into the clinic. The therapeutic space, which is private, is a problem insofar as it is privatising, but it is also a secure contained space. It is refuge from demands made by capital, and from political demands of any kind, whether reactionary or ostensibly 'radical.'

Organisation: Collectivising Work through Networks

15. The Red Clinic is committed to the collectivising of experience, of those directly involved and those we work with. That means building a 'critical mass' of practitioners and activists. We need to think therapeutically and politically about what the boundaries are between the inside and outside of the clinic and between therapists and clients. A critical mass includes different kinds of critical mass engaged in different kinds of task, organising, and linking and learning from each kind of practice.
16. Organisational work involves education and the integration of what we learn into the development of the clinic. The monthly online panel events organised through the Learning Cooperative need to be organically linked to reading and discussion groups. There needs to be an accumulating corpus of material resources for those joining us to read and discuss. This is part of the historical memory of the project as part of the longer history of communist therapeutic practice.
17. We can build a 'service' and that will at some point need a material base, but we are also a network. We need to be able to build different kinds of network that are appropriate to the different kinds of work we do. This needs to be formulated in such a way that it is open to change. The development of the network or networks should have the potential to challenge and go beyond their assigned place and transform what is expected of them. Local initiatives and autonomous groups are part of this process.
18. At the same time, dialectically linked to the locally grounded initiatives and a crucial aspect of the communist nature of the project, is

that it is internationalist. Our internationalism means that we think of ourselves in relation to global struggles, open to a collective dimension of our work that is as important as the historical dimension. This is facilitated by online work, but that online communication has its own limitations. How we are concretely practically 'internationalist' is a recurring question for us.

Practice: What We Can Realistically Provide Now

19. We are linking in practice with existing initiatives and working towards the development of online forums and exchanges. These are overlapping networks that we want to support and that we want to feed into our own work. This means working out with these other initiatives in different parts of the world what is specific about them, and what differences we enable in order to maintain ourselves and offer something distinctive to them.
20. We are giving support as well as supervision and providing psychotherapy. The work of the Arabic-speaking groups we set up in Palestine, for example, has posed questions about what it is to work under occupation and what we can do practically to support therapists who are engaging in radical work. We will be collectivising that experience and conceptualising it, making it available while maintaining the safety and security of our colleagues.
21. We can provide support for radical therapists and trainees as a network, a space to think through contradictions in theory and practice. We break the isolation and privatisation of distress and therapeutic experience, primarily focusing now on what we can actually do. That is, we cannot pretend to bring therapy to the people. We can operate as a relay point through which others can, in a minimal way, offer therapy in a radical way and challenge their own institutions, at least survive inside them.
22. This provides the potential basis, one that is not immediately available while we build a critical mass of practitioners and activists, for formulating what we could offer to activist organisations such as political campaigns and trades unions. We are starting to formulate

this while functioning as a support base for those who are already part of collective communist activity inside and outside of the domain of the clinic.

References

Parker, I., & Pavón-Cuéllar, D. (2021). *Psychoanalysis and revolution: Critical psychology for liberation movements.* 1968 Press.

Pospihalj, D. (2022). For a communist clinic. *Sublation media.* https://sublationmedia.com/for-a-communist-clinic/

Psychoanalysis and Revolution website: https://psychoanalysisrevolution.com/

Red Clinic website: https://www.redclinic.org/

Titus, J. S. (2024). Assistance for the mind: Remembering and rebuilding radical praxis in the clinic. *Parapraxis Magazine.* https://www.parapraxismagazine.com/articles/assistance-for-the-mind

9

Working as a Therapist in an Unjust Mental Health Care System

Joel Vos

Introduction

Note: Case studies have been anonymised, pseudonyms used, and facts significantly altered to make them unrecognisable, and informed consent was achieved.

> *You know what? I cannot take it anymore! The lack of resources, bureaucratic nonsense, and endless paperwork—it's all a giant obstacle course preventing me from giving our clients the care they deserve. Do not even get me started on the inequitable access and stigmatization our clients face, even before they reach our service. It is infuriating to see them struggle because of the systemic injustices in our mental health care services and society. We need real change, and we need it now!*

J. Vos (✉)
Department of Counseling, Metanoia Institute, London, UK
e-mail: Joel.Vos@metanoia.ac.uk

Sarah has been my clinical supervisee for the past two years. She is currently in her third placement of her training in Counselling Psychology. When I first met Sarah, she was filled with hope and enthusiasm, perhaps naive, with an idealized view of our field. Over time, I witnessed her hope become despair as she became aware of the structural injustices within the mental healthcare system. Instead of sugar-coating the reality and pretending that the system is flawless, I created a safe space for Sarah to express her emotions, including her anger, and acknowledge the harsh realities she encounters daily working with clients. As Sarah grapples with unanswered questions and frustration, I am here to provide unwavering support and understanding as her clinical supervisor.

This chapter explores some of the many injustices that therapists, such as Sarah and her clients, face in mental health care systems. For instance, Social Injustice (SI) may manifest as a systemic failure to provide fair and equitable access to mental health services, support, and resources for individuals with mental health problems. SI encompasses the prevalence of disparities in treatment, stigmatization of mental health conditions, inadequate funding, and lack of comprehensive and inclusive care options. These injustices often result in marginalized communities and individuals facing barriers to receiving the care and support they require, perpetuating a cycle of inequality and diminished well-being.

Those looking for a detailed overview of critical psychology and injustices in mental health care may want to read our book 'Mental Health in Crisis' (Vos et al., 2019). This chapter will focus on the question, 'How can we work as therapists in an unjust mental health care system?' I will treat therapists working in unjust mental health care systems as victims of SI. I will review the stages of Social Justice Oriented Interventions: safety creation, skills training, recognition of SI, reformulation in terms of the Integrated Cycle of SI, interventions to break the cycle of SI, recovery, and building resilience. I will ask you the questions and suggest the interventions I did with Sarah.

Safety Creation

Breathe, relax. You are safe here. I invite you to join me in this nurturing environment where you can be yourself and explore what is going-on. Are you, your colleagues, and clients safe in your work? How realistic is your assessment of safety? Is the unsafety caused by your personal life situation, your physical workplace situation, your experience of the workplace, or society in general? Do whatever you need to feel safe (see Table 9.1). If you do not feel safe, your clients will not feel safe.

Personal Safety

This is not about your life-situation or life-story. Despite this, you must look after yourself before you look after others. For example, did you have a verbal disagreement with your partner before you came to work? You can count on having a client struggle with a similar argument today or even starting an argument with you. This seems to be Murphy's Law of

Table 9.1 Examples of safety-creating actions

- Do not engage with clients or colleagues if there is an immediate physical threat to yourself or others; create physical safety first.
- Do exercises to feel safe when you arrive at your workplace and before seeing each client, such as breathing, orienting, grounding, shaking, mindfulness, and safe space visualization exercises.
- Talk with your manager, clinical supervisor or coach in the workplace
- Find peers in the workplace, set up social events and informal support groups ('Let's have a drink together after worktime!')
- Use a clinical supervisor outside your workplace
- Use a personal therapist
- Catharsis: Netflix, sports, nature, music, hobbies, friends, love, sex
- Break: self-care, holiday, sickness leave
- Activate your social network
- Share your feelings and concerns with colleagues, and if needed, write a complaint/concern letter to the management (stronger together than alone)
- Join a trade union; speak with a union rep
- If needed, lawyer up, at least to inform yourself
- Join or organize protest groups or social movement
- Write to a member of parliament/minister/secretary
- Recognize a mental health urgency, e.g., talk with your family doctor

therapists: clients always know how to find weaknesses and put their fingers in wounds that have not entirely healed. You incorrectly think you have resolved all your personal struggles. Welcome to the reality of therapists. We all have had moments when we thought our past was past, but our clients triggered something in us, reminding us of what we have not yet processed sufficiently. Spot your countertransference and opportunities for catharsis outside of work. You know best what you need to do to create your personal safety. Moreover, do not forget self-compassion and self-care, which therapists often seem to forget, possibly due to their personal life scripts that frequently brought them into this profession.

Explicit Systemic Safety (Physical)

Feeling safe starts with the physical work situation. Ensure you do not feel physically threatened. If you do, for example if a client is aggressive towards you, ensure that there are colleagues and safety procedures to protect and support you.

Implicit Systemic Safety (Emotional, Social)

Although we may be physically safe, we may feel emotionally unsafe in the workplace. Recognize the symptoms of unsafety, such as stress and trauma responses, tensed muscles, and startling. Your body may tell you, "You are not safe." Even though the threat may be imagined, you may still experience an automatic fight/flight/freeze/fawn/flop response. Notice your body responses. Do you notice a pattern? What is it that makes you feel unsafe? Can you leave your work behind when you close your office door? These are the types of questions you may ask your clients. Ask them yourself, and be honest in your answers, as they may give you the first clue about your needs and SI in your workplace.

Skills Training

What professional skills do you need to survive in the context where you work? Identifying the emotional skills, we may need to develop may be more difficult. To identify these needs, we must start by critically reflecting on our relationships towards our clients, their mental health struggles, how they and their struggles fit within their social context, and all their possible relationships at all possible levels (Fig. 9.1; cf., Vos, 2023). This critical reflection may be fostered by keeping personal journals,

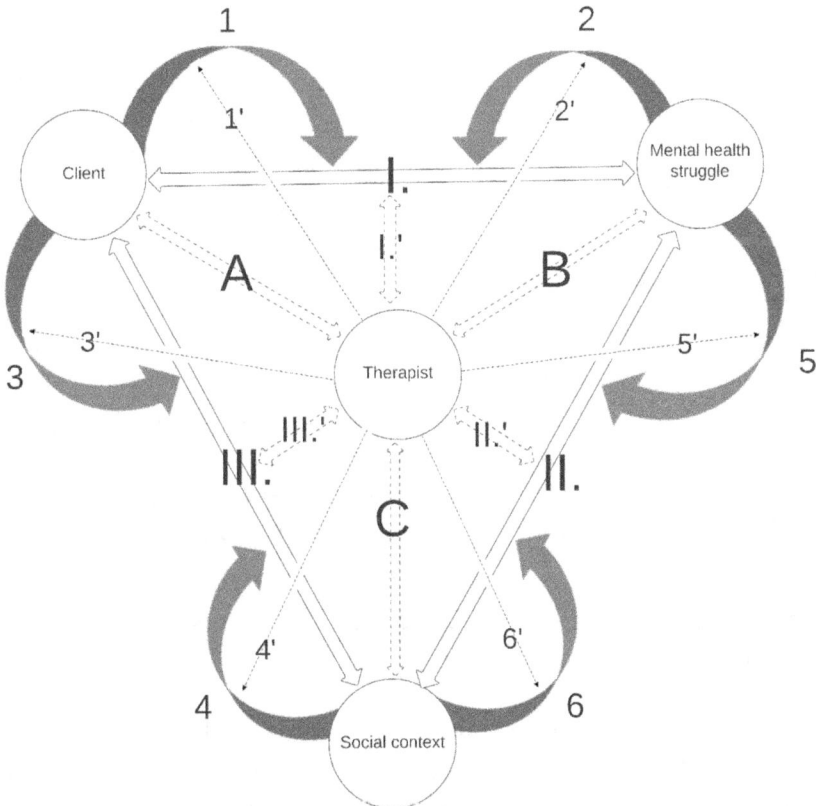

Fig. 9.1 Visualization of the therapist's systematic critical self-reflection and reflexivity (Based on Vos, 2023)

regular supervision, multidisciplinary team meetings, and personal therapy. These reflections may help identify the skills we need to learn or the SI we need to tackle in our service or broader social system.

Furthermore, we may ask ourselves ten fundamental self-reflective questions to identify the multi-faceted nature of SI in mental health care (Vos, 2020, 2021).

What Meaning Does SJ/SI Have?

What meanings are at stake in the workplace? Is it just about our salary or physical situation (materialistic type of meaning), the ability to enjoy (hedonistic meaning), personal development and expression (self-oriented meaning), broader injustice in our relationships with clients, colleagues, managers, or society in general (social meaning), challenges to universal, ethical, or religious/spiritual meanings (large meaning), or abstract values (existential-philosophical meanings)?

How Do Therapists Approach SJ/SI?

How do you know what is just or unjust in the workplace? For example, do you unquestioningly follow what your teachers, supervisors and books told you (traditional approach), act mechanically (e.g., automatic pilot, ticking boxes), or do you critically listen to what your intuitions tell you what is just and unjust in unique situations? Reflect on your approach, and if possible, train your critical intuition to sense injustice.

What Is the Relationship Between Therapists and the System?

Do you let yourself be defined by the expectations and constraints of the system, which may load you with unrealistic demands, feelings of guilt, shame, and the imposter syndrome (social determinism)? Or do you develop your own therapeutic style and express your individuality as much as possible based on your critical intuition of what truly matters (individual determinism)? Or do you consider yourself a mixture of both, developing your individual critical approach within the structural constraints?

How Does SJ/SI Develop?

How did you develop your sense of SJ/SI regarding working with clients with mental health problems? This most likely originated long before your therapy training and may involve early-life messages and decisions. How much is your sense of justice a reflection of the present or your life-story?

How Much Freedom Do Clients and Therapists Have to Address SJ/SI?

How much time and resources do you have to address SJ/SI in your workplace? How accessible are your services to diverse populations? Can you give the number of sessions clients need, or is there a pre-given limit? Can you develop a therapeutic approach tailored to the client's strengths, needs, and preferences? Can you help them with questions about SJ/SI that may go beyond the traditional role of therapists? Do you merely help them eliminate psychological symptoms (negative freedom), or do you also empower and allow them to explore their options to realize their potential (positive freedom)? What limits your professional freedom?

What Is the Impact of SJ/SI on Existential Well-Being?

Can you address the client's existential needs and help them live meaningfully? How meaningful and fulfilling is your work?

What Is the Effect of SJ/SI on Mental Health?

Can you sensitively address specific vulnerabilities in clients and help groups with specific mental health needs? In yourself, what emotions do you notice in the workplace? Particularly notice a silence in the heart of a storm when you are calm despite obvious SI. This may indicate that you may be suppressing or splitting your genuine feelings of injustice. SI/SJ is a multi-faceted phenomenon in our work as therapists. We may want to train our competencies and intuitive sensitivity towards the reality of SJ/SI in the workplace, its multiple meanings, and its development in interactions between society and the individual. Instead help clients develop freedom not only from their memories/feelings of SI, but also freedom towards actively creating a more meaningful and fulfilling life.

Interpersonal Relationships

What is going on in your relationships with your clients, and how do these relationships reflect your workplace and the broader societal structures? To what extent and how are you doing injustice to your client, albeit unintentionally? How does your mental health system do injustice to them and to yourself? How do your clients cope with the fact that the people they look to for safety and security in mental healthcare may be the same people who are causing harm (again), and how do you cope with this realization? How do you cope with relational ruptures with clients? Instead of playing a game to rescue your ego, can you do justice by acknowledging that you were wrong or have not done enough, and engage in an authentic encounter from human to human.

Team Relationships

What relationships do you have with your colleagues? Notice group dynamic processes and any changes in these, such as the implicit creation of norms and roles within a team. How cohesive is the group, or is it more like a loose organization? What subgroups, conspiracies, gossip, and myths exist? What is presented as justice but is actually unjust? Who decides what is just and unjust? How are newcomers treated, and what roles are they allocated, or are they given the freedom to develop their identity and position? How are relational ruptures repaired? How do the team dynamics reflect the broader structures in the health care system or society, or are they unique to this team? Do the team dynamics reflect the projections and splitting of clients discussed in the team? What is your role in the team, and how does this reflect your other roles in life and your family of origin?

Thus, the team and mental health service play a crucial role in the ability of therapists to do justice to their clients and meet their needs. Unfortunately, whereas victimized clients may struggle to get recognition from their perpetrator and community, this may be re-enacted by the health care system. Consequently, clients may express anger at the failures of the mental health system, which their broader lack of recognition may fuel. The therapist is often the symbolic representation of the mental health care system or the community that has failed to protect the client. Therapists may need to hold their clients' anger towards the system and society in general, even if they feel frustrated about these themselves. For individual therapists to be able to hold their client's emotions and offer them a reparative space, they may first need to receive recognition, healing, and reconciliation at the professional team level.

Reductionism

Nobody is perfect. Therefore, you will most likely take shortcuts and sometimes be unjust to some clients. How could you become aware of and prevent structurally doing injustice to your clients? Try to be aware of your assumptions of SI/SJ, and if possible, be transparent and repair ruptures. To what extent are you splitting in your therapeutic work, for example, by seeing some as 'the perfect client' and dreading seeing others? How do you know your client's problems, experiences, and priorities are theirs, not your projections? To what extent do your clients help you boost your ego? How strong are your ego boundaries? Can you see the situation from the other person's perspective and walk in their shoes (mentalization)? Do you feel dependent or merging with colleagues (insufficient ego-boundaries)? To what extent are these mechanisms also visible in other areas and periods of your life? Have you sufficiently learned these skills, or could you benefit from personal therapy to improve these?

Vicious Cycles

What self-fulfilling cycles are you stuck in at your workplace? Do your clients discuss similar topics? What themes do your colleagues, supervisors and managers pick up in your work? What patterns in the workplace do you find boring or upsetting, and what do you find the most exciting? Are your responses directed to the present situation, or do they reflect broader frustrations? How could you break these cycles?

Embodiment

How do you feel physically at work, and is this different from when you are at home or with friends? The answers may give an initial impression of the embodiment of SI/SJ in the workplace. What are your dominant emotions and concerns? Are these emotions about what is truly bothering you, or are there other authentic emotions? How does your body feel and move, and what do your bodily sensations tell you about how safe your workplace feels? How could you listen more to your body in the workplace and make authentic decisions that align with your authentic feelings?

Conclusions

Based on the previous reflections, identify when, where, and to what extent SI emerges in your workplace and which skills and knowledge you need to foster SJ. You may ask your clinical supervisor, personal therapist, or close friends/partner to critically reflect on this, as nobody can see their blind spots.

Recognition

Reflect on some examples of minor or major injustice in your workplace. What happened? What was then-and-there realistically possible and impossible? How does this injustice hinder something important or meaningful for you in your job, and possibly in your life? How did or does this impact you? Imagine the situation in detail. What is this memory's most challenging aspect? Try to go to the most painful, uncomfortable, or helpless part. Try to focus on this emotion and to locate the feeling in your body. If it feels too much, focus on a safe part of your body before you return to the specific sensation. Do any images, memories, or thoughts arise, regardless of whether they relate to your work, personal life, or life history? What can you realistically do here-and-now to feel safer in your body and emotionally?

This section will hurt, at least if you have never fully engaged in critical self-reflection. Only you know the reality of SI in the specific health care service, system, and society that you are in. If we want to assume our responsibility for solving the problems of the mind and the problems of the world, we need first to solve the problems in our field. Critically reflect on your work situation, preferably with peers or a personal therapist or clinical supervisor.

Therapy as Disciplinary Measures

Some critical psychologists have argued that talking therapies emerged to discipline individuals and ensure they fit social or political norms. Examples include the historical negative diagnostic labels of individuals deviating from the status quo. In the early days, psychiatric institutions functioned as ways of segregating individuals who deviated from status quo (Vos, 2020). Such practices disregard patient autonomy and rights, such as involuntary hospitalization or treatment without informed consent. This often puts pressure on therapists to balance a client's safety and well-being with their client's right to autonomous decision-making (Knapp, 2015). This may also include instances of excessive force or violence by law enforcement or mental health professionals in handling individuals experiencing mental health crises, leading to harm and trauma. Ask yourself: To what extent does your work with clients implicitly or explicitly aim to discipline individuals? Are your clients able to give full consent? Do you stimulate their autonomy? What broader powers (physical, social, explicit and implicit) bring and keep your clients in therapy?

Therapy as Manipulation

Sigmund Freud developed his ideas about talking therapies in close collaboration with his in-laws, the aristocratic and capitalist Bernays family (Vos, 2020). Bernard Bernays developed the terms and practices of 'propaganda' and 'public relations' to help sell products. Hitler, Goebbels, and Stalin explicitly applied Bernays' ideas. Propaganda aims to manipulate the thoughts and emotions of individuals to make them behave in a way that an elite prefers (Vos, 2020). Propaganda and talking therapies used many similar techniques. An excellent example of this is how, in his early work, Freud recognized the reality of sexual abuse of his clients, but he dismissed these as the client's imaginations and projections in his later work. Economists and politicians explicitly used the Bernaysian-Freudian philosophy to impose capitalist-liberal ideas onto the general population, which was described as 'neoliberalism' in the Lippman-Colloquium in 1938. These ideas have continued to be used by neoliberals, neoconservatives, and Third Way Politicians (Vos, 2020), as well as politicians who used psychological 'nudging' techniques during the COVID-pandemic (Vos, 2020, 2021). Thus, the early talking therapies reinforced patriarchal and aristocratic structures and suppress a widespread call for justice for victims with the help of psychological techniques that have been applied in politically questionable ways.

To what extent does your work with clients mute their dissent and call for social change? What socio-economic class-related values do your practices reflect? How do political and economic powers benefit from your success in helping your clients? What are your implicit and explicit goals for providing therapy? Do these goals help your clients or the powers puppeteering them? To what extent can clients differ from the ideal therapy outcome? To what extent do you offer the bare minimum to help clients become effective cogs in the socio-economic machine?

Lack of Funding

In general, many mental health practitioners complain about insufficient funding and resources, leading to long wait times, limited treatment options, or inadequate support services. This is particularly the case for long-term mental health care and minority groups. In the US, individuals struggle to access mental health care without a job or health insurance. Even if national health services offer mental health care to everyone on paper, they usually only offer the number of sessions deemed the minimum to achieve, on average, some positive effects instead of providing the number of sessions that all individuals need (Vos et al., 2019). Health services also seem to have become hyperspecialized with specific inclusion and exclusion criteria. For instance, in the UK's national health service, so-called complex cases with comorbidities often seem to be referred to private or charity mental health care or have to wait years to get the urgent care they need. Associated with the structural lack of funding are policies and practices that result in individuals with mental health conditions being disproportionately represented in the criminal justice system rather than receiving appropriate care. How do you cope with this lack of funding? Do all individuals receive the care they need from you? If you lead a practice, do you offer different rates or free therapy to increase accessibility?

Privatization and Commercial Interests in Mental Health Care

Across the globe, mental health care is increasingly provided by private profit-driven health care services. This privatization trend is stimulated by economists, such as Layard and McDaid, who are experts on finance but not on the content of care and client needs (Vos et al., 2019). Decisions about mental health care are often made by policymakers who are paid by the pharmaceutical industry, like 82% of the UK National Institute for Health and Care Excellence board having direct ties with BigPharma (Vos et al. 2019). Reorganizations of mental health care systems are often based on ideal situations, but not systematic research. Research published by the original developers of the UK's Improved Access to Psychological Therapies (IAPT) reported client recovery rates of over 50%; whereas independent research indicates around 9% (Vos et al., 2019). The Surviving Work Survey, amongst a representative sample of 1500 therapists, mainly in IAPT, complained about underpayment, powerlessness and fears, high workload, performance management, worries about quality-of-care, and concerns about the IAPT model (Vos et al., 2019). Thus, economic ideals such as privatization and commercialization may be at odds with therapeutic and SJ ideals. How do private and commercial interests impact your service and client work? What clients does your service reject, why, and how can they still receive care? Who tells you which client needs what care, and how do you know this advice is in the client's best interest?

Lack of Attention to Diversity

As mentioned before, many countries have disparities in access to mental health services based on factors such as income, race, ethnicity, or geographic location. Furthermore, mental health problems are still associated with stigmatization and discrimination, potentially resulting in inadequate care or social exclusion. Many mental health care systems have also been criticized for not adequately addressing the cultural needs and perspectives of diverse populations, leading to ineffective or inappropriate treatment. For example, Black and other ethnic minority groups are more likely to be forced into involuntary care and diagnosed with psychosis in western, dominantly white countries (Vos et al., 2019). There is also an apparent failure to address the unique mental health needs of marginalized populations. How diverse are the clients that you see in your service? How do you relate to individuals who are different from you, and how do you make them feel welcome and affirm their identity? How have you learned/trained to work with diversity? How can you increase accessibility and affirmative practices?

Overemphasis on the Medical Model

Mental health care services have been criticized for an overreliance on medication and a lack of holistic, client-centered approaches in treatment, disregarding the importance of social, environmental, and psychological factors (Vos et al., 2019; Davies, 2013, 2017). Where are your service and practices on the continuum, ranging from the absolute medical model to the absolute client-centered model? How do you justify your position on this continuum? How could you improve your service and individual care? What type of service is the most just?

Focus on Narrow Outcomes

Service audits and clinical trials usually report positive and average outcomes, but they do not specify adverse events which

> regard negative changes in physical and/or mental health in social or professional life relevant to the client, therapist, or others, such as new, recurrent or worsening symptoms, suicidality, aggression, drugs use, or medication. Treatments fail in 5–20% of clients, 3–15% worsen, and 50% do not experience significant positive change or drop out. Due to various factors, misunderstandings may remain unresolved and lead to clients quitting therapy. [Furthermore], whereas meta-analyses indicate that even though most clients report a reduction in mental health problems and few adverse effects, this does not automatically mean that they also experience more positive emotions and improved quality of life, including happiness, positive relationships, and meaning in life. (Vos, 2023, p. 56)

How do you and your service know that your clients benefit from your therapy? Do you seriously reflect on clients who report a decline or even kill themselves, what this may say about your practice, what your blind spots are, and how you could improve your practices? What defines positive outcomes? Do you only look at psychiatric diagnoses or also consider the client's quality-of-life, their ability to live a meaningful and fulfilling life, and their self-defined therapy goals? Focus your therapy on your clients' goals, strengths, and meanings in life (Andresen et al., 2011; Rapp & Goscha, 2011; Slade et al., 2017).

Individualization of Problems

If you cannot cope with society's injustices, go into therapy to learn to accept SI and to fall in line with other ideal, obedient citizens. This is the stereotypical criticism by critical psychologists of mental health care services (Andresen et al., 2011) Research indicates that the more unequal a society and the lower the social mobility are, the more mental health problems people report, and the more people use mental health care services. Does this mean that people in more unequal or socially immobile/regressive countries have more 'mental disorders' or does this imply that their stress levels accurately reflect their socio-economic reality? When we treat our clients' mental health problems, are we merely suppressing and hiding the ails of inequality and potentially stopping people from complaining, demonstrating, and demanding radical socio-economic change?

Critical psychologists have argued that by focusing on individual mental health problems, societies deflect from the underlying socio-economic causes. The individualization of problems is associated with the problem of fragmentation between mental health care and other social services, leading to challenges in addressing the complex needs of individuals with mental health conditions. For example, many clients in psychotherapy may also benefit from seeing a social worker, debt specialist, or clergy, and they may benefit from aligning care across these disciplines. To what extent does your service or your work with clients individualize problems that are actually collective? Do you help clients see how their issues relate to the socio-economic system? How much do you refer your clients to other professions? How could you improve your referral and multidisciplinary collaboration? SI clients particularly benefit from reconnecting with the community. To what extent do you explicitly help clients struggling with SI reconnect with the community, and how could you improve this?

In conclusion, SI-aware therapists may want to ensure that their therapy is not provided as an explicit or implicit disciplinary measure or manipulation; is accessible; and tailored to the unique needs, strengths, and preferences of diverse clients rather than merely systemic or financial resources. Most of all, therapists should explicitly address SI and systematically help clients achieve more SJ.

Reformulation as Integrated Cycle of Social Injustice

I would not be surprised if some of my previous questions felt challenging, confrontational, frustrating, shaming, or confusing. Such feelings are a normal response to the abnormal situation that many mental health care services find themselves in. Like many others, you were possibly trained and started working in this system, considering many things to be normal that, in retrospect, seem ethically questionable. You may be experiencing a so-called 'moral injury,' which is psychological distress resulting from actions or inactions that conflict with your ethical or moral values. The good news is that your emotions and self-criticism show your healthy sense of SJ and may help you make better future decisions. Yes, I also know that you may feel frustrated and helpless about the constrictions that your mental health care service or system imposes. Try to focus on what you can still do despite these limitations (see Fig. 9.2).

Structurally Unjust Context

Reflect on all aspects in the immediate and broader context of your therapeutic practice that may create an injustice to your clients, as described above. What lies in your power to change, and what does not?

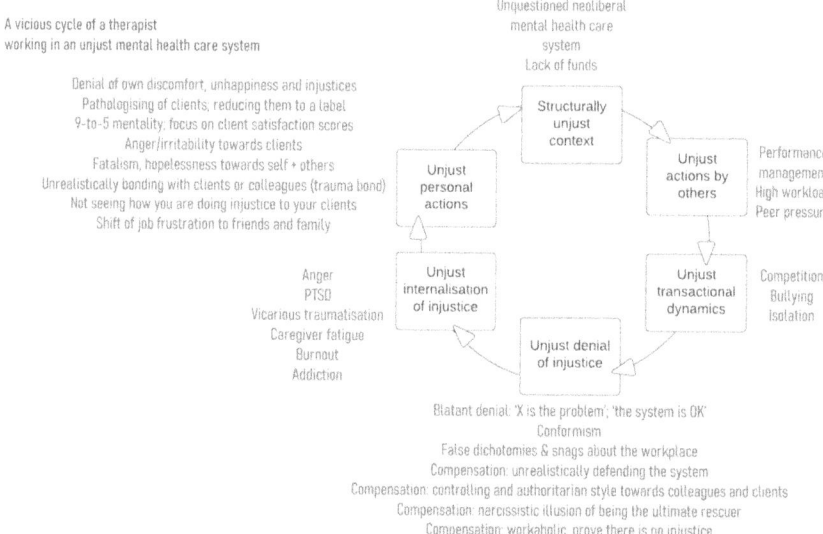

Fig. 9.2 Example of a vicious cycle in mental health care

Unjust Actions by Others

What practical actions do others do that impact your care? Think of performance management, high workload, peer pressure, and limited funding by health insurance or national health services. What lies in your power to change, and what does not?

Unjust Transactional Dynamics

What interpersonal interactions/transactions feel unjust to you and your client? Think of competition, bullying, and isolation in the workplace. What lies in your power to change, and what does not?

Unjust Denial of Injustice

How is SI denied in your clients and your service? This may involve group dynamics, unchosen group roles, such as egos and scapegoats or favourite and worst clients, by yourself, colleagues, and clients. Blatant splitting may include reasonings, such as 'X is the problem, not the system.' As an overcompensation of the felt SI, some individuals may unrealistically defend the service or system, impose a controlling or authoritarian style, or create narcissistic illusions of the ultimate rescuer or prosecutor. On the other side, individuals may flee into a passive victim role, become a workaholic, and try to prove there is no SI. What lies in your power to change, and what does not?

Unjust Internalization of Injustice

How do you, your colleagues and clients internalize the systemic injustice? For example, do you show anger, stress, PTSD, vicarious traumatization, caregiver fatigue, burnout, or addiction? What lies in your power to change, and what does not?

Unjust Personal Actions

How do you (and your colleagues and clients) reinforce the vicious cycle of SI in your workplace? For example, you may focus merely on getting your salary or self-development and not contributing to helping others or SI in general. You may unquestioningly follow what others tell you or act on automatic pilot and deny your critical intuition. You may focus on your lack of freedom and assume being completely determined by your situation. You may merely focus on helping your clients get rid of their psychiatric diagnosis but not contribute to them realizing their broader potential and living a more meaningful life. You may disproportionally pathologize your client's normal responses to abnormal socio-economic situations and reduce them to a label. You may start splitting and develop unhealthy ego boundaries in relationships with clients or colleagues. You, your colleagues, or clients may get stuck in rigid roles and relational games, such as trying to be the rescuer, prosecutor, or victim. This may include showing anger, irritability, fatalism, hopelessness, or boredom towards clients or colleagues, as well as the development of unhealthy bonds (trauma bonds). You may also shift your work frustrations to your personal life, family, and friends.

Before consciously noticing these patterns, you may experience bodily discomfort or shift emotional stress and problems to secondary emotional issues. These personal actions may keep the service or system unquestioned and continue as it is. What lies in your power to change, and what does not? What can you do to stop the vicious cycle?

Interventions to Break the Cycle of Injustice

Start with self-care and self-compassion. What may feel like an abnormal response may be a very normal response to a very abnormal situation. Try to get a larger perspective on the situation to see the bigger context and the realism and helpfulness of your response. Remember that your feelings most likely reflect your professional role in this situation, not your professional potential, personal life, personality, life-story, and potential. Be aware of what is in your power to change and what is not:

Look at your answers in the 'Integrated Cycle of Social Injustice' section. What are the most critical underlying problems? Focusing on these critical problems, how could you formulate clear, achievable goals to change these? What practical steps do you need to achieve these goals? Focus on goals and steps in your power, particularly those that keep the vicious cycle going. Look after your mental health and prevent internalization of problems in the service/system. This may also include working on unprocessed SI in your life-story. What are helpful responses to change the SI? Most of all, do not deny the injustice that may be going on and that you may be contributing to by refraining from active change, such as systemic racism.

Recovery and Building Resilience

Psychotherapists can build personal resilience by engaging in self-care practices, seeking supervision and support from colleagues, cultivating a strong support network, practising mindfulness and reflection, and staying connected to their sense of purpose and values in their work.

Tolerate Personal Discomfort If that Improves Justice

Learn to embrace the discomfort that critical self-reflection and reflexivity may bring. In this discomfort, the seeds of justice may grow and bear fruit. As Nelson Mandela (1990) said, learn that "courage is not the absence of fear, but the triumph over it. The brave man is not he who does not feel afraid, but he who conquers that fear" (p. 32). Get out of your comfort zone. The more you are in it, the less likely you will do full justice to the other and yourself.

Stay Sensitive to Injustice

Therapists may stay sensitive and empathic to topics of social injustice by continuously educating themselves about social issues, engaging in self-reflection to understand their own biases, and actively listening to their clients' experiences. It is crucial for therapists to remain open to learning from their clients and to validate their experiences without imposing their perspectives. Working with SI is not about 'winning' or 'rescuing' but about listening with compassion and understanding, recognizing our shared human needs and vulnerabilities, and setting aside our ego and needs. Additionally, seeking supervision and support from colleagues can provide a space for processing difficult emotions and experiences, preventing emotional numbing. Engaging in advocacy and social justice efforts outside of their therapeutic practice can help therapists stay connected to broader societal issues and maintain their sensitivity and empathy.

Never Let Go of Your Fundamental Values

A poor person should not need to justify their right to a roof over their head and food in their belly. Similarly, a person with mental health issues should not need to justify their right to tailored professional mental health care. Because each individual is worth living a meaningful life (Vos, 2020).

Innovate

Get out of your comfort zone and of your comfy chair—literally. Examine how you can move your service into the community, where people need support, and experiment with innovative care tailored to your client's strengths, preferences, and cultures (Thornicroft, 2011).

Boundaries

Setting healthy boundaries is crucial for maintaining emotional and psychological well-being, allowing therapists to establish clear limits in their professional relationships and balancing empathy and professional detachment. By setting boundaries, therapists can protect themselves from emotional exhaustion, burnout, and compassion fatigue while fostering a safe and ethical environment for their clients. Additionally, healthy boundaries help establish a framework for effective communication, build trust, and maintain professional integrity, ultimately contributing to the overall quality of care.

Prevent Splitting

Therapists can prevent the use of splitting as a coping mechanism by engaging in regular self-reflection and introspection to identify and address their biases and emotional reactions. Seeking supervision and consultation with colleagues can provide an external perspective and help therapists gain insight into their thoughts and emotional responses. Additionally, ongoing professional development and training in cultural competence and diversity can help therapists develop a more nuanced understanding of complex issues, reducing the likelihood of resorting to splitting as a coping mechanism. Finally, practising mindfulness and self-awareness can help therapists recognize and manage their emotional reactions healthily and constructively.

Prevent Burnout

Therapists may prevent burnout, compassion fatigue, and vicarious traumatization by prioritizing self-care practices, setting healthy boundaries, seeking supervision and support from colleagues, and engaging in regular self-reflection and mindfulness. Therapists must maintain a healthy work-life balance, engage in activities that bring them joy and relaxation, and seek support from their own therapist or mental health professional when needed.

Diagnose Broadly

A holistic assessment should include the client's emotional issues and sense of self, biology, emotions, daily life, community, society, and global issues (Fig. 9.3). When assessing a client's case, do not unnecessarily pathologize and individualize the client's problems, but be holistic. Examine powers, threats, traumas, interpersonal reciprocal processes, SI, contributions to the cycle of SI, and opportunities to break these. Also, reflect on how clients' answers may reflect their expectations or power position towards the health care system, you as a person or as a symbolic authority figure (Vos et al., 2019). Assessment and diagnostic systems should be used to recognise SI/SJ, such as the Power-Threat-Meaning Framework endorsed by the British Psychological Society (Johnstone & Boyle, 2018). The Power-Threat-Meaning Framework is an alternative to the traditional diagnostic mental health model. It focuses on understanding the impact of power, threats, and meanings in a person's life rather than labelling and categorizing symptoms. Its core questions are: What has happened to you (how is power operating in your life?), how did it affect you (what kind of threats does this pose), what sense did you make of it (what is the meaning of these experiences to you?), and what did you have to do to survive (what kinds of threat response are you using?).

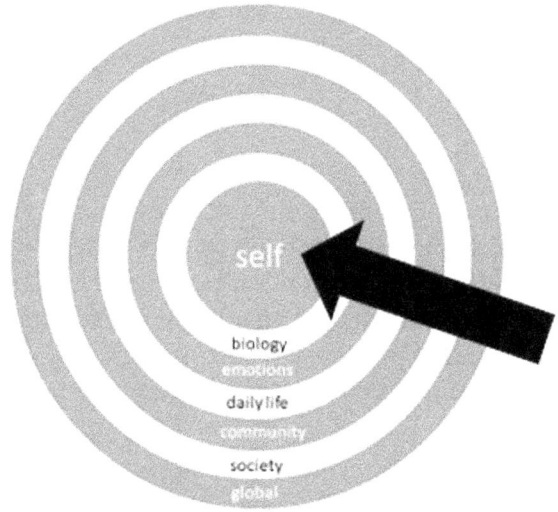

Fig. 9.3 Social model of mental health care (Vos et al., 2019)

Tailor Client's Goals

Therapists can tailor therapy to clients' needs, goals, and preferences by engaging in collaborative goal-setting discussions. This involves actively involving clients in identifying their therapy goals, ranging from specific behavioural changes to broader personal growth objectives. By asking clients to set therapy goals, therapists can gain insight into their unique aspirations and concerns, allowing for a more personalized and client-centered approach to treatment. Additionally, therapists can adapt their therapeutic techniques, interventions, and treatment plans to align with each client's individualized goals and preferences, fostering a more effective and meaningful therapeutic experience. For example, focus on their strengths (Rapp & Goscha, 2011) or offer therapy to help clients live a meaningful and fulfilling life despite life's inevitable challenges (Vos, 2018).

Address Social Injustice

Explicitly acknowledge SI in the client's life-experiences and help them to set and achieve SJ-related therapy goals, such as Social-Justice Oriented Interventions.

Adjust Therapeutic Methods to Address SI

Creatively adjust your therapeutic method and tools to address SI explicitly. For example, behavioural therapists often ask clients to keep a diary that includes their situation, thoughts, emotions, and behaviour. This may also include the situation's meaning, resources, and existential threats (Vos, internal report). Explicitly ask clients to identify their lack of resources/power and how realistic and helpful the threats are.

Discussion

This chapter addressed the challenges therapists face within an unjust mental health care system. It offered a comprehensive framework for addressing SI through Social Justice Oriented Interventions. It emphasized the importance of therapists feeling safe and secure in their personal and professional lives. Based on systematic research, this chapter offered self-reflective questions and practical strategies, although this framework requires further validation through empirical research. Furthermore, the chapter focused on individual therapists, whereas more fundamental social structures and power dynamics may need to be addressed.

Therapists may want to prioritize personal safety and well-being to effectively address SI in client interactions, engage in self-reflective practice to understand the impact of SI on clients and themselves, and embrace mindful self-compassion to prevent burnout and enhance resilience. Clinical supervisors and lecturers/trainers may incorporate theory and practical tools to address SI in therapeutic practice, encourage therapists to creatively adapt therapeutic approaches to tackle SI, and foster a culture of self-reflection and self-compassion.

Mental health professionals are responsible for improving both their clients and the broader society in which they operate (Wise, 2013). That is, they fulfil a vital role by supporting individual clients in the therapy room so that the clients may become more empowered to fulfil their potential in society. The impact of therapists should not be underestimated, as socio-economic and political development starts with facilitating an individual's practical and emotional freedom (Sen, 2001; Vos, 2020).

Structural transformation of mental health care into a justice-oriented system may require patience and political skills (Fairweather et al., 2013). However, one day and one client at a time, therapists contribute to the revolutionary change that the mental health care system desperately needs (Kinderman, 2019; Vos et al., 2019). Furthermore, the nature of SI is such that it isolates and makes victims believe that they are fighting on their own. As a therapist, look around and connect with people with a similar sense of justice. Fighting collectively for SJ is like a flock of birds in flight. When one tires, another takes the lead, ensuring their journey continues uninterrupted. You are not alone. As long as we are flying, we are moving and not stuck in one place. Find hope by looking towards our joint destination of a more just system and society.

References

Andresen, R., Oades, L. G., & Caputi, P. (2011). *Psychological recovery*. Wiley.
Davies, J. (2013). *Cracked*. Icon.
Davies, J. (2017). *The sedated society*. Palgrave.
Fairweather, G. W., Sanders, D. H., & Tornatzky, L. G. (2013). *Creating change in mental health organizations*. Elsevier.
Johnstone, L., & Boyle, M. (2018). *The power-threat-meaning framework*. BPS.
Kinderman, P. (2019). *A manifesto for mental health*. Springer.
Knapp, S. J. (2015). *Ethical dilemmas in psychotherapy*. APA.
Mandela, N. (1990). *The struggle is my life*. Popular Prakashan.
Rapp, C. A., & Goscha, R. J. (2011). *The strengths model*. OUP.
Sen, A. (2001). *Development as freedom*. OUP.

Slade, M., Oades, L., & Jarden, A. (Eds.). (2017). *Wellbeing, recovery, and mental health*. CUP.
Thornicroft, G. (2011). *Oxford textbook of community mental health*. OUP.
Vos, J. (2018). *Meaning in life: An evidence-based handbook for practitioners*. Bloomsbury.
Vos, J. (2020). *The economics of meaning in life*. University Professors Press.
Vos, J. (2021). Systematic pragmatic phenomenological analysis. *Counselling and Psychotherapy Research, 21*(1), 77–97.
Vos, J. (2023). *Doing research in psychological therapies: A step-by-step guide*. Sage.
Vos, J., Roberts, R., & Davies, J. (2019). *Mental health in crisis*. Sage.
Wise, E. H. (2013). *Ethical and legal issues for mental health professionals*. Taylor Francis.

Part IV

Context

10

For the Breathless to Breathe: Frantz Fanon's Clinic

Leswin Laubscher

Introduction

"Radical" is a rather easy epithet and descriptive for Frantz Fanon. More often than not, such an association is of a negative sort, in general and for Fanon in particular, used to designate an extremist, a kind of dogmatic or ideological fringe. Impervious to moderating reason, such radicals are assumed to hold harsh and unbending positions, threatening to the well-being of a compromising and accommodating polis. Inasmuch as we acknowledge, even valorize, the radical descriptive for Fanon, our understanding differs, privileging as it does the etymological unconscious of the word, as the "root or ground" of the thing, the thing "vital to life" (from the Latin, *radicalis*). As such, Fanon *is* radical, but in a way that serves as exemplar for science and practice in general, of a thoroughgoing theory and praxis that is creatively, critically, and courageously reflexive,

---

L. Laubscher (✉)
Clinical Psychology Department, Duquesne University, Pittsburgh, PA, USA
e-mail: laubscher@duq.edu

© The Author(s), under exclusive license to Springer Nature Switzerland AG 2025   179
J. Hook, F. Gruba-McCallister (eds.), *The Revolutionary Psychologist's Guide to Radical Therapy*, The Politics of Mental Health and Illness,
https://doi.org/10.1007/978-3-032-02399-5_10

open to possibility and a more fulfilling, ethical, just, and loving world. Indeed, it is by a focus on such roots that it becomes possible not only to call out the rot that betrays fulfilling growth for the tree, but also to act, to cull dead roots and parasitic organisms from its violent restraints on the promise "for ourselves and for humanity" to "develop a new way of thinking, and endeavor to create a new man"[1] (Fanon, 2004, p. 239).

Thus it is also possible to contest thinking "the radical" as that singular exception whose insights and actions are well beyond reach for the rest of us. Whether in the guise of hero or villain, the radical (say Nelson Mandela or Florence Nightingale, Jesus or Mohammed, Ché Guevara or Greta Thunberg) is perceived as one whose actions and beliefs places them outside the orbit of "common" and everyday lives and concerns where school fees, rent, or the care of aging parents vie for privileged attention. The point is that we assume an almost insuperable psychic distance between "mere mortals" and "the radical." The consequence is either to bridge this distance by giving up our critical and agentic faculties to "join" the radical in cultish incorporation, *or* that we separate ourselves so completely from the supposedly unattainable example in order to carry on tilling our monadic place in the sun.

If Fanon teaches us anything, however, it is that we can all be radicals inasmuch as we can reflect, and act. "To educate man to be actional, preserving in all his relations his respect for the basic values that constitute a human world, is the prime task of him who, having taken thought, prepares to act" (Fanon, 1967a, p. 158). In fact, as the quote already suggests, it is not simply that we *can* act, but that it is incumbent upon us that we do, as an ethical demand, imposed on us by the other and humanity itself. We reflect, we act, we serve because it is how we redeem our humanity, how we justify ourselves before the other. Our response is our responsibility, to the other and ourselves. It is a call prior to ontology, and the very resonance by which we recognize ourselves as human.

Much of Fanon's inspiration, if not the most prominent motivation for the "radical" and "revolutionary" descriptor, derives from the political. Social theory and sociology, cultural studies, critical phenomenology,

---

[1] I have retained Fanon's gendered references in direct quotes. They are, of course, to be considered in light of a contemporary corrective, which I subscribe to and abide by in all other instances.

philosophy, post- and decolonial studies (among others) have all been nourished by his insights, as has the practical work of political activists and non- governmental organizations (Burman, 2021; Laubscher, 2025). Psychology, at least the mainstream and Western versions, however, has been slow at best, or wholly ignorant, at worst, of his psychological contributions and promise (Laubscher et al., 2021). But if general psychological attention is sparse, deliberate engagement with his psychiatric and psychotherapeutic innovations is even less so[2]—at least until relatively recently. In the wake of Jean Khalfa and Robert Young's magisterial collection of Fanon's clinical writings (Fanon, 2018a), including papers from journals which have long been out of print, there has been a resurgent flurry of attention to Fanon's clinical practice (e.g. Gaztambide, 2021, 2024; Gibson & Beneduce, 2017; Goozee, 2021; Hook, 2020; Siegel, 2023; Turner & Neville, 2019). For many, "until the publication of his clinical papers (in English) we had no idea how deep Fanon's theorization of the psychopathology of colonization/decolonization ran in his dialectics of revolution" (Turner & Neville, 2019, p. 42). Perhaps, considering that Fanon "regarded himself essentially as a psychiatrist and practiced and researched psychiatry almost continuously, whether in France, Algeria or Tunisia" (Khalfa, 2021a, p. 1), it should not come as complete surprise. This chapter also focuses on Fanon's clinical writings, and whereas it does so in an introductory and synoptic manner, it should still highlight that the radical of Fanon's theory and politics also marks his clinical praxis.

Voici L'Homme[3]

Having committed to the marching orders for this chapter—to provide some exposition of Fanon's clinical practice, and to wrestle with the ways such practice might be challenging of, and instructive to, our contemporary own, I should thus "get on with it." I could certainly do so, were I to

---

[2] A few earlier exceptions include Bulhan (1985), McCulloch (1983), Razanajao et al. (1996) and Keller (2007).
[3] Whereas the section heading is an admittedly elliptical (and ironic) reference to the question of the biographical, "Behold the man" is also purposely metaphorical, overdetermined for its judg-

write about Freud, Jung, or Rogers. Almost every paper on Fanon in "mainstream" journals or books, however, finds itself somehow compelled to lead with some introduction to "the man" alongside, or in preparation for, his theory and philosophy. One might argue that there is a straightforward reason for this: many (most?) readers don't know much about him, and/or their psychological training omitted him from considered mention.

There is a complication, though, to such an explanation. Fanon is neither "new" nor "unfamiliar" to psychology, scholarship, and activism in academic "…departments and on the streets of the Global South and the inner cities of the Western north—indeed, wherever an oppressive or racist context serves to prod and prompt recourse to the wisdom of his insights and scholarship" (Laubscher, 2025). Most Black teens and young adults knew who 2Pac (Tupac Shakur) was, and found an inspirational connection to his music well before White teens and young adults "discovered" him (a dynamic also true for James Baldwin, Maya Angelou, Erykah Badu, and others). To speak about 2Pac then would demand a similar biographical pressure as Fanon's erasure from the western psychological canon[4] does to an audience who would mouth "Fanon who?", "the violence guy?", or "never heard of him."[5] If, now, commenting on the Chicago riots of 1967, David Caute remarks that "every brother on a rooftop can quote Fanon" (Caute, 1970, p. jacket copy), and Abu Jamal notes that "every (Black) panther was told it was his/her duty to read *The Wretched of the Earth*" (Abu-Jamal, 2019, p. 7), or that Fanon would resurface in George Floyd's wake, and at many Black Lives Matter protest marches, emblazoned on ubiquitous posters as "we revolt because we can no longer breathe,"[6] the fact of his erasure betrays a structural dynamic and politics. We can ask, as Lewis Gordon does, "How many biographies

---

ment of the radical, from Pontius Pilate's presentation of Jesus to the rejecting and mocking crowd (*Ecce Homo*), through Nietzsche's announcement of the Dionysian philosopher.

[4] See Laubscher (2025) and Laubscher et al. (2021) for additional commentary on Fanon's absence from psychology.

[5] All of these are actual responses to Fanon's mention at formal and informal scholarly gatherings.

[6] The quote is often misattributed and erroneously rendered. It is not from *The Wretched of the Earth*, but from *Black Skin, White Masks*, and reads as follows: "It is not because the Indo-Chinese has discovered a culture of his own that he is in revolt. It is because 'quite simply' it was, in more than one way, becoming impossible for him to breathe" (Fanon, 1967a, p. 226).

10 For the Breathless to Breathe: Frantz Fanon's Clinic   183

of Frederick Douglass, W. E. B. du Bois, and Fanon do we need before it is recognised that they also produced *ideas*? It is as if to say that white thinkers provide *theory* and black thinkers provide *experience* for which all seek explanatory force from the former" (Gordon, 2015, p. 5, emphasis in original). Already, we challenge readers of this book to consider the omissions of their training and knowledge less as benign oversight than a structural politics to which their science provides scaffolding support.

But there are also other reasons why so many of us feel drawn and compelled to introduce Fanon with the biographical, truth be told even if the audience "knows" his theory and story. At first glance there may be similarity to the way we introduce some speaker at a learned conference.: We list publications or academic awards, to demonstrate the speaker's bona fides to speak knowledgeably about the topic. I believe, for Fanon, the difference is that the authority of his story and his voice, for all its uniqueness, derives from the recognition of ourselves in it, all the wretched and damned of the earth ("the Black man's alienation is not an individual question" [Fanon, 1967a, p. 11]). To read and recount that oft quoted primal scene of *Black Skin, White Masks*, of a white child reacting to Fanon's presence—"Mama, see the Negro! I'm frightened" (p. 112)— also echoes in my daily experience on a bus, where the open seat next to me, or next to some other black man, is always the last to be filled, if it is at all. It sounds in the apprehension at every police car in our rearview mirror and as we carry every other black and brown person with our entry into the boardroom or the lecture hall. "Wherever he goes, the Negro remains a Negro" (Fanon, 1967a, p. 173).[7]

Notwithstanding, much of Fanon's story will have to be the reader's responsibility. Whereas I make some biographical references in the sections to follow, the betrayal of a life by such brevity can be ameliorated by introductory recourse to one or more of the existing biographies of

---

[7] Sheehi and Sheehi (2021) relays reading a section of *The Wretched of the Earth* aloud, to a group of training-clinicians and their Palestinian supervisors (who had never heard of Fanon before) in the city of al-Nasirah (Nazareth), whereafter "... there was utter silence ...," a silence which "... held seven decades of colonial trauma, thick with affect that had not been spoken" (pp. 184–185). This scene was replicated in my own experience, coming across Fanon in apartheid South Africa, and it remains true in my classes, for students of color from Delhi to Detroit, Lima to Lagos.

Fanon, especially that of Macey (2012), Cherki (2006), and most recently, Shatz (2024).[8]

He was born on July 20, 1925, on the small Caribbean island of Martinique, a French colony then, as it remains to this day (albeit rebranded as a "special territorial collectivity of the French Republic"). Bearing the mark of his enslaved African ancestors on his skin, the colonial project saw to the grammar of the psyche: "In the Antilles, the black schoolboy who is constantly asked to recite 'our ancestors the Gauls' identifies himself with the explorer, the civilizing colonizer, the white man who brings truth to the savages, a lily-white truth" (Fanon, 2008, p. 126). Aware, as a teenager already, of racism and colonial privilege, as well as the argument against participation in World War II (as "a White man's war"), Fanon nonetheless joined the Free French Forces, expressing the view that "whenever human dignity and freedom are at stake, it involves us, whether we be black, white, or yellow. And whenever these are threatened, in any corner of the earth, I will fight them to the end" (Recounted by his friend and fellow soldier, Marcel Manville, cited in Cherki, 2006, p. 10). It was a belief, however, that was to be severely tested by the racism he encountered on the front. The ideals of the republic—*liberte, egalite, fraternite*—did not apply to its Black subjects. "I've been deceived, and I am paying for my mistakes," he would write to his brother Joby (quoted in Macey, 2012, p. 101).[9] At the end of the war, entertaining "serious doubts about his identity as a Frenchman" (Bulhan, 1985, p. 28), Fanon enrolled at the University of Lyon to study medicine and psychiatry.

---

[8] Earlier biographies include Caute (1970), Gendzier (1973), Geismer (1971). Additionally, a more intimate record of Fanon's life is provided by his brother, Joby (J. Fanon, 2014).

[9] Similar experiences were also commonly recounted by African American soldiers. Historian Matthew Delmont (2022) documents several such instances, including allowing Nazi prisoners to eat with White American servicemen, ride in the same train car, or attend movie screenings with them when their fellow Black soldiers were not. Not unlike Fanon, such incidents led scores of Black American soldiers to question their identification with, and belonging to, the United States.

Four (Clinical) Steps[10] in Place

We edge up to Fanon's clinical writings by the image of four "steps." They are not discrete. Neither are they to be thought linearly, as in a movement from one place to another, from an origin to a destination markedly different from its commencement. Yet the stepping in place *is* progressive, as a demonstration that reveals the march—like dressage, the stepping performance of which illustrates the possibility of the impossible. Each step recapitulates the ones before as it simultaneously prepares the ones to follow, actually not unlike therapy. Then, by its emulation and reinvention for our times, it might just be possible to step *out* of place to the radical possibility of Fanon's new humanism to come.

The Theoretical Step

Alongside his training in medicine, Fanon's education at Lyon included a rigorous and extensive exposure to phenomenology, existentialism, and psychoanalysis. He also read voraciously beyond the prescribed curriculum, for example many of the so called Négritude writers, philosophers such as Marx and Hegel, works of anthropology and sociology (Levi-Strauss, for example), but also drama, poetry, and literature. A prominent bookseller, Raymond Péju, writes that Fanon "was curious about everything ... most especially about the human sciences and poetry" (Letter from Peju, cited in Fanon, 2018a, p. 387). I dwell on the variety of Fanon's reading because the manner of his major "work in psychology,[11]" *Black Skin White Masks* (2008), uses all these influences and crosses all these disciplinary boundaries quite deliberately. There is no program-

---

[10] There is a deliberate allusion here to (one of) the French word for step (*pas*), and the complex ways in which the word can be used; For example, as adverb when it forms the negative form of the verb (*je ne sais pas*), as noun where it refers to the positive of a physical step (*faites un pas en avant*), or as expression to qualify and express particular nuance (*pas mal*). Jacques Derrida's use of *pas* is one I am particularly mindful of for the ways its deployment signal the movement of *différance* and the deferral of meaning's final, apocalyptic arrival.

[11] A common distinction would have *Black Skin White Masks* as his "psychological" work, and *The Wretched of the Earth* his "political". This is a lazy and banal distinction, hence the quotation marks—the psychological threads through his whole oeuvre, as does the political: the point is precisely about the psychological in the institutional, and the institutional in the psychological.

matic psychology as such, which he admits to: "I shall be derelict" and leave the straitjacket of disciplinary method and grammar "to the botanists and the mathematicians" as "there is a point at which methods devour themselves" (Fanon, 1967a, p. 12). This is not a negative. Quite the contrary, it serves as a radical model for what a rigorously academic, but creative and reflexive psychology could be.

Fanon intended *Black Skin, White Masks* to serve as his doctoral dissertation, but it was rejected as unsuitable—defying as it did all existing academic and scientific norms (Cherki, 2006; Macey, 2012). So, in a space of a few weeks, he wrote a more "traditional" dissertation, "Mental alteration, character modifications, psychic disorders and intellectual deficit in spinocerebellar heterodegeneration: A Case of Friedreich ataxia with delusions of possession" (Fanon, 2021b). Even here, however, in a dissertation that takes a supposedly clear biological issue, a hereditary neurological illness, he emphasizes that the biological of the illness must be considered alongside the social and the cultural for any fuller scientific meaning. Indeed, the epigraph for the dissertation, a quote from Nietzsche ("I speak only of *lived* things and do not simply present cerebral processes"),[12] powerfully supports this view and acts as herald, really, for all of Fanon's life.. As strategically as his argument unfolds, it sounds a clear warning to the attempt (and seduction) that reduces the psychological to the neurological. Even if mental illness has a neurological origin, it "develops in a socially determined relational space which in turn explains the form it takes" (Khalfa, 2021a, p. 8). One may classify the neurological into neat categories, but cannot do so for its psychiatric correlates. A tree or an ashtray, Fanon argues, is on a hill or a table, but such facts "loses all stability" with a human being, who "always exists in the process of" and with others (Fanon, 2021b, pp. 54–55).

Returning to *Black Skin, White Masks*, which Fanon clearly characterizes not only as "a work in psychology," but as "a clinical study" (Fanon, 1967a, p. 12), the point is precisely to demonstrate how racism and colonialism permeates and structures the psyche and material being-in-the-world. The colonial and racist world is a violent one, structurally and

---

[12] Fanon attributes the quote to *Alzo sprach Zarathustra*. It is actually from a preparatory manuscript for *Ecce Homo*. "Lived" is emphasized in Fanon's quotation.

overtly, with direct psychic effects (Robcis, 2020), lived and felt in the body, the imagination, and relationships (Desai, 2014; Pitts, 2022). As such, one cannot assume established ontological truisms, for example that, skin color notwithstanding, we are fundamentally all the same, all "human." "Ontology—once it is finally admitted as leaving existence by the wayside—does not allow us to understand the being of the black man" (Fanon, 1967a, p. 110). Indeed, Fanon's analysis of lived experience lays bare the Black's appearance as a "phobogenic object," crafted as it were from myth, history, and "a thousand details, anecdotes, stories" (p. 111) of primitivism, cannibalism, savagery, backwardness, and wonton, instinctive violence. Prereflective and prelinguistic, the Black is present before they "actually" arrive. Even "children know that innocence is not black" (Sexton, 2011, p. 116).

The desire to live as a human being cannot be reconciled by an unconscious constitutively alienated (Siegel, 2023), and by a life of exile from an ontological universal. It is a banishment most visibly branded onto the body, which is not "what it should be, the body of a man" (Khalfa, 2021b, p. 48). The corporeal of Merleau Ponty's (1968) body in relation to the world, one of agency, freedom, and temporality, is "nullified and rendered naïve by the Black experience" (Weate, 2021, p. 168). A historico-racial schema overlays the corporeal, and a "livery that the white man has sewed for him" (Fanon, 1967a, p. 138) renders a world wherein "the Negro suffers in his body quite differently from the white man" (p.138). "Overdetermined from the outside," "a slave...to my appearance," carrying the weight of a "corporeal malediction" (p. 95), the Black is "abraded into nonbeing" (p. 109) and a carceral existence from where "passage to existence finds itself lost in a profound obscurity, where everything slips away" (Marriott, 2018, p. 315).

There are worlds more to *Black Skin, White Masks*, but for our focus on the clinical, let us emphasize Fanon's use of lived experience, his own as autoethnographic case study of sorts, as well as readings of literature, descriptions of others, observations of friends, family, passersby, for his insights. By the test of the material and the everyday, received theories and practices are evaluated, modified or discarded. Thus, phenomenology and psychoanalysis are both used and revised, its truth measured by the recognition that, "beside phylogeny and ontogeny stands sociogeny"

(Fanon, 1967a, p. 11). As such, psychic conflict is less the repetition of individual and familial trauma than the intrusion of the social and of material and lived experience, a clinical extension being for example that dream interpretation must concede "the rifle of the Senegalese soldier is not a penis but a genuine rifle, model Lebel 1916" (p. 106). Every practice, as methodology and procedural act, has to be rethought for its relation to the epistemological and ontological assumptions it shelters.

An often neglected early publication of Fanon's, "The North African Syndrome" (Fanon, 1967b), also provides insight for its express linkage of theory and clinical practice. Fanon recounts, as a training medical student, accompanying established physicians to predominantly Muslim neighborhoods in Lyon, that Western medicine would often find no significant illness among those patients—in spite of friends and family being convinced the patient was at death's door. Not only did these doctors find "…no lesional basis" for the complaint, "…no consistency, no reality," but more often than not, the patient would "spontaneously" recover a few days later, providing evidence for the assumption of the North African as "a simulator, a liar, a malingerer, a sluggard, a thief" (p. 7). For Fanon, however, the symptoms may not have been physiological, but they were no less real. He calls it the "North African Syndrome," characterized by the North African in France, "threatened in his affectivity, threatened in his social activity, threatened in his membership in the community" (p. 13). One for whom the "encounter with himself" is in a neurotic mode, emptied out as he is, "without life, in a bodily struggle with death, a death on this side of death, a death in life" (p. 13). In the frustration of western psychiatrists to offer a functional and causal diagnosis, they resort to medicalized jargon to cover an a priori attitude. The North African is an intellectual child, the north African is constitutionally lazy, unable to reason, to govern themselves.

The lesson of this first step is that there is no radical therapy without radical theory, and that radical theory emerges from lived and embodied existence in time and place. To be a radical is to examine the root assumptions of our science, and its expression in what we do and how we understand others. And to reflect on how others die and suffer as a challenge to how we live and act in the world.

The Sociotherapeutic Step

Not long after receiving his medical degree, Fanon took up psychiatric residency in central France. Here his paths would cross with Francois Tosquelles, for whom "radical" and "revolutionary" is as bespoke a fit as any.[13] Tosquelles's "Institutional Psychotherapy" (which Fanon more frequently referred to as *socialthérapie*—social therapy) sought nothing less than the complete restructuring of the psychiatric hospital as a site for radically transformative clinical interventions (Gibson & Beneduce, 2017; Luxon, 2021b; Vergés, 1996).

Of institutional psychotherapy's innovations, one is struck by its comprehensiveness and its practical reorganization of lived space. For example, patients were organized into a self-managed union of sorts (known as "the Club") (Robcis, 2020), tasked with overseeing and planning activities and life at the hospital For example, regular general meetings with all hospital stakeholders provided feedback, critique, suggestion; workshops on printing, pottery, cooking were part of "ergotherapy"; uniforms were abandoned, making doctors, nurses and patients indistinguishable from one another; a wide range of cultural activities (films, concerts, theatre) was offered. A newsletter, run by an editorial board comprised of patients and staff, had both a theoretical-therapeutic and practical function. Transformation also extended to physical architecture—the walls separating the patients' "cells" were demolished, as were those separating the hospital from the surrounding village.

One might recognize some of these changes in contemporary practice, even offer that whereas they might have been radical in the 1940's and 1950's, they are more common today. However, these are mostly isolated "enrichment" events, a "distraction," or borne from a certain patronizing "goodwill" humanism. They are not, as was the case with Institutional

---

[13] François Tosquelles qualified as a psychiatrist in Spain and became the head of the Republican Army's psychiatric services core during the Spanish Civil War. Sentenced to death by Franco's regime, he escaped Spain in 1939 by crossing the Pyrenees on foot. In France, Tosquelles quickly joined the French resistance, and after the war worked to transform psychiatry, striving to turn the asylum into a caring community where everyone—patient and staff—would have a treatment say and responsibility. Camille Robcis (2016, 2020) provides an excellent introduction to Tosquelles's story and influence.

Therapy, integrally connected to the transformation of the institution as much as the patient. Nor are they seen as methodological extensions of an epistemological sociogenics or an ontology of justice and/as care. The consequence is that such piecemeal activities almost always catch its overseers off guard when the activity produces its own revolutionary and radical potential—as when the inmates challenge the administration of the prison or its practices, or patients insist on inviting a speaker on alternative/indigenous healing.

Institutional therapy's practices are inexorably linked to theory, as theory is to therapy. The activity both engenders and facilitates symbolic and psychotherapeutic meanings. Thus the piece of weaving or sculpture the patient fabricates does "not have a therapeutic value in itself, but it was invested with affective, economic, and social values" (Tosquelles, quoted in Robcis, 2021, p. 44) which allows for "new vectors of transference, different forms of identifications, and alternative social relations" (Robcis, 2020, p. 314). As such therapy is broader than the individual therapeutic office or the formalized group therapy session, but part and parcel of the whole where alternative social interactions and roles open defenses and transferences, and where meaning making could be facilitated. The hospital becomes "a space for disalienating encounters" (Gibson & Beneduce, 2017, p. 14), one where patients can play a deliberate part in their own recovery (Shatz, 2024). It becomes, in Tosquelles oft repeated phrase, a *collectif soignant*, a "healing collective."

Fanon thrived at St. Albans, enthusiastically participated in all its activities, and lent his name to those of Tosquelles and his colleagues as pioneering patronym for Institutional Psychotherapy (or, as he preferred, socio-therapy). This clearly aligned with his theoretical views, especially the notion of madness as less a function of consciousness than a pathology of freedom. As such, the hospital becomes a place for the mentally ill "seeking after lost meaning" (Fanon & Asselah, 2018, p. 447), a place to engage in "inter-human encounters" and activities in the service of a "rediscovery of the ego and the world" (Tosquelles & Fanon, 2018, p. 294), a place to "explore the affect that attaches to recollection, and to work towards verbalizing the unspeakable" (Luxon, 2021a, p. 187). For the cure of the patient, a cure of the institution was needed.

The Decolonial Step

In 1953, after passing the exam qualifying him to work as a *médecin-chef* (director of a psychiatric hospital), Fanon travelled to Blida-Joinville in Algeria, then the largest psychiatric institution in North Africa (Macey, 2012; Robcis, 2021). The hospital was overcrowded, underfunded, and had the look and feel of a prison. To "cure the hospital" by the tenets of socio-therapy was an immediate imperative.

Thus, in the sections of the hospital Fanon oversaw (he was one of five supervising psychiatrists, each tasked with separate divisions of the hospital), he immediately set out to reframe the "social architecture" of the hospital and instituted radical reforms similar to, but also more extensive than, those at St. Albans. Uniforms and a long list of disciplinary protocols were cast aside ("formulating disciplinary rules and regulations at a psychiatric hospital is a therapeutic absurdity" [Fanon, 2018b, p. 348]). Training (and retraining) of staff was emphasized including the demand to be respectful, warm and friendly. It involved not only general ways of relating, but was also theoretical, for example teaching them about transference and countertransference, urging them to keep notes of interactions with patients, to learn about patients' singular lives as individuals and before they took ill, and to be constantly vigilant of themselves and their interactions such that "…medical staff, nurses and patients were to learn to take responsibility at each instant, for each of their acts, and to continuously produce their present" (Khalfa, 2020, pp. 90–91). In addition, in order to "institute the social" and create space to "re-learn the gestures of the outside" (Fanon, 2018b, p. 331), Fanon set up a café, instituted daily meetings with patients, set up ergotherapy stations, created a new library, and arranged activities such as trips to the beach, drama and singing performances, and a movie club.

Of particular importance was a newspaper (*Notre Journal*—"Our Newspaper"), to be edited and published by patients. Fanon held a specific theoretical sensitivity to language. The therapeutic of the newsletter was cast in the notion that "to write means to want to be read…to want to be understood" (Fanon, 2018b, p. 325). The newspaper was to function as a particularly important object of care (Egalité, 2024) by which bonds of community and a therapeutics of disalienation could be supported. In an editorial for the newspaper, Fanon writes that "On a ship, it is commonplace to say that one is between sky and water; that one is cut off from the world; that one is alone. This journal, precisely, is to fight against…that solitude" (Fanon, 2018b, p. 315). The newspaper "livens up the boat," informs about "on board" happenings and "next ports of call," but also about "news on land," which is important, because soon "passengers will meet up again with their parents and friends, and return to their homes" (p. 315).

Another emphasis of the reforms at Blida-Joinville was Fanon's emphasis on the therapeutic use of the body. Again, not altogether surprising given the theoretical and philosophical centrality of Fanon's body "as the knot of lived experience" (Luxon, 2021b, p. 99), as a dialectic between body and world, and all the ways racism and oppression locks the Black in their bodies. From the theory of embodiment, and clinical theoretical explorations of the body in insomnia, agitation and violence, for example, there is also the practical therapeutic in the "benign" deployment of bodily energetics, of facilitating an energizing tension and raising bodily tension in activity.

These reforms were instantly successful. At least with the ward of "European women." With Muslim men, however, it was a "total failure" (Fanon & Azoulay, 2021, p. 199). Patients remained indifferent, reform initiatives felt like a burden, and there was no participation in the production of the newsletter, nor was it read. The ergotherapy stations, theater, movies all failed to move Arab patients to any collective or shared sociality and the atmosphere on the Muslim ward remained "oppressive" and "stifling." One might conclude, as colonial psychiatrists like Antoine Porot and John Carothers have, that the failure of such reforms provide evidence for the North African's "neuronal immaturity," lack of "emotivity," "labile" psychomotor functions, lack of "curiosity of mind," and "idleness" of the frontal lobes (Carothers & Porot, quoted in Fanon, 2018b, pp. 406–408).[14]

---

[14] Fanon lists and responds to the ethnopsychiatry of the so called Algiers school and the racism of colonial psychiatrists in all of his major works (e.g. 1965, 2004, 2008).

For Fanon and Azoulay, however, it was an opportunity to reflect on the process of social therapy itself: "we had naively ... adapted to this Muslim society the frames of a particular Western society" (Fanon & Azoulay, 2021, p. 204). It was not simply that the film, or the journal, in itself, did "humanizing" and relational work, but that the artifact and the action had meaning within a particular context, within specific cultural frames of reference and lived experiences. Activities evoke and reflect a world, such that rethinking social therapy would demand restructuring it from "the social morphology and forms of sociability" of the society in which it finds itself (p. 206). This stance is neither of cultural essentialism, nor simple cultural relativism, but to consider the dynamic "total social fact" of a culture in history and material existence.

Hence Fanon and Azoulay set out to learn from the people they served. They started to travel throughout Algeria, visiting local *douars* (villages) to learn about daily life outside the walls of the hospital. They attended local ceremonies and events, participating in and studying exorcism rituals by *marabouts* (religious leaders) and the mental health frameworks occasioned by belief in *djinns* (supernatural beings from Arabic mythology) (Khalfa, 2021a; Luxon, 2021b). The result was what Gibson and Beneduce (2017) calls Fanon's "critical ethnopsychiatry" which would ask what would institutional therapy look like for the Algerian context, specifically.

Almost immediately, Fanon started to encourage his staff (as he did too) to learn Arabic (Cherki, 2006). The recognition, now, that "out of the two hundred and twenty patients in our unit, only five knew how to read and write in Arabic and two, how to read and write in French" (Fanon & Azoulay, 2021, p. 212) explained the indifference to the newsletter. Social gatherings for Muslim patients were religious or familial. Hence social activities were now arranged around Muslim feasts and holy days (Robcis, 2021). Many of the patients had never been exposed to theater, an artifact of the city, but were familiar with professional and itinerant storytellers, and the recitation of oral epics (Egalité, 2024). Thus such storytellers and Muslim singers were hired and invited to the hospital. Weaving, one of the ergotherapy options, was perceived as "woman's work." Hence agricultural work, more familiar to the men, was now presented as an alternative option (Robcis, 2021). The movies were too "western" in subject matter and plot, and were now replaced with action packed ones. Games which sought to support social interaction were not recognizable to the men, and/or were considered affairs for a child.

Perhaps, though, one could cite two "breakthrough" reforms. From the observation of social life outside the hospital came the knowledge that Muslim men, at the end of the day, tended to congregate at a café to drink tea, engage in lively discussion, and play dominoes or cards. Thus, Fanon started a "Moorish café" (*Café Maure*) where staff and patients would do the same. Secondly, and a particularly proud accomplishment for Fanon, staff and patients built a soccer pitch on the hospital grounds, still in use today. Soon enough, patient involvement grew as institutional psychotherapy "had literally *instituted* the social" (Robcis, 2020, p. 320, emphasis in original) in a deterritorialized, disalienating, and decolonial way.

The practical went hand in hand with a theoretical analysis of colonization on the psyche, but a theory from the ground up, from the lived everyday of peoples' lives. It is a critically reflective attunement that also extends to the tools of therapy. Using the Thematic Apperception Test (TAT), for example, Fanon and Geronimi (2021) noted that European women were well able to engage with it, while the responses of Muslim women were "unorganized," "a dry enumeration" with no narrative, "no stage, no drama" (p. 279). In fact, the only card that elicited the imagination was the blank, white card. In the world of these women, the pictured scenes were wholly unfamiliar such that a violin might be a coffin or the crosses of the cemetery. "Imaginary life cannot be isolated from real life: the concrete, objective world is what constantly fuels, enables, legitimates and founds the imaginary" (p. 282). Consequently, Fanon set out to design a projective test appropriate to the world of the Maghrebi Muslim, a project which sadly never came to fruition as the war for liberation would shortly overtake hospital activities.

The social death of the colony cannot be replicated in the asylum. Treatment must recognize the patient's relationship to history and the dynamic processes and relationships of experience within a colonized and raced world (Luxon, 2021a), which is also to say its politics. "Psychiatry must be political" (Charles Geronimi, quoted in Khalfa, 2021a, p. 26), and "all political leaders should be psychiatrists as well" (Fanon, quoted in Bhabha, 2004, p. xxxvii).

The Ethical Step

In 1956, the National Liberation Front (FLN) of Algeria was nearly two years into an increasingly brutal war for national independence from French occupation. Blida-Joinville could not avoid its location within the system and the conflicts of its surround. Both torturer and tortured, colonizer and colonized, occupied the same space for treatment, and the colonial state made demands on the staff to extract confessions from "terrorists" and "troublemakers" even as Fanon and several of his staff provided support to the FLN in the form of food supplies and clandestine shelter (Cherki, 2006). In fact, Blida-Joinville was on the state's radar as a hotbed for "radicals," and staff were harassed, interrogated, and several detained. Some were tortured and killed (Cherki, 2006). Fanon himself received death threats and survived a bomb explosion outside his home (Lee, 2015). At the end of 1954, the FLN reached out to Fanon, not because he was a political activist, nor on the strength of his philosophy or theories, but because they needed a psychiatrist to help their recruits deal with mental problems (Hudis, 2015). Two years later, the situation at the hospital had become untenable enough for Fanon to tender his resignation. He was promptly expelled from Algeria, and settled as an exile in Tunisia, where he took up a fulltime leadership role in the FLN, but also continued his clinical work. The latter included treatment of combatants, refugees, and soldiers on the battlefront (several of these became the case studies in the last chapter of *Wretched of the Earth*), and starting a psychiatric day hospital in Tunisia, the first of its kind in Africa.

Fanon's resignation letter proceeds from an easy truth: that neither his efforts nor his enthusiasm has been spared as he poured every ounce of his activity into serving his patients. But he was forced to ask, now, "what are a man's enthusiasm and care if daily reality is woven with lies…and scorn for humankind" (Fanon, 2021a, p. 286)? What if psychiatry, as the tool with which to nurture the human back from alienation to freedom, succeeds only in sending the patient back into the pathogenic, to live "permanently alienated in his own country…in a state of absolute depersonalization" (p. 286)? For Fanon, for any clinician with a conscience, "there comes a time when tenacity becomes morbid perseveration" (p. 286), "a time when silence becomes a lie" (p. 287). What is one's responsibility as a healer—or better still, who does one serve—if the task is to patch and dress the wound in order to send the soldier right back out to die? It is common to frame Fanon's choice as a political one, which it is, but it is also about medical interests of care in conflict with colonial interests, and where one cannot serve both.

This tension is also ours, and of our times. We are all faced with the question of the ethical in the distance between its demand and our (inevitable) collusions, betrayals, and silences. It is an ethics that was always present, from Fanon's earliest question already, in the *North African Syndrome*: "Have I not, because of what I have done or failed to do, contributed to an impoverishment of human reality? The question could also be formulated in this way: 'Have I at all times demanded and brought out the man that is in me?'" (Fanon, 1967b, p. 5).

Whereas Fanon's decision reflects a deliberate turn to political activism, the political work itself can be thought psychologically, "as a radicalization of his therapeutic work and its perspective on worldmaking, not a rejection of it" (Siegel, 2023, p. 25). That is, as working towards a collective psychological liberation within which the truly individual could be free to flourish. Decolonization, after all, "bears on being," fundamentally altering it in the veritable "creation of new men. The 'thing' colonized becomes a man through the very process of liberation" (Fanon, 2004, p. 2).

Afterlife of Fanon, Or, "Stepping up"

In December 1960, while traveling to Mali as an FLN representative, it became apparent that Fanon was ill. The diagnosis was leukemia. After an unsuccessful treatment stint in Moscow and the intercession of a CIA operative (which would provide fodder for all kinds of conspiracy theories), Fanon traveled to Washington, DC. His illness, however, had progressed too far already, and on December 6, 1961, at the age of 36, Fanon died in a hospital in Bethesda, Maryland. Only a few months after his burial in Algeria, in July of 1962, Algeria won its independence from France.

Why Fanon today? This is not a new question—the eminent cultural studies scholar, Stuart Hall, asked it nearly thirty years ago already (Hall, 1996). At one level, there is a range of obvious lessons to be learned, some of which this chapter hopefully gestured towards—a critical and sociogenic theory and praxis rooted in context, or the importance of embodiment and the psychoaffective, for example. At another level, the question matters given that racism remains an essential and structural element of American life and culture. In a scholarly paper such as this, one might be expected to provide evidence of such a claim, perhaps list corroborative research and statistics. I shall be derelict, and will offer instead: ask any Black or Brown person.

All such responses, and more (we have barely scratched the surface !) are true, appropriate, and important for our present. But there is another form of the question, one Nigel Gibson, upon receiving the Frantz Fanon Prize at the Caribbean Philosophical Association in 2009, prompts us to think in the after of Frantz Fanon's life: *Whether we are relevant to Fanon?* By dint of our thought and our actions have we honoured his legacy, narrowly, and the future of a new humanism, broadly. If the call to actional praxis is the fact and condition of BE-ing, it is so by an ethical call for us to be radicals as therapists and human beings, in the therapy room and in all the spaces of our lives where "to be truly radical is to make hope possible rather than despair convincing" (Williams, 1989, p. 118).

"We are nothing on earth if we are not in the first place the slaves of a cause, the cause of the peoples, the cause of justice and liberty" (Fanon, letter to Roger Taieb, quoted in Cherki, 2006, p. 165).

References

Abu-Jamal, M. (2019). Frantz Fanon and his influence on the Black Panther Party and the Black revolution. In D. Byrd & S. J. Miri (Eds.), *Frantz Fanon and emancipatory social theory* (pp. 7–26). Brill.

Bhabha, H. (2004). Foreword: Framing Fanon. In F. *Fanon, The wretched of the earth* (pp. xiii–xlvii). Grove Press.

Bulhan, H. A. (1985). *Frantz Fanon and the psychology of oppression*. Plenum Press.

Burman, E. (2021). Frantz Fanon and revolutionary group praxis. *Group Analysis, 54*(2), 169–188.

Caute, D. (1970). *Fanon*. Fontana/Collins.

Cherki, A. (2006). *Frantz Fanon: A portrait* (N. Benabid, Trans.). Cornell University Press.

Delmont, M. F. (2022). *Half American: The epic story of African Americans fighting World War II at home and abroad*. Penguin.

Desai, M. (2014). Psychology, the psychological and critical praxis: A phenomenologist reads Frantz Fanon. *Theory & Psychology, 24*(1), 58–75.

Egalité, N. (2024). Our Newspaper as care: Narrative approaches in Fanon's psychiatric clinic. *Journal of Medical Humanities*. (Advance online publication), https://doi.org/10.1007/s10912-10023-09834-w

Fanon, F. (1965). *A dying colonialism* (H. Chevalier, Trans.). Grove Press. (Original work published 1959)

Fanon, F. (1967a). *Black skin, white masks* (C. L. Markmann, Trans.). Grove Press. (Original work published 1952)

Fanon, F. (1967b). *Toward the African revolution* (H. Chevalier, Trans.). Grove Press. (Original work published 1964)

Fanon, F. (2004). *The wretched of the earth* (R. Philcox, Trans.). Grove Press. (Original work published 1961)

Fanon, F. (2008). *Black skin, white masks* (R. Philcox, Trans.). Grove Press.

Fanon, F. (2018a). *Alienation and freedom: Frantz Fanon* (S. Corcoran, Trans.; J. Khalfa & R. J. C. Young, Eds.). Bloomsbury Academic. (Original work published 2015)

Fanon, F. (2018b). Our Journal: Editorials of the weekly ward journal of the Blida-Joinville psychiatric hospital, December 1953–December 1956. In J. Khalfa & R. J. C. Young (Eds.), *Frantz Fanon: Alienation and freedom*. Bloomsbury.

Fanon, F. (2021a). Letter to the resident minister. In J. Khalfa & R. J. C. Young (Eds.), *Frantz Fanon: The psychiatric writings* (pp. 285–288). Bloomsbury Academic.

Fanon, F. (2021b). Mental alteration, character modifications, psychic disorders and intellectual deficit in spinocerebellar heterodegeneration: A Case of Friedreich ataxia with delusions of possession. In J. Khalfa & R. J. C. Young

(Eds.), *Frantz Fanon: The psychiatric writings* (pp. 39–114). Bloomsbury Academic.

Fanon, F., & Asselah, S. (2018). The phenomenon of agitation in the psychiatric milieu: General considerations, psychopathological meaning. In J. Khalfa & R. J. C. Young (Eds.), *Frantz Fanon: Alienation and freedom*. Bloomsbury. (Original work published 1957)

Fanon, F., & Azoulay, J. (2021). Social therapy in a ward of Muslim men: Methodological difficulties. In J. Khalfa & R. J. C. Young (Eds.), *Frantz Fanon: The psychiatric writings* (pp. 195–294). Bloomsbury. (Original work published 1954)

Fanon, F., & Geronimi, C. (2021). TAT in Muslim women: Sociology of perception and imagination. In J. Khalfa & R. J. C. Young (Eds.), *Frantz Fanon: The psychiatric writings* (pp. 277–283). Bloomsbury. (Original work published 1956)

Fanon, J. (2014). *Frantz Fanon, my brother: Doctor, playwright, revolutionary* (D. Nethery, Trans.). Lexington Books.

Gaztambide, D. J. (2021). Do Black lives matter in psychoanalysis? Frantz Fanon as our most disputatious ancestor. *Psychoanalytic Psychology*, 38(3), 177–184.

Gaztambide, D. J. (2024). *Decolonizing psychoanalytic technique: Putting Freud on Fanon's couch*. Palgrave Macmillan.

Geismer, D. (1971). *Fanon*. Dial.

Gendzier, I. L. (1973). *Frantz Fanon: A critical study*. Vintage Books.

Gibson, N., & Beneduce, R. (2017). *Frantz Fanon, psychiatry and politics*. Rowman & Littlefield International.

Goozee, H. (2021). Decolonizing trauma with Frantz Fanon. *International Political Sociology*, 15, 102–120.

Gordon, L. (2015). *What Fanon said: A philosophical introduction to his life and thought*. Fordham University Press.

Hall, S. (1996). The after-life of Frantz Fanon: Why Fanon? Why now? Why Black skin White masks? In A. Read (Ed.), *The fact of blackness: Frantz Fanon and visual interpretation* (pp. 12–37). Institute of Contemporary Arts, London & Bay Press.

Hook, D. (2020). Death-bound subjectivity: Fanon's zone of nonbeing and the Lacanian death drive. *Subjectivity*, 13, 355–375.

Hudis, P. (2015). *Frantz Fanon: Philosopher of the barricades*. Pluto Press.

Keller, R. C. (2007). Clinician and revolutionary: Frantz Fanon, biography, and the history of colonial medicine. *Bulletin of the History of Medicine, 81*(4), 823–841.
Khalfa, J. (2020). Rereading Frantz Fanon in the light of his unpublished texts. *Aisthesis, 13*(2), 87–96.
Khalfa, J. (2021a). Introduction: Fanon, revolutionary psychiatrist. In J. Khalfa & R. J. C. Young (Eds.), *Frantz Fanon: The psychiatric writings from alienation and freedom* (pp. 1–38). Bloomsbury Academic.
Khalfa, J. (2021b). My body, this skin, this fire. In L. Laubscher, D. Hook, & M. Desai (Eds.), *Fanon, phenomenology, and psychology* (pp. 48–64). Routledge.
Laubscher, L. (2025). Frantz Fanon: Toward a new humanism. In L. Hoffmann (Ed.), *APA handbook of humanistic and existential psychology: Vol. 1. History, research, philosophy, and theory*. American Psychological Association.
Laubscher, L., Hook, D., & Desai, M. (2021). Of bodies that matter: Fanon, phenomenology, and psychology. In L. Laubscher, D. Hook, & M. Desai (Eds.), *Fanon, phenomenology, and psychology* (pp. 1–19). Routledge.
Lee, C. (2015). *Frantz Fanon: Towards a revolutionary humanism*. Ohio University Press.
Luxon, N. (2021a). The disalienating praxis of Frantz Fanon. *Cultural Critique, 113*, 165–193.
Luxon, N. (2021b). Fanon's psychiatric hospital as a way station to freedom. *Theory, Culture & Society, 38*(5), 93–113.
Macey, D. (2012). *Frantz Fanon: A biography*. Verso Books. (Original published 2000)
Marriott, D. (2018). *Whither Fanon? Studies in the blackness of being*. Stanford University Press.
McCulloch, J. (1983). *Black soul, white artifact: Fanon's clinical psychology and social theory*. Cambridge University Press.
Merleau-Ponty, M. (1968). *The visible and the invisible* (A. Lingis, Trans.). Northwestern University Press. (Original work published 1964)
Pitts, A. (2022). An "Extension of the occupier's hold": Frantz Fanon on psychiatry, carcerality, and etiology. *Chiasmi International, 24*, 293–310.
Razanajao, C. L., Postel, J., & Allen, D. F. (1996). The life and psychiatric work of Frantz Fanon. *History of Psychiatry, 7*(28), 499–524.
Robcis, C. (2016). Francois Tosquelles and the psychiatric revolution in postwar France. *Constellations, 23*(2), 212–222.

Robcis, C. (2020). Frantz Fanon, Institutional Psychotherapy, and the decolonization of psychiatry. *Journal of the History of Ideas, 81*(2), 303–325.
Robcis, C. (2021). *Disalienation: Politics, philosophy, and radical psychiatry in postwar France*. University of Chicago Press.
Sexton, J. (2011). The social life of social death: On Afro-pessimism and Black optimism. *Tensions, 5*, 1–47.
Shatz, A. (2024). *The rebel's clinic: The revolutionary lives of Frantz Fanon*. Farrar, Straus and Giroux.
Sheehi, S., & Sheehi, L. (2021). *Psychoanalysis under occupation*. Routledge.
Siegel, N. (2023). Fanon's clinic: Revolutionary therapeutics and the politics of exhaustion. *Polity, 55*(1), 7–33.
Tosquelles, H., & Fanon, F. (2018). Indications of electroconvulsive therapy within institutional therapies. In J. Khalfa & R. J. C. Young (Eds.), *Frantz Fanon: Alienation and freedom*. Bloomsbury. (Original work published 1953)
Turner, L., & Neville, H. A. (Eds.)(2019). *Frantz Fanon's psychotherapeutic approaches to clinical work*. Routledge.
Vergés, F. (1996). Chains of madness, chains of colonialism: Fanon and freedom. In A. Read (Ed.), *The fact of Blackness: Frantz Fanon and visual representation*. Bay Press.
Weate, J. (2021). Fanon, Merleau-Ponty, and the difference of phenomenology. In L. Laubscher, D. Hook, & M. Desai (Eds.), *Fanon, phenomenology, and psychology* (pp. 162–174). Routledge.
Williams, R. (1989). *Resources of hope*. Verso.

11

Working as a Therapist with Victims of Social Injustice

Joel Vos

Introduction

Note: Case studies have been anonymised, pseudonyms used, and facts significantly altered to make them unrecognisable, and informed consent was achieved.

John, a twenty-year-old black transman, asked for my therapeutic support to overcome symptoms of Post-Traumatic Stress Disorder (PTSD) caused by racism and transphobia. John responded well to exposure therapy and cognitive interventions. Once he began a session enthusiastically, "I solved my problems! I asked the police to drop their investigations into the ongoing abuse, even though the bullies still hang around my housing estate, continuing their shouting and spitting. However, I am now coping so well with their abuse that they no longer upset me. The police procedures are just making the situation more difficult." John's statement

---

J. Vos (✉)
Department of Counseling, Metanoia Institute, London, UK
e-mail: VosJoel.Vos@metanoia.ac.uk

made me feel as if I had failed as a therapist, even though my clinical supervisor reassured me, saying, "Do not worry. You fulfilled your therapeutic duty by alleviating your client's PTSD."

Did I unintentionally contribute to and perpetuate systemic injustice by helping John accept rather than challenge the status quo? Am I accountable for contributing to the culture of acquiescence to injustice? Should we start demonstrating and demanding firm measures to stop the structural racist and transphobic abuse? Treating psychiatric symptoms like PTSD without addressing the underlying injustice is akin to a surgeon proudly declaring, "The surgery was successful, but the patient died." Indeed, something within John seemed to have died—the fire, the passion for justice. Whereas some justice-related emotions may be disproportionate or unhelpful, such as a call for revenge, other emotions, such as asking for social change, may be helpful and proportionate. Labelling all emotions as a vice that needs to be eradicated may isolate the victim, and continue or aggravate Social Injustice (SI) (Nussbaum, 2016).

Imagine that we could give our clients a pill to remove all their emotions connected to their experiences of SI, but without changing the SI itself—like taking a 'soma' in Huxley's *Brave New World*. Imagine that this pill would effectively resolve their worries and emotional turmoil, enabling them to continue their daily life, numbing the emotional impact of the SI that is still ongoing. Should such a solution be offered? I am confident that our governments and health insurance providers would eagerly embrace this as a cost-effective means of addressing mental health crises; while maintaining the existing socioeconomic and political order. However, by doing so, we would potentially forfeit a fundamental aspect of our identity: the resilience and strength we develop by overcoming adversity. Moreover, SI would persist without the fury to trigger change. We may also lose a significant portion of our capacity for empathy and the creation of genuine communities, which are often built on a shared understanding of one another's pain.

Thus, as therapists, our work inherently involves Social Justice (SJ). However, to what degree do therapists inadvertently replicate or attempt this hypothetical pill to numb the pains of SI? At what point does therapy become more harmful than beneficial to clients and society?

11 Working as a Therapist with Victims of Social Injustice   205

The pill is merely a thought experiment. Social justice is a complex phenomenon emerging from social, interactive, and internal dynamics, which cannot be addressed by merely solving the victims' feelings. Social Justice (SJ) and non-violence include, for example, negotiation and fairness, economic partnership, shared responsibility, responsible parenting, honesty and accountability, trust and support, respect, and non-threatening behavior (Herman, 2023). In contrast, SI and violence may include coercion, threats, emotional and economic abuse, male privilege, using children, minimizing, denying, blaming, isolating, and intimidating (Herman, 2023).

This chapter is based on the intuition that therapists frequently neglect SJ/SI, especially when their mental health care system does not comprehensively examine SI/SJ (Vos et al., 2019). Disregarding SJ/SI may neither serve our clients' or society's interests. I argue that it is no longer sufficient to call therapy bona fide when it only has empirical evidence for its ability to remove a psychiatric label, such as 'PTSD,' as it should also be able to address the social injustice associated with that label (Vos, 2023). Therapeutic success should be measured by the amount of injustice addressed, clients empowered, and justice achieved.

Social Justice Is Multi-faceted

To understand what is at stake, we need to imagine the totality of SJ/SI. While this may seem impossible, we can attempt to gain a comprehensive understanding through Systematic Pragmatic Phenomenological Analysis (Vos, 2020, 2021). This approach involves asking ten fundamental questions, following philosophers such as Heidegger, Foucault, and Lacan, to develop a comprehensive understanding of a phenomenon. See Table 11.1.

How Real Is SJ/SI?

Therapists may address SJ/SI merely as the client's perception or negative thoughts of the situation (SJ/SI as imagination), address this as a

Table 11.1 Systematic-pragmatic-phenomenological-analysis of social justice

Formal name	Applied question	Formal examples
Ontological status	How real is social justice, or is it merely imagination and symbols?	Reality Symbol Imagination
Type of meaning	What meaning does social justice have?	Materialistic Hedonistic Self-oriented Social Larger Existential-philosophical
Approach to meaning	How does an individual approach social justice?	Traditional Functionalistic Phenomenological (also called critical-intuitive)
Relationship between individual and society	Where in society does an individual experience social justice?	Social determinism Social individual interactionism Individual determinism
Development over time (social history)	When in history does an individual experience social justice?	Historiography Historiology
Emergence of individual meaning (individual history)	Who develops social justice?	Psychology Pedagogy Anthropology
Sense of freedom	Whose freedom does social justice involve?	Symbolic vs realized freedom Negative vs positive freedom Individual vs structural freedom
Existential well-being	Why do individuals experience social justice?	Existential questions and concerns Realistic sense of freedom and limitations Mental health problems
Impact on daily life	Which impact does social justice have on daily life?	Quality of life Life satisfaction

symbolic ritual (SJ/SI as a symbol), or instead, they may acknowledge the reality of the client's lived experiences (SJ/SI as reality). For instance, Freud initially acknowledged the reality of his clients' stories of sexual abuse, which he later dismissed as mere imagination and symbols. Even though clients may present SJ/SI as imaginary/symbolic, therapists should explore the underlying reality. This means understanding how the imaginations/symbols have evolved, such as rationalizations and fantasies about justice and revenge, which may prevent the client from truly facing and feeling the pains of SI.

What Meaning Does SJ/SI Have?

SJ/SI may have different meanings, as it may refer to a materialistic unjust situation (materialistic type of meaning, e.g., salary, housing, education, socioeconomic opportunities); the inability to enjoy our life (hedonistic meaning, e.g., work/private time, pleasure, entertainment); struggles with personal development and expression (self-oriented meaning, e.g., self-care, self-development); broader injustice in relationships, community, and society (social meaning, e.g., family, care for vulnerable, equality, trade union solidarity); a universal, ethical, religious/spiritual experience (large meaning, e.g., climate change); or abstract reflections (existential-philosophical meaning, e.g., principles of freedom, responsibility, democracy). A therapist should examine what meaning(s) SJ/SI has to a client, not assuming any meanings.

How Do Individuals Approach SJ/SI?

Individuals may engage in SJ/SI by following their tradition (e.g., obeying social expectations, rules, laws, class), acting mechanically (e.g., automatic pilot, using values that seem opportunistic, random, mindless), or in a more critical-intuitive/phenomenological way. Therapists should not merely address SI/SJ, as their tradition or mechanical therapy culture requires this from them, but let their intuition critically guide them in exploring the experiences and options of their clients.

What Is the Relationship Between Individuals and the Society?

SI-victims often present unrealistic feelings of guilt and shame (individual-determinism), possibly as a way to imaginarily/symbolically reclaim control over their lives impacted by SI (social-determinism). Similarly, therapists may see individual clients as victims entirely determined by SI/SJ (social-determinism), or as active agents fully responsible for their perceived SI/SJ (individual determinism). However, the social responsibility model (Young, 2010) argues for a realistic dynamic model of social-individual interactionism, whereby SI/SJ emerges in the interaction between individual and community.

How Does SJ/SI Develop?

We may see SI/SJ as historically fixed facts or as organically evolved perceptions. From a critical-realist, neurobiological perspective, therapists may argue that the immediate reality of the pain of SI is undeniable, even though our perceptions, responses, and coping styles may differ, as described below.

How Much Freedom Do Clients and Therapists Have to Address SJ/SI?

Frankl argued that even if we cannot change our adverse situation or structural injustice—as in his experience in the concentration camp—we may change how we respond to it. This individual freedom allows individuals to keep hope, survive, and maintain a sense of mental well-being (structural/individual freedom). SJ may imply the absence of SI (negative freedom) and the client's empowerment and self-realization (positive freedom). Therapists may help clients develop freedom, social and individual, positive and negative, within their constraints and opportunities (Vos, 2015).

What Is the Impact of SJ/SI on Existential Well-Being?

Studies indicate that SJ/SI is associated with existential well-being, such as living a meaningful and fulfilling life despite life's SI. SI may undermine our assumptions about the world's fairness, benevolence, and controllability, which we need to feel safe and stable (Janoff-Bulman, 2010). Therapists may help clients live meaningfully despite their struggles.

What Is the Impact of SJ/SI on Mental Health?

Research clearly shows that victims of structural SI are more likely to struggle with mental health problems. Groups at particular risk include LGBTQI+, BAME, women, neurodivergent, and disabled individuals (Vos et al., 2019). Therapists should sensitively explore SI in these groups.

In conclusion, SI/SJ is a multi-faceted phenomenon. Therapists may want to reflect on the extent to which they address SI/SJ in their totality. They may want to train their competencies and intuitive sensitivity towards the reality of SJ/SI, its multiple meanings, and its development in interactions between society and the individual. And thus help clients develop freedom not only to liberate them from their feelings/memories of SI, but also freedom towards actively creating a more meaningful and fulfilling life.

Social Justice Is Social

Therapists often seem to conceptualize SJ from the traditional liberal theory of justice, focusing on individual rights and equal treatment (Rawls, 1999). For example, a therapist could acknowledge how John was maltreated, help him overcome PTSD, and develop assertiveness skills to claim his rights. However, this may not address the broader systemic discrimination and marginalization that John faces outside the therapeutic setting.

Traditional-liberal theories often operate under the assumption of universal equality, overlooking the specific challenges and systemic barriers individuals face because of their intersecting marginalized identities. This can result in a failure to adequately address the client's experiences of systemic oppression, including racism and transphobia, which are not solely based on individual actions but are deeply embedded in societal structures. As a result, traditional-liberal therapists may not fully empower the client to confront and challenge the broader societal injustices that significantly impact their well-being. As John told me, his individual bullies may end up behind bars, but others are likely to replace them, as the racism and transphobia he faces are more structural.

When a river floods, you examine upstream to identify what is obstructing its source. The social responsibility model of Iris Marion Young (2010) acknowledges that many individual experiences of injustice are embedded in social, economic, and political structures, including collective and intergenerational trauma. SI is not merely a subjective experience that may be solved by changing our perceptions or memories, but an objective fact that may require actions beyond the therapy room. The individual experience of injustice is embedded in the context of broader structural injustice. SI involves not only one perpetrator and one victim, but is structural and complex, involving many individuals contributing minor or major parts. The complexity is, for example, revealed in the fact that most criminals are victims themselves (Leschied, 2008; Rhee & Waldman, 2002). John's bullies may be individually penalized for discriminating John, but their bullying may have been caused by the broader racist, homophobic culture and the bullies' own unresolved issues. As John told me, not merely the bullies but society as a whole should be penalized. We need to move from individual guilt to collective social responsibility. If one thinks about racism by examining only one wire of the cage, or one form of disadvantage, it is difficult to understand how and why the bird is trapped. Only a large number of wires arranged in a specific way, and connected to one another, serve to enclose the bird and to ensure that it cannot escape (Young, 2010, p. 56).

Young highlighted how SI may not merely consist of intentional and blatant injustices, such as a physical assault or calling names, but also tiny steps, such as micro-aggressions or even well-intended but insensitive responses. Evil is not an abstract category but consists of minor individual actions that we were taught and never properly questioned (Arendt,

2006). For example, when I, a cis-man, asked John—with my best intentions—to explain his experiences of his transgender identity and journey, I may have unintentionally given him the message of 'being different,' reinforcing his sense of SI. Young's model asks therapists to radically question themselves about their (un)intended contributions to their client's SI. It calls for therapists to recognize and actively work to rectify these structural injustices inside and outside the therapy room.

The psychologist Judith Herman (2023) made similar conclusions based on her research with SI victims:

> For those who are the most directly victimized, the complicity and silence of bystander-friends, relatives and neighbors, not to mention officials of the law, feel like a profound betrayal, for this isolates them and abandons them to their fates. Survivors can perhaps accept the fact that some people are predators or psychopaths who seek absolute power. But what about all those who collaborate: the enablers, the apologists, those who profit from the subjection of others? What about all those who collude implicitly: the people who prefer not to know the truth or choose not to help, the people who say, "It's none of my business," and those who are just looking out for themselves? What about those who blame the victims for disturbing the peace? Often, survivors feel the bitterness of these betrayals more deeply than the direct harm inflicted by perpetrators....Acknowledgement on a massive scale means recognition by individual perpetrators and the complicity of all the people who enabled them....Survivors need many kinds of reparative action from their communities, ranging from immediate help and support in a crisis to broad education programs for prevention...They want bystanders to take a stand, recognize that a wrong has been done, and unambiguously denounce the crime...They want assurances that they did not deserve to be abused. (pp. 37–38)

As SI and trauma are interpersonal, SJ and recovery also require an interpersonal approach. Social structures enabled and allowed John's perpetrators to bully him, isolating and othering him. John may never feel OK, regardless of how much therapeutic insight he gains, as long as his community does not actively validate his identity. Herman argues that healing from SI does not merely require work at an intrapsychic level one-to-one between perpetrator and victim, but also at the community level.

In line with London (2014), she describes how an unwritten agreement of reciprocity exists within our community, guiding our actions. When this trust is breached, the community is expected to empathize with the victim, offer support, and hold wrongdoers responsible for their actions. Through these collective efforts, the community reaffirms the victim's sense of belonging; while conditioning perpetrators' ongoing membership on genuine displays of remorse and willingness to rectify their wrongs. Herman describes how the community may facilitate healing, for example, via legal proceedings, community support, advocacy groups, and political action.

However, Herman recognizes that society is often far from ideal. For example, the legal system frequently gives victims a passive role as merely a witness in the court's prosecution of the perpetrators, "as a cog in something turning…for your peace of mind, be prepared to throw any illusions about justice you might have had out the window…there was no way for me to say to him, Why did you do this? Or for him to acknowledge what he did and take responsibility. There was no opportunity for a personal exchange" (Herman, 2023, p. 46). The individuals in Herman's book were already helpless victims of a crime whose emotions did not matter to the perpetrators. The system subsequently reinforced their sense of passivity and disregard for their feelings. Thus, the public need for prosecution via impersonal legal methods may contradict the victim's need to redevelop a sense of agency.

There have been experiments that have given victims a more active role, such as mediation, reconciliation, and restorative justice. However, the outcomes are mixed, possibly because these interventions must be sensitively tailored to the individual, not allowed by bureaucratic legal systems (Daly, 2017). Restorative justice, whereby victims face and forgive their perpetrators, is also frequently hampered by the perpetrators' refusal of a genuine apology, possibly because they see their actions as justified (Konstan, 2010). The social expectation of forgiveness may create new forms of oppression: "Exhorting victims to forgive their abusers is always so much easier than confronting the abusers and putting a stop to the violence" (Herman, 2023, p. 76).

Those who have been wronged might find it difficult to accept that obtaining validation from their offenders may never occur. Waiting for a genuine apology may keep victims trapped in a dependency role towards the perpetrator, who retains power over the victim by refusing a genuine apology. This may hinder the healing process and reconnection of the victim within society. Thus, the healing process should not hinge on wrongdoers' acknowledgement of their experiences. Victims might have to grieve and regain their autonomy by letting go of unrealistic expectations about SJ. Their community may support them in this process by recognizing their shortcomings in allowing or facilitating SI, protecting victims and preventing this from reoccurring.

Therapists may play a crucial role in exploring how clients may achieve some sense of justice, develop realistic expectations, and reclaim their agency. Alongside the individual healing process, therapists may help clients explore recognition, healing, and reconciliation at the community level.

Social Injustice Is Cyclical

Young does not perceive SI as a one-time perpetrator-against-victim action, but as a chain of minor actions contributed by many individuals. This may inadvertently include some unhelpful responses from the victim. Herman highlights the community's contribution to the etiology and recovery from SI. Although not explicated by Young and Herman, SI may include vicious cycles. For example, a woman may struggle with the glass ceiling, undermining her self-esteem and subsequent ability to fight the ceiling (Vos et al., 2019). Similarly, victims of narcissistic abuse may feel so helpless that they start enabling the narcissists and develop a trauma bond.

In my community work in Israel and Palestine over many years, I discovered the steps in how PTSD may become a vicious cycle: (1) the aggressor oppresses, threatens, or uses violence against a victim; (2) the aggressor causes SI; (3) the victim experiences an automatic stress response; (4) the automatic response may be unhelpful, for example, because the victim responds aggressively, shows weakness by fleeing or freezing, or threatens the aggressor with legal prosecution; (5) the victim's response triggers aggressors to feel oppressed, threatened, or victimized, to which they may respond with additional oppression, violence, or threats. Therefore, when I work with political activists in crisis zones, I start with psycho-education, explaining how their anger in response to the SI may be justified but unhelpful, as this may reinforce the vicious cycle of SI (Vos, 2020). Thus, I acknowledge how they have been victimized; while I simultaneously help them cope more constructively with their trauma so that they do not inadvertently trigger new traumas.

We must differentiate between primary responsibility for SI in the past (causing the injustice and initial survival responses there-and-then) and secondary responsibility in the present (responding to the injustice here-and-now). Victims are not at fault for the perpetrator who started the conflict. A victim may not have had any other options to respond than how they did there-and-then and possibly still do not. Stress and trauma responses are not deliberate decisions, but resemble conditioned reflexes. When our actions are driven by automatic reactions, we lack control in that instant. Recognizing this is not about evading accountability, but about being realistic about the past.

Whereas victims may not have had a choice in the past, they may have some choice now to prevent the cycle from worsening or at least they may try to avoid this. This secondary responsibility needs clear demarcation from their primary responsibility, as perpetrators and society often seem to conflate these to deflect from the real cause of SI. Society frequently employs nuanced methods to suggest that those who suffer from SI are to blame for their own experiences and responses without explicitly stating 'it was your fault.'

It is possible to take ownership of our lives in the here-and-now without implying that we have invited injustices upon ourselves. Therapists may want to help victims acknowledge and develop self-compassion that they were not responsible for the original SI. Their responses are understandable while allowing them to see that they may have some freedom here-and-now to break the SI cycle. "Between stimulus and response, there is a space. In that space, we have the power to choose our response. In our response lies our growth and freedom" (Frankl, 1955, p. 23).

Social Justice Is Embodied

Young suggests the subtle nature of SI. If there is one key insight my work with SI victims has provided, it is that the physical impacts of SI far exceed the stress and psychological symptoms that are immediately apparent. Since the early 2000s, authors such as van der Kolk, Porgess, Levine, Ogden, and Maté have increasingly focused on the body's role in coping with traumatic SI experiences.

SI victims often present with secondary emotions seemingly unrelated to the underlying traumas and SI. For example, John spent several sessions talking about his burnout in his work before he was able to acknowledge that his worries were really about racist and transphobic abuse in his neighborhood. Talking about burnout seemed safer than talking about his more authentic emotions. I helped him identify, express, and explore his underlying primary emotions, such as his anxiety, sadness, anger, images, and memories. However, his emotions about the abuse still felt theoretical and abstract to me, disconnected from his body language, which showed a much larger intensity. Therefore, I asked him to focus on his feelings, movements and sensations in his body, such as his cringed posture and fidgeting. I asked him to focus on these embodied sensations and stay with them. John found this very difficult, as he seemed to have developed the habit of coping with his physical fears in response to the structural abuse by shifting his attention away from his body, for example, towards his work or rationalization, presenting a false self to others. By staying with his bodily sensations, he discovered how he had initially developed this habitual response due to bullying at secondary school. By creating this insight, processing this initial trauma, and feeling safe to accept his experiences, he was able to recognize the intensity of the pain of the bullying and discrimination.

Thus, therapists may want to unpeel the layers clients may have built to hide their pains, as the body keeps the score of the SI (van der Kolk, 1994). For example, instead of showing shame and vulnerability, clients often respond with denial, anger towards others, social withdrawal, or depression, even though the underlying issue regards their sense of vulnerability and shame (Elison, 2006). However, this work of phenomenological unpeeling (Vos, 2017; Vos & Van Rijn, 2024) may require multiple therapy stages, as trauma treatment often consists of creating safety and relational trust, building affect regulation skills such as developing somatic stress relief techniques (e.g., breathing, grounding, orienting), emotional and embodied processing, and recovery of a meaningful life and some sense of SJ.

Furthermore, as SJ/SI is both embodied and interpersonal, therapists should also be conscious of their somatic processes. For example, sitting confidently and looking clients directly in the eyes may unintentionally reinforce a sense of unjust power dynamics, conveying that they are unsafe. As a clinical supervisor, I sometimes ask my supervisees to see muted videos of their sessions so that we can analyze the nonverbal transference, countertransference, and projective identification of SI/SJ in their clients and themselves.

Explanations of Reductionism

The previous sections show how clients, therapists and society may not always recognize the multi-faceted, multi-agent, embodied reality and subjective meanings of SJ/SI. Instead, people seem to reduce SJ/SI to simplistic, intellectual black-or-white models of victim-versus-perpetrators. Why do they reduce SJ/SI?

From an object-relations perspective, this may be described as splitting, which involves seeing others and oneself polarized as either all-good or all-bad: 'the perpetrator is 100% responsible, and the victim is 0% responsible.' This black-or-white splitting seems unrealistic. For example, research shows that most perpetrators have been the victim of SI themselves (Leschied, 2008; Rhee & Waldman, 2002) and that it is ineffective to focus on the prosecution of the individual perpetrator. For example, deterrence, such as fines or imprisonment, is often counterproductive, as it may lead to shame, guilt, discrimination, and socioeconomic struggles that increase the risk of recidivism (Dularif, 2019; Pratt, 2017). In contrast, psychological treatment, community projects, and reconciliation programs seem more effective (Beaudry, 2021; Nugent, 2004). Furthermore, this black-or-white splitting that focuses on legally prosecuting the perpetrator often requires the victim to wait long and endure the legal procedures' uncertainties, stress, and helplessness (Herman, 2023).

Furthermore, offering psychotherapy to victims of SI without addressing the causes of SI may inadvertently make them feel guilty. For example, in the UK, some job seekers at JobCentrePlus, who may be unemployed due to economic conjunctures, are required to undergo therapy. This may implicitly tell them that they are at fault and not society, and reinforce their helplessness (Vos et al., 2019). Victim support without addressing broader structural injustice revictimizes victims.

Object-relations therapists have also argued that, particularly when individuals do not have integrated representations of the self and others, clients may project undesirable feelings or traits unto others and externalize internal conflicts and anxieties. Projective identification means unconsciously inducing others to experience feelings or traits that one cannot tolerate within oneself. Therapists must be aware of and reflect on these SI/SJ-related processes.

Why do individuals create false dichotomies and projections? Clients may find it emotionally easier to split the world into black-or-white and project unwanted feelings than to integrate the complexities of social reality into complex representations of themselves and others. Splitting may occur when the experience of SI shatters one's fundamental assumptions about the world, exceeding their affect regulation skills. Also it may trigger a regression to an early child-like state and/or any pre-existing psychological vulnerabilities and unresolved emotional issues. This is particularly true for clients who have not been able to develop integrated self-other representations and mature affect regulation skills in their early life (Schore, 2015). Similarly, those with insufficient ego-boundaries and individuation-separation may struggle to differentiate actions by others and themselves and their complex interactions. This struggle may be visible in either unrealistic self-praise (narcissism) or self-undermining (depression).

For example, Adler and Reich suggested that individuals may never have learned to cope with their sense of inferiority constructively. Consequently, SI-victims may respond to SI by avoidance or denial, overdependence on others, or overcompensation by adopting an attitude of superiority, selfishness, or authoritarianism. Research on Terror Management Theory confirms that threatening situations, particularly those explicitly or implicitly threatening mortality and physical integrity, may trigger responses of denial/avoidance, including holding rigidly onto conservative values (Burke, 2010).

We develop our sense of SJ/SI via preverbal, embodied interactions in early-life (Schore, 2015). For instance, a child might fail to establish a basic sense of justice and emotion-regulation if caregivers do not consistently address their concerns and distress sensitively, such as not being fed when crying out of hunger. In early childhood, we learn that others are trustworthy and that we are worthy, not merely from the amount of praise we receive but mainly from how others attentively respond to our difficulties (Vos & Van Rijn, 2024). Children from narcissistic parents and emotional neglect may suffer from life-long hypersensitivity to injustice, for instance, reflected in symptoms of Complex-PTSD. Neurodivergent children may develop hypersensitivity to injustice because they have often been misunderstood. These are the preverbal, embodied experiences of SI/SJ, which may be triggered or re-enacted when encountering SI in later life. Consequently, a typical response to traumatic experiences, particularly in individuals with early-life neglect and trauma, is a disconnection from body sensations and primary emotions, which may, for example, cause a client to rationalize/intellectualize SI.

Individuals may use many psychological mechanisms, such as splitting, to cope with the embodied reality of SI. Consequently, they may present a false self and play relational games like 'Nothing is wrong,' 'I am strong, and 'Blame-me-instead' (Vos & Van Rijn, 2024). Such games may become so profound that they may drive an individual's purpose in life, such as Mother Theresa imposing extremely rigid SJ ideas onto others. Games seem to prevent the players in that game from feeling hurt too much. Such games are often socially reinforced, as bystanders prefer games over feeling hurt and being reminded of their implicit involvement as bystanders. Similarly, legal systems and parliamentary investigations may offer superficial games that address SI, but prevent feeling the deep, actual pain, as victims often complain about a lack of SJ after such investigations.

Offering psychological therapy to an SI victim may also be a game that allows society to acknowledge SI without addressing its causes. While national health services and health insurance may offer sessions to treat psychiatric diagnoses, healing from SI requires intimacy instead of games in an authentic therapeutic relationship. Therapists should, therefore, examine how they can offer true intimacy that facilitates clients to lower their need to play games and split. This requires that therapists acknowledge their own experiences and defense mechanisms against SI. If therapists do not resolve their own experiences of injustice, they may, for instance, play the game of 'the rescuer' with clients. This game may function as a narcissistic defense against their own overwhelming emotions and bodily sensations (Miller, 2009).

Systematic Literature Review of Social Justice

How are the concepts of SJ reflected in psychotherapy research? I conducted a scoping literature review with the search terms 'social justice,' 'injustice,' and associated terms within the fields of psychology, psychotherapy and psychiatry, in Web-of-Knowledge and PsycInfo (Vos, 2022; references may be requested from the author). Reflexive-thematic-analysis indicated seven groups of social injustice.

Structural Injustice

This included studies on structural injustice (n = 209 articles), inequality (n = 7256), privilege (n = 18,567), traumatic life experiences (n = countless), and insecure attachment (n = countless). These studies indicated how social position and life experiences may affect our perception of SJ/SI.

Specific Unjust Actions by Others

Micro-aggressions (n = 45) are brief, everyday exchanges sending denigrating messages to particular individuals because of their group membership. Denial of micro-aggression could lead to internalized aggression. Factual and perceived discrimination are unjustified distinctions between people based on the groups/classes/identities to which they belong or are perceived to belong. This includes institutional discrimination and institutional/secondary victimization (n = 54), which are harmful acts to vulnerable individuals in an institution or those depending on authorities. Other unjust actions by others include economic/political propaganda and marketing to influence what individuals perceive as meaningful and just (Vos, 2020).

Unjust Transactional Dynamics

There may be an imbalance between giving and receiving in relationships. Early-life imbalances may predict later-life imbalances ('relational ethics;' n = 354). Other examples include the drama triangle (n = 24), a destructive interactional pattern between the roles of persecutor, victim, and rescuer. Co-dependency (n = 232) refers to imbalanced relationships where one person enables another person's self-destructive tendencies and/or undermines the other person's relationship. Specific examples include folie-a-deux and mass-psychosis (n = 232).

Unjust Internalization of Injustice

The structurally unjust context and actions of others may impact an individual's well-being, for example, via situational and minority stress (n = 2158), shame, guilt (n = 731), PTSD and Complex-PTSD (n = countless). This may also include internalizing values from the economic/political system which may be labelled as Capitalist and Communist Life Syndromes, similar to the Stockholm Syndrome (Vos, 2020).

Unjust Denial of Injustice

SI may be denied by victims, perpetrators, and society, for example, via defense mechanisms ($n = 1693$) or the contemporary pejorative terms of 'wokeness' ($n = 47$) and 'cancel culture' ($n = 51$).

Unjust Personal Actions

Several studies show how SI-victims may inadvertently contribute to SI, for example, via repeating personal and intergenerational histories ($n = 703$), moral injury ($n = 277$), and trauma-bonding ($n = 12$).

Philosophical Concepts

Theoretical studies were excluded, such as Arendt's concept of the banality of evil, Buber's I-Thou/I-It-relationships, Heidegger's care, and Levinas' alterity.

Although informative, each of these SJ/SI studies only addressed specific components of SJ/SI. Unlike the social responsibility model, they did not explain how they dynamically relate and interact. Therefore, I hypothesize an Integrated Cycle of Social Injustice (Fig. 11.1). This model asserts that a structurally unjust context increases the likelihood of unjust actions by individuals. This may lead to unjust transactional dynamics, denial, internalization, and personal actions, subsequently reinforcing the cycle of injustice.

Social Justice-Oriented Interventions

Based on the Integrated Cycle of Social Injustice, therapists may help clients identify each step in the cycle and empower them to find possible places to break the cycle without blame/guilt. I loosely developed the integrative-therapeutic model of Social Justice Oriented Interventions (SJOI). SJOI aims, like Niebuhr's Serenity Prayer states, to recognize the

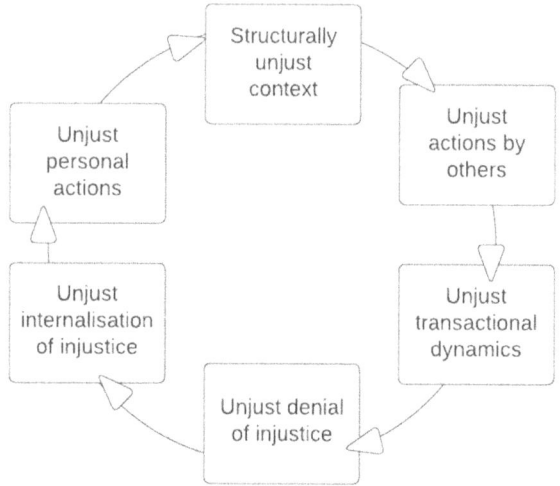

Fig. 11.1 Cycle of social injustice

client's victimhood ('things I cannot change'), develop skills to prevent and change injustice ('courage to change'), and stimulate realism without victim-blaming or splitting ('wisdom to know the difference'). A feasibility study of 21 clients receiving between ten and twenty-one sessions in a private therapy clinic suggested significantly large effects on PTSD, anxiety, and depression (measured pre-post-therapy with PCL-5, GAD-5, and PHQ-9) and subjective satisfaction (Elliott's Client-Change-Interview) (unpublished internal report). SJOI consists of seven stages, extending the previously mentioned stages of PTSD treatment.

Safety Creation

The therapist creates a safe environment where the client feels secure by offering a supportive relationship. The aim is to let the client know, not only rationally but also experientially, that the current factual context is safe, not threatening/harmful, and to facilitate mature affect regulation, for example, via exercises like breathing, mindfulness, and safe space visualization. Psycho-education can empower clients and instill a sense of agency. This stage includes assessing immediate physical safety (e.g., risks by others, housing, medical, food) and psychological risks (e.g., suicide, harm), activating their social network, involving other experts/social workers, and offering psychological first-aid if needed.

Skills Training

Before clients can recognize and process SI, some may need to develop fundamental psychological skills, such as paying attention to their body (Levine, 2010), breathing or grounding (Dana, 2018), and self-compassion (Gilbert, 2010). Be particularly aware of the needs of clients who seem to be regressing to a child-like state. Complex-PTSD or victims of childhood abuse or neglect may benefit from training in interpersonal and affect regulation skills (Cloitre, 2020). These skills may help clients to create healthy boundaries to contain their emotions.

Recognition

The therapist shows compassion and genuine care, fostering self-compassion and self-care for the client's account of SI. Explore what SI means to them, how they approach this, how it developed, how much freedom they had, and its impact on their existential, social and mental well-being. Whereas the therapist may recognize the reality of SI, the client may not recognize it, for example, due to avoidance/denial, rationalizing, splitting, or projection. The therapist kindly supports clients in connecting with their embodied hurt. For example, therapists may ask clients to describe moments of injustice that are not too stressful. They may ask about the facts (What happened?) and realistic resources in that situation (What was realistically possible and impossible?). They may ask to imagine the situation in detail, such as exploring all senses (Where were you, who was there, what did you see/feel/smell?), and to express their emotions.

If clients present a secondary emotion or rationalization, therapists may explore the most difficult/challenging aspect until they identify a more primary emotion (Vos & Van Rijn, 2024). Subsequently, therapists may ask clients how the experience of SI feels in their body and whether there are any tensions or wishes for movement in their body. Therapists may ask clients to pay attention to these somatic experiences and return their focus to a safer place in their body when that becomes too much ('pendulation;' Levine, 2010). Therapists may ask clients whether they have images or memories connected to their embodied experiences. They may ask for automatic thoughts about themselves, others, and SJ/SI. These explorations may help to recognize the embodied reality of SI.

Reformulation as Integrated Cycle of Social Injustice

The therapist may offer psycho-education about the cycle of injustice so that clients can take responsibility and develop a sense of control in the here-and-now without blame/guilt/shame about the past. For each step and the connection between steps in the cycle of injustice, the therapist may generate as many examples as possible of actions by the client and others that may have contributed to the cycle of injustice, highlighting clients' realistic lack of freedom in the past and their freedom in the present. Often, this requires cognitive reframing, e.g., 'an abnormal reaction to an abnormal situation is a normal response;' 'your reaction was a response to the unjust situation.' Therapists may ask for examples of how they may respond differently in future situations. This process may help clients develop a realistic, integrated understanding of SI/SJ, highlighting agency and opportunities for hope and change.

Interventions to Break the Cycle of Injustice (Including Processing)

Identify realistic and important goals to break the cycle of injustice (see Fig. 11.2). Focus dominantly on goals that help reconnect individuals with their community. For example, consider how the community may be included in breaking this cycle, for instance, via community support, advocacy groups, and political campaigns. Rank goals in order of achievability and importance, break-down the most realistic/important goals

11 Working as a Therapist with Victims of Social Injustice

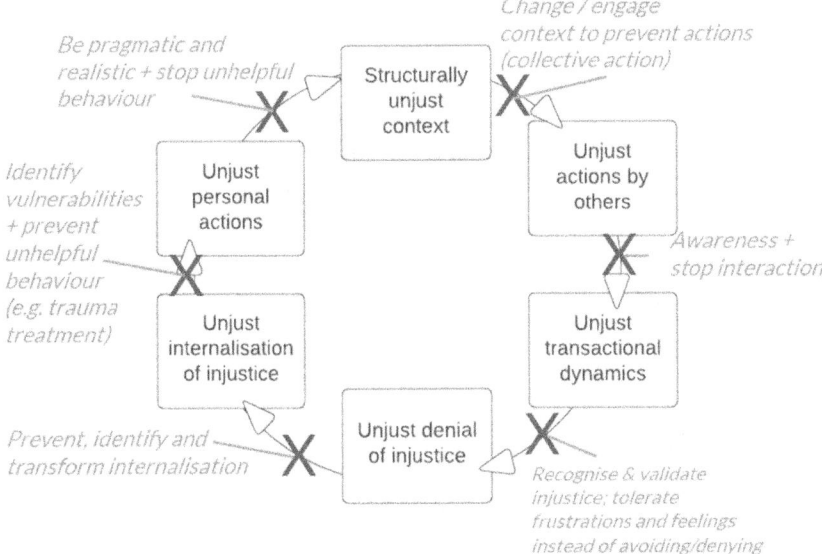

Fig. 11.2 Example of breaking the cycle of social injustice

into specific steps, and help the client make these changes in daily life. This step may include the therapist offering to reach out to other experts, social workers, debt support workers, etc., and meeting and educating others in the client's social network. This stage may also include additional therapy. For example, clients may need further treatment to overcome PTSD-symptoms (e.g., Eye Movement Desensitization and Reintegration, exposure-therapy), distance themselves from overwhelming emotions and thoughts (e.g., mindfulness), improve unhelpful, unrealistic thought patterns and behaviors (e.g., Cognitive-Behaviour-Therapy, Interpersonal-Therapy), and stimulate self-esteem and self-compassion (e.g., compassion-focused therapy). Individuals may need to train assertiveness skills, create boundaries, change toxic relationships, and move from unhealthy living and work situations.

Recovery and Building Resilience

Therapists should not automatically stop when clients no longer report mental health problems or have interrupted the SI cycle ('negative freedom'). They may want to identify and plan how clients may cope with inevitable future SI (relapse prevention) and explore their positive freedom to build resilience, a fulfilling social network, and a meaningful life (Vos, 2018). This may include helping clients identify bigger life goals and breaking them down into specific steps, such as education/training and joining social groups.

Discussion

When a puzzle piece does not fit, you look at the bigger picture, not just the piece. Similarly, working with SI victims requires therapists to look at the totality of the client's SI. Therapists should enhance their skills and intuitive grasp of SJ/SI, recognize their varied interpretations, and understand how these perceptions evolved from a dynamic interplay between societal structures and individual experiences. They should assist clients in moving beyond merely coping with past injustices to actively construct a life filled with meaning and satisfaction, empowering them to thrive and fulfil their personal and communal aspirations. Psychotherapists are encouraged to actively engage with clients in discussions on achieving a sense of justice and setting realistic expectations. This involves facilitating processes of healing and reconciliation that consider both community and individual levels without implying that clients are responsible for the injustices they have faced. Failing to address SI's complex, somatic, and interpersonal nature may inadvertently perpetuate clients' tendencies towards avoidance or denial, thus feeding into the SI cycle.

Therapists are advised to foster safety, genuine compassion and care, which may reduce clients' reliance on defensiveness and games. This requires therapists to recognize their pains and overcome their defense mechanisms so that they do not bring their unresolved needs into the therapy room and offer genuine authenticity and compassion towards their clients. For instance, therapists who adopt the role of rescuer to solve their own issues or boost their ego, rather than genuinely helping their clients, turn their act of healing into a narcissistic game.

This chapter has outlined the ideal therapeutic model for working with SI victims. However, many therapists may be unable to implement these practices due to limited time and resources within their mental health care service. Through their actions, however small, therapists may trigger a butterfly effect of positive change:

> A small action, or even a brief thought or sense of meaning, may create a chain of effects and cause structural injustice. The good news is that the same may lead to structural justice. (Vos, 2022, p. 32)

References

Arendt, H. (2006). *Eichmann in Jerusalem*. Penguin.
Beaudry, G. (2021). Effectiveness of psychological interventions in prison to reduce recidivism. *The Lancet Psychiatry, 8*(9), 759–773.
Burke, B. L. (2010). Two decades of terror management theory. *Personality and Social Psychology Review, 14*(2), 155–195.
Cloitre, M. (2020). *Treating survivors of childhood abuse and interpersonal trauma*. Guilford.
Daly, K. (2017). *Restorative justice*. Routledge.
Dana, D. (2018). *The polyvagal theory in therapy*. Norton.
Dularif, M. (2019). Is deterrence effective? *Problems and Perspectives in Management, 17*(2), 93.
Elison, J. (2006). Investigating the compass of shame. *Social Behavior and Personality, 34*(3), 221–238.
Frankl, V. E. (1955). *The doctor and the soul*. Simon & Schuster.
Gilbert, P. (2010). *Compassion-focused therapy*. Routledge.
Herman, J. (2023). *Truth and repair*. Hachette.
Janoff-Bulman, R. (2010). *Shattered assumptions*. Simon & Schuster.
Konstan, D. (2010). *Before forgiveness*. Cambridge University Press.
Leschied, A. (2008). Childhood predictors of adult criminality. *Canadian Journal of Criminology and Criminal Justice, 50*(4), 435–467.

Levine, P. A. (2010). *In an unspoken voice*. North Atlantic.
London, R. (2014). *Crime, punishment, and restorative justice*. Wipf.
Miller, A. (2009). *The drama of the gifted child*. Basic Books.
Nugent, M. E. (2004). *The changing nature of prosecution*. APRI.
Nussbaum, M. (2016). *Political emotions*. Belknap.
Pratt, T. C. (2017). *Taking stock*. Routledge.
Rawls, J. (1999). *A theory of justice*. Simon & Schuster.
Rhee, S. H., & Waldman, I. D. (2002). Genetic and environmental influences on antisocial behavior. *Psychological Bulletin, 128*(3), 490.
Schore, A. N. (2015). *Affect regulation and the origin of the self*. Routledge.
van der Kolk, B. A. (1994). *The body keeps the score*. Penguin.
Vos, J. (2015). Meaning and existential givens. *Palliative & Supportive Care, 13*(4), 885–900.
Vos, J. (2018). *Meaning in life: An evidence-based handbook for practitioners*. Bloomsbury.
Vos, J. (2020). *The economics of meaning in life*. University Professors Press.
Vos, J. (2021). Systematic pragmatic phenomenological analysis. *Counselling and Psychotherapy Research, 21*(1), 77–97.
Vos, J. (2022). Social justice in psychological therapies. *Psychotherapy Research Conference*, Leeds, 3–5 May.
Vos, J. (2023). *Doing research in psychological therapies: A step-by-step guide*. Sage.
Vos, J., Roberts, R., & Davies, J. (2019). *Mental health in crisis*. Sage.
Vos, J., & Van Rijn, B. (2024). *Handbook of transactional analysis psychotherapy*. Sage.
Young, I. M. (2010). *Responsibility for justice*. Oxford University Press.

# 12

Radical Youth Work: A Community Based Approach to Working with Youth, Young Adults and Families

Weston Robins

Mental Health: The Industry

I embarked on my journey in early 2020, when I took my entire life savings and decided to open the Eternal Strength Center for Radical Youth Work. After spending the previous fifteen years working in and around the mental health industry and field in various roles, I became increasingly dissatisfied with nearly every aspect of them. From the ages of seventeen to twenty- three I struggled with anxiety, depression, substance abuse, and suicidality. After three arrests, emotional turmoil and incomprehensible demoralization, I began to move in a different direction at the age of twenty-four and made a choice to devote my life to holistically healing myself and working to offer a sacred space for other youth, young adults and families to do the same.

W. Robins (✉)
Eternal Strength, Radical Youth Center, Alpharetta, GA, USA
e-mail: drwes@eternalstrength.com

© The Author(s), under exclusive license to Springer Nature Switzerland AG 2025
J. Hook, F. Gruba-McCallister (eds.), *The Revolutionary Psychologist's Guide to Radical Therapy*, The Politics of Mental Health and Illness,
https://doi.org/10.1007/978-3-032-02399-5_12

Working early on in psychiatric hospitals and intensive outpatient facilities, I began to see the reality of the mental health care industry and the multilayered sociopolitical nuances of the system which perpetually kept youth, young adults and families stuck in a cycle of labeling, diagnosing, medicating and treating symptoms. This left families in a perpetual place of deep pain, shame, guilt, and desperation. I worked tirelessly to find organizations whose focus was humanistic and holistic and who held ethical integrity at the forefront of the therapeutic care. However, this search proved fruitless. Very few organizations and businesses operated with these humanistic standards and care. Rather, what I uncovered was a slew of burnt out mental health workers blindly assessing, coding, diagnosing and treating clients with solution-focused methodologies that only seemed to contribute to their clients being stuck, disempowered and challenged.

I don't place the entirety of onus on the practitioners, as I often encountered amazing humans who were pursuing their licensure in counseling, alongside seasoned practitioners who had integrated their love for psychology into their work. Sadly, the mental health industry is a billion dollar money making machine and many of these amazing healers have been lured into its grips. A system that profits on the back of people believing they are sick, damaged, and diseased and that their cure lies in medication or traditional therapy. Similar to the film *Serpico*, where Al Pacino plays a rookie New York City police officer who discovers the entire law enforcement department is corrupt and unethical, I was beginning to uncover the corrupt businesses who claimed to care. Instead they focused on gross profit margins and engaged in treatment that was unethical, anti-therapeutic and even negligent.

I Believe In A Better Way

I have always had a love/hate relationship with psychology, a field at its best full of beauty in exploring human behavior. My family lineage is strong in the field, my mom holding a Master's in Behavioral Analysis and my maternal grandmother her Ed.D. in Psychology. I respect deeply

Alan Watts, Ram Dass, Carl Rogers, Erich Fromm, Carl Jung, Irv Yalom, Bell hooks, R. D. Laing, Franco Basilglia, and Rosi Braidotti. They all challenge the authorities and the socio-politically corrupt aspects of society and culture at large. However, the sad reality is that current political power has turned mental health treatment into a vicious, gluttonous, and exploitive money making machine. Psychology has one of the darkest and most oppressive histories of any field. We may never repair the evils and abuse committed by psychiatry, i.e., ECT, asylums, lobotomies. Yet we must also face the cold hard reality that even though psychology is not placing people in straight-jackets and asylums and giving them lobotomies anymore, we are most certainly still dehumanizing people on a consistent basis.

My sacred work with youth and families was fulfilling, but every day I was hearing more from families and youth about unethical programs, abusive psychiatric facilities, and money hungry outpatient programs. Cold and callous, these programs attempted to hire good healers, but created a business hierarchy with greed and power at the top. Business owners treat their therapists and staff like disposable productivity machines, imposing overwhelming caseloads with little to no training, direction or support. In my work with youth and families, I have never viewed a client or family as a paycheck or as a lesser human being than me. I can only hope that if that day were to ever occur, I would have the wisdom, patience and insight to look within myself and see what led me to exhibit dehumanization.

Co-Collaborative Community Work

The families and clients I have seen and continue to serve have saved my life, quite literally. Over the course of the last fifteen years, I have seen some of the most beautiful, compassionate, dedicated, intelligent, creative, and amazing human beings. I am grateful for them allowing me to hold space and enter into a sacred relationship of psychotherapy and counseling with me. It was the clients and the families I served that began to shape my vision and give me the fuel I needed to start working toward building a unique community youth center/mental health holistic growth facility. But years before, it was an idea, a seed planted in my young psyche that was percolating all these years.

When I was eight years old one I discovered a film, *Breakin' 2 Electric Boogaloo*. The main characters were Turbo and Ozone, the coolest breakdancers on the block and they meet a classically trained ballerina named Kelly. Together the three of them work to build "The Miracle," a community youth, music/arts/rec center that is inclusive, loving and holistic. My eight-year-old self was hooked. I wanted to be Ozone more than anything. So much so, that I had my mom make me an Ozone jacket by buying fabric paint and helping me write Ozone on the back with an awesome boombox!

In early 2020, it was my chance to be my community's Ozone and build "The Miracle." Because after seven years in private practice listening to hundreds of families tell me in tears the thousands of dollars they had spent on wilderness therapies, residential treatment centers, educational consultants and intensive outpatient and partial hospitalization programs, I became committed to helping these families find a better way to healing and growth. I talked to each of them about their journeys and asked what helped and what hurt. I listened intently and took notes on the family's journey, treatment and clinical recommendations. I was appalled at the repetitive patterns I began to see. Families being fed into a mental health system only to be spit out left monetarily depleted and emotionally worse off. Something was way off and had to be changed. I knew then, and still believe, that I would spend the rest of my life fighting for truth, love, compassion, and true client care. It is my hope that through my center, I can be more a part of the solution and stop contributing to the problem.

Eternal Strength is a one of a kind community youth and family center with comprehensive and holistic mental health care and support. Every day we work diligently to create a space of love, care and compassion for families and youth struggling with the challenges of growth and development. We see each family we serve as our neighbor and community. They help teach us as we co-collaboratively help their families grow and heal in the directions they seek. We also have a nonprofit branch called Cosmic Lamb where we regularly scholarship clients and families who are financially struggling to help them receive the services and support they seek. If we can better teach, train and guide healers in a study of true character development, integrity and ethics, I believe we can start to make a massive shift and reduce the toxicity which currently plagues our industry.

Radical Youth Work

Pinpointing the exact origins of the term "radical youth work" is challenging, as it likely emerged gradually within the discourse of youth, youth work and other related fields. The term has gained prominence as a descriptor for approaches within youth work that prioritize co- collaborative community work, social justice, activism, and systemic change. While it's difficult to attribute the term "radical youth work" to any one single individual, it likely emerged in the context of social movements, academic discussions, and grassroots initiatives focused on youth empowerment and social change. Scholars, activists, and practitioners who have been influential in shaping critical perspectives on youth work and advocating for transformative practices may have contributed to the development and popularization of the term.

Some key figures and movements associated with radical perspectives in youth work include Paulo Freire and his work on critical pedagogy; the youth empowerment movements of the 1960s and 1970s; and critical youth work scholars, such as Howard Sercombe and Mark Smith. These individuals and movements have advocated for approaches to youth work that challenge oppressive structures, promote critical consciousness, and empower young people to become agents of social change. As the concept of radical youth work has evolved, it has been further shaped by ongoing dialogue, activism, and research within the field. However, the most comprehensive writing and theoretical research on radical youth work has been done by Dr. Kathleen Skott-Myhre, Chair and Professor of Psychology for the Department of Anthropology, Psychology, and Sociology at the University of West Georgia and Dr. Hans Skott-Myhre, tenured professor in Human Services at Kennesaw State University.

Radical youth work can never truly be defined in one sentence. Rather, just like any malleable practice, it must grow and expand. Radical youth work is a vulnerable choice of the power of love over the love of power (Skott-Myhre, 2011). It is a theoretical praxis blending of heart, soul and co-collaborative work with youth, where youth and youth worker are both transformed by the experience. No one can ever teach you what it means to be a radical youth worker. You must define this for yourself, find your own path, and locate your individual voice as you engage with youth on their journey. However, many grounding tools can be used and there must always be a focus on doing what is in the best interest and greatest good of the youth.

Radical youth work requires bringing authenticity and love to the youth, never shying away from speaking your truth, and always taking time to ask yourself "What do youths need that will help them grow and expand their perception of self?" The role of a radical youth worker is unique and extremely sacred. Many highly trained professionals are unable to play the role of a radical youth worker due to the confines of their traditional practice. A radical youth worker is someone who is actively working on their own holistic growth and uses their journey of growth to guide and help youth in a co-collaborative relationship of mutual liberation.

Core Tenets/ Foundation of Radical Youth Work

- Co-collaborative work with youth workers and youth which emphasizes social justice, critical consciousness and grassroots organizing.
- Empowering youth to become active agents of change in their own lives and their communities at large.
- Honoring youth voice and creating spaces for youth to explore truth, justice, socio-cultural, and socio-political issues while questioning dominant narratives and social systems.
- Critically thinking about the individual's experience and the world at large.

Key Conceptualizations of Radical Youth Work

- Mutual Liberation

    - Working collaboratively to achieve maximum creative life force and expression.
    - Working on common projects and true self-expression and examination.
    - Carving spaces to have discourse and dialogue about all aspects of society, culture and the human condition.
    - Walking hand in hand to understand commonalities of lived experience and struggle and growth.
    - Co-collaborative community formation.
    - Fighting against tactics of exclusion or domination/discipline.

- Common Political Purpose

    - Working together towards common political purpose.
    - Creating new forms of community that serve the common desires, needs and aspirations of those currently mis-categorized into the distinctions of youth and adults.
    - Examining youth and adult relations to better understand the ways young people and adults live and work together, i.e., love and community.

- Flattening of the Developmental Hierarchy

    - Challenging the traditional view of youth development as a linear progression from dependence to independence.
    - Recognizing young people's unique voice, perspective, lived experience and skills that can positively influence and impact sociocultural change and growth.
    - Challenging the notion that adults are always the experts and youth are always the learners and seeking reciprocal relationships with youth to learn from one another and work together towards common goals.

- Creating sacred spaces where youth and adults can explore identities, beliefs and experiences working toward a mutual critical consciousness.
- Providing voice and autonomy to youth to express their truth.

- Embracing Co-Collaborative Creative Life Force Expression

  - Fostering Creative Life Force or the energy that drives and sustains creativity and innovation.
  - Using this force to generate new ideas, perspectives, and solutions to problems.
  - Expressing this energy through various channels including: art, music, writing, poetry, theatre, film/media creation & production, and forms of activism and social expression.
  - Utilizing Creative Life Force as a liberatory practice to empower youth and youth workers to explore their identities and beliefs in new and innovative ways for social change.

The above scaffolding and framework is what begins to curate the soup that is radical youth work. But cook it how you want, figure out your own special recipe, add spices, think of new unique dishes, and begin to have dinner parties with your ideas. Work with youth requires work with yourself and that is the most radical part of it! If you can learn to sit with a youth, a family, a human for that matter, you can over time begin to recognize the youth energy that we all embody- emotions, feelings, dreams, ideas, fears, trepidations. We are all human.

In radical youth work, youth and youth worker share and co-collaboratively begin to explore the arenas of development, psychology, family, society, and existence. An invitation for two souls to connect and understand life and existence together as equals, sharing similar struggles and existing in the same modern Westernized and traumatized society. If radical youth worker and youth together seek freedom from oppression, marginalization, indoctrination, and the mental health industry, what possibilities lie on the horizon?

Well, that depends on you…whoever is reading this. If these words call to you, you may be being called to do some of the most sacred work that can be done, becoming a radical youth worker! Taking work with youths a step further by joining hands with them and walking beside them through the fire of their radical pilgrimage of growth. Ego identity formation, peer exploration, societal judgement, technological symbiosis, the goal is to help our youth and, in turn, have them help us in a relationship of mutual liberation. Can we come together and expand our consciousness and unite towards love, acceptance, compassion, cooperation and connection? I believe in the end, loving and compassionate relationships are what save our souls from despair.

Eternal Strength provides radical youth work with community engagement, humanistic counseling and experiential mentoring. We weave these areas together and pull from a deep theoretical lineage including humanistic psychologies, Batesonian systems thinking and Deleuzo-Guattarian conceptual frameworks and lay them all on the antipsychiatry movement.

Rehumanizing Mental Health

Humanistic psychology emerged in the mid-twentieth century as a response to the limitations of behaviorism and psychoanalysis, championing the inherent worth and potential of individuals. Pioneered by figures such as Abraham Maslow and Carl Rogers, it emphasized subjective experience, personal growth, and self-actualization. Humanistic psychology focused upon the following suppositions:

- Humans have free will or personal agency.
- All individuals are unique and have an innate drive to achieve their maximum potential.
- A proper understanding of human behavior can only be achieved by studying humans – not animals.
- Subjective reality is the primary guide for human behavior.
- Psychology should study the individual case (idiographic) rather than the average performance of groups (nomothetic).
- Whole persons should be studied in their environmental context.

- The goal of psychology is to formulate a complete description of what it means to be a human being (e.g.. the importance of language, emotions, and how humans seek to find meaning in their lives).

These deep seated truths are used as our foundation of working humanistically with youth. Integrating the humanistic heart into youth work is a unique blend that we are co-curating at the Eternal Strength Center for radical youth work. All of our therapeutic care is deeply rooted in humanistic psychologies and person-centered therapeutic care. We believe that all people should be treated with dignity, appreciation and care, especially the youth and families that trust us to provide them sacred spaces of therapeutic support. The potentiality for true humanistic care is unlimited. If we could envision a world where citizens and community members of all backgrounds began to stand with truth, integrity, ethics and compassion for one another, we would have the potential to make true systemic change. Our youth hold the key to that change. Can we learn from our youth and teach them simultaneously, learning how to relate at a core understanding of our mutual humanity?

Can Batesonian and Transcontextual Thinking Save Us?

So much of our world is studied through analysis and compartmentalization. We often feel that in order to understand something, we need to separate it from its context so that we can truly see it clearly and directly. However, this scientific reductionism, although useful in many ways, often times leaves out the complexity and abundance of context at play. If we are truly to learn systemically it is crucial that we begin to explore the relationships and interconnected webbing of our world. Nora Bateson writes:

> I found that what I needed for the work I was doing around systemic learning demanded that I have another species of information–that could handle multiple contexts in motion. One in which the information itself is alive. Ecologies are not static, and within them many organisms respond and calibrate to each other's responses in varying timings. (Bateson, 2022, pp. 13–14)

Nora Bateson defines warm data as the information that is alive within the transcontextual relating of a living system. Transcontextual simply stated is the ways in which multiple contexts come together to form complex systems. Bateson's father, Gregory Bateson's work as an anthropologist, ecologist and philosopher began to touch on the extreme importance of context. Bateson stated "context is all" emphasizing that true meaning only begins to emerge from the contextual webbing in which communication takes place.

How can we begin to explore this warm data and its potential usage in our work with youth and families? Bateson (1978) states "…the major problems in the world lie in the difference between how man thinks and how nature works" (p. 14). Existence is a priori to the categories we have constructed. Biology, sociology, anthropology, etc. are all various lenses from which to examine life. But we missing massive amounts of nuance and complexity by compartmentalizing our study. To work with youth and families, it is critical we think from a transcontextual perspective and examine the relationships between ecology, media, spirituality, health, education, technology, family, and history. For too long we have neglected warm data research in our psychological studies. We need to begin to explore the interconnectedness and interdependencies of our world.

Warm data goes beyond traditional data and statistics, which often focuses on isolated pieces of information.

> Theory is beautiful. But it is not enough. Until the theory lives in your breakfast, in your walk, in your spine, in your kiss, in your memories, in your laugh and your tears–it will remain disintegrated. This is why we do warm data: its more than a lovely intellectual exercise. (Bateson, 2022, p. 15)

Warm data is an invitation to see the true complexity and interconnected nature of reality and existence. For it is only when we explore the relationships and the liminal space in between that we begin to see more clearly the fabric of reality and life. When we talk about a family, there is no way to pull the family out of the larger contexts in which it exists.

Aphanipoiesis and Radical Youth Work

With each human we encounter we are met with the possibility that lies in our communication with one another. Bateson (2022) speaks of aphanipoesis, a term she coined that combines the roots of afani (unseen) and poiesis (becoming). It is defined as an unseen coalescence toward vitality or coalescence of experience becoming unseen. She describes it as the experience of how one person's story changes my story. There are ways in which we communicate with one another that reveal aspects of the unseen. We feel and experience them vibrationally and relationally. A felt sense or knowing exists in our encounters with each other, providing us complex sensory information that allows us to maneuver in our world. The rich ecology of communication evermoving and flowing in our relationships with one another is aphanipoiesis.

In radical youth work (Skott-Myhre, 2008a, 2008b, 2016, 2020; Skott-Myhre & Skott-Myhre, 2008), it is necessary to give respect and reverence to the unseen and the becoming. Youth and youth workers join in a mutual invitation to understand one another and connect relationally. How do our stories shape and change ourselves and each other? In my work as a critical and antiauthoritarian psychologist, I am continually fascinated at the stories and narratives we tell ourselves about our world, our identity, our existence, and our relationships. Youth share the stories they have constructed about their identity, health, illness, and life. In radical youth work, it is critical that we suspend any agenda or reductionistic methodology to diagnosis or categorize youths. Rather we must join them in a mutual exploration of themselves. Diving deep to understand their way of being in the world, while being vulnerable about our own ways of being. In this space in between lies an unseen coalescence toward vitality.

Much traditional developmental psychology views the adolescent development process as a linear set of achievable psycho-social stages. We need to not view youth as inept and deficient in knowledge of self, while viewing adults as teachers. This hierarchy and power imbalance is beyond dangerous in relational and humanistic healing work with youth. If clinicians and practitioners believe they are able to teach youth how to be in the world, we are beyond lost in our understanding of human existence. Each of us must learn how to be in the world in our own way. Bateson (2016) observes:

> Each one of us is a crooked tree, reaching for water and light, bending ourselves around obstacles, scary thoughts, hurtful moments, darkness and thirst, finding a way to breathe in the sun and hold the soil, our branches are kinked and twisted, because that is what it took to be here, the ways of learning to be in our worlds, have shaped responses, our many experiences are speaking through every gesture. Our loves, and broken paths, a tenderness, a criticism, learning always, yearning always, in a crooked beauty…to be home for those who may find comfort in the asymmetry of our belonging, a nest cradling new life, tucked into an old log teeming with creatures, learning to be in each other's reshaping. (p. 101)

Learning to be in each other's reshaping is drastically different than trying to bend the limbs of a tree to be shaped the way you feel it needs to be. How can we see youth as trees and see ourselves as crooked trees and thus see the beauty of our becoming, of our growth, of our asymmetry? Paradoxically, it is only when we accept our crooked ridges that we begin to grow toward vitality. Roger's (2015) radical acceptance speaks of the importance of allowing and accepting our flaws in order to enrich our holistic growth. For it is the resistance or denial of our crookedness that keeps us stuck and stagnant. However, this requires bravery and courage needed to allow a tree to grow as it needs, not the way in which you think it needs to.

In order to keep our relationality alive and authentic we must always have curiosity and gratitude for the person in front of us. Rather than dissecting, analyzing and attempting to behaviorally correct, we must dance with one another. For it is only when we dance that we loosen and reveal the spaces in between, the cracks and the unseen. Rather than becoming a detective and taking a bright flashlight to our youth and families, we must invite them to dance and make music together. When this occurs, the gaps are revealed and this is where the hope of systemic transformation is waiting. Now we dance with one another in ontological and epistemological melodies and improvisation, seeking to see the other as a flow of growth, rather than define them as a stagnant entity.

The Deleuzo-Guattarian Tool Kit

Deleuze and Guattari's work provides a powerful critical deconstruction of the entire field of psychology and psychiatry. Through true comprehensive ontological critique of the history of psychology, a worthy field that is also steeped in a dark history of dehumanization, Deleuze and Guattari (1987) offer a new path and trajectory, a horizon that holds promise for a better tomorrow. Their work offers many conceptual tool kits to explore and examine existence and life. Together, they pave new ways to think, explore, and understand philosophy, existence, and human behavior.

Deleuze and Guattari speak of rhizomes, a unique botany analogy comparing standard psychology and psychoanalytic thinking and study to arborescent thought, shaped like roots and trees. Deleuze and Guattari encourage rhizomatic thought, a spontaneous untraceable growth and expansion of free form explorations. A rhizome has four distinct principles:

> (1 and 2): any point of the rhizome can be connected to any other, it is non-hierarchical, 3: rhizomes have the principle of multiplicity, 4: rhizomes have the principle of a signifying rupture (if a single point of the rhizome is destroyed, it will start up again on an old line or a new line). (Deleuze & Guattari, 1987, pp. 6–7)

It is with this rhizomatic creative energy that we can reconceptualize our co-collaborative work with youth to a radically different experience of healing and growth, using the following acronym of RETINA, Rhizomatic/Experiential/Therapeutic/Imperceptible/Nomadic/Assemblage:

Rhizomatic–We seek to make maps not tracings. We are invested in experimentation with the real, not a copy or imitation, but a true organic production.

> To be rhizomorphous is to produce stems and filaments that seem to be roots, or better yet connect with them by penetrating the trunk, but put them to strange new uses. We're tired of trees. We should stop believing in

trees, roots, and radicles. They've made us suffer too much. All of arborescent culture is founded on them, from biology to linguistics. Nothing is beautiful or loving or political aside from underground stems and aerial roots, adventitious growths and rhizomes. (Deleuze & Guattari, 1987, p. 15)

Experiential–We utilize experiential radical youth work. We engage and journey into the unknown through a phenomenological approach to experience of relationship to shift our understanding of ourselves and the world around us. We see experiential therapy as an open-ended process that explores what's new and what's coming into being rather than something already experienced and known. We see experiential therapy as true discovery of the self and the other. The elements with which we experiment are desires, forces, powers and their combinations, not only to 'see what happens,' but to determine what different entities (bodies, languages, social groupings, environments) are capable of.

Therapeutic–We believe in the healing nature of relationship and connection. Our therapy is a mission to establish a relational set of capacities with young people and through these relationships establish deep and meaningful interactions and encounters that allow for the maximum degree of creative possibilities for each human soul.

Imperceptible–We seek to become imperceptible. Becoming imperceptible is part of Deleuze's ethic of becoming. It means striving to transcend one's ordinary perception and subjectivity and deconstruct aspects of oneself in order to experience profound change. It involves looking at life beyond what is visible and familiar.

Nomadic–We embrace a nomadology in our utilization and engagement of space. Our experiential center for radical youth work is a land, a space, a sacred territory of engagement and relationship. Traveling is our default mode of relating to space, we move, explore, experience, and flow through space together on a journey of exploration and freedom. The center is our territory to traverse through, not a stagnant space to occupy or own. We are all nomads on a journey of growth and Eternal Strength is our watering hole, meeting place and tribal community clubhouse that carves lines of connection on our souls path to expansion and growth.

Assemblage–We are carving and creating a new assemblage of love, trust, connection and expression. Our function is to transform one another into our highest selves through relationship and community.

Another concept of Deleuze and Guattari is schizoanalysis, an alternative approach to traditional psychoanalysis, which they felt pathologized and medicalized differences in thought and behavior. Schizoanalysis seeks to explore the multiplistic nature of subjectivity and the unique thought and behavior expressions of all human beings. Schizoanalysis aligns well with the principles of radical youth work because it rejects the notions of a normative psyche. It offers an acceptance and curiosity about the fluid and diverse nature of the human experience, providing a more inclusive and empathic understanding of youth and families.

Anti-Psychiatry

Last, but not least, promise is held in the positive potential for systemic disruption of the Anti-Psychiatry movement. The Anti-Psychiatry movement was a social and political movement that emerged in the 1960's and 70's as a response to the widespread use of dehumanizing medical and psychiatric treatments for mental illness. The movement was characterized by critique of psychiatric diagnoses, treatments, and institutions, and argued that these practices were oppressive, dehumanizing and often ineffective.

R.D. Laing's (2018) work focused on the social and interpersonal factors that contribute to mental illness. Laing argued that mental illness was often a response to environmental and social factors and could be understood as a meaningful and rational response to these conditions. In his approach to family therapy, Laing emphasized the importance of understanding the interpersonal dynamics within families and their influence on individual psychological well-being. He believed that mental illness often arises from dysfunctional family relationships and societal pressures.

There is much that we can continue to learn from Laing and the entire others critical of psychiatry including the current work of Levine (2022), Moncrieff and Kirsch (2015), Akomolafe (2017), and Johnstone (2014).

They are transcontextual thinkers and activists fighting for humanistic care and holistic health and growth for self, family, society, and world at large. If we can stay open in our thinking, learn and grow with youth, and employ a critical, humanistic, radical, and transcontextual approach, we have the capacity to change the world for the better in unimaginable ways. The potential to alleviate unnecessary suffering remains possible. However, we must start with ourselves and get to a place of health and healing within. Then, we can begin to share this light with others, teaching them how to do the same. We are woven into the fabric of the universe together as one.

So it seems as if we have the tools, the energy and the vision. Now is the time for revolt. The time to think critically and see from and through a transcontextual lens. We must do better for our families, parents, children, humanity, and our planet. We can heal once we begin to recognize and harness the power of our words, emotions, thoughts and actions. For it is we that have the power as people to stand up and fight for our freedom, rights, and minds. A revolution of consciousness is the call to action. Begin to dream of a world you want to live in and then do everything you can to create it around you and your community at large. Together we can keep pushing forward towards a beautiful horizon of love, acceptance, tolerance, compassion, community, and positive evolution and growth. A place where our mental health is woven into our physical, spiritual, and collective health as human beings.

References

Akomolafe, B. (2017). *These wilds beyond our fences: Letters to my daughter on humanity's search for home.* North Atlantic Books.

Bateson, G. (1978). *Steps to an ecology of mind: Collected essays in anthropology, psychiatry, evolution, and epistemology.* University of Chicago Press.

Bateson, G. (2000). *Steps to an ecology of mind: Collected essays in anthropology, psychiatry, evolution, and epistemology.* University of Chicago Press.

Bateson, N. (2016). *Small arcs of larger circles: Framing through other patterns.* Triarchy Press Limited.

Bateson, N. (2022). *Unpsychology: An anthology of warm data*. Raw Mixture Publishing.
Braidotti, R. (2011). *Nomadic theory: The portable Rosi Braidotti*. Columbia University Press.
Deleuze, G., & Guattari, F. (1987). *A thousand plateaus: Capitalism and schizophrenia* (B. Massumi, Trans.). University of Minnesota Press.
Deleuze, G., & Guattari, F. (1988). *A thousand plateaus: Capitalism and schizophrenia* (B. Massumi, Trans.). Bloomsbury Publishing. (Original work published 1980)
Duke, K., Gleeson, H., Dąbrowska, K., Herold, M., & Rolando, S. (2021). The engagement of young people in drug interventions in coercive contexts: Findings from a cross-national European study. *Drugs: Education, Prevention and Policy, 28*(1), 26–35.
Johnstone, L. (2014). *A straight talking introduction to psychiatric diagnosis*. PCCS.
Klingemann, H. (2020). Successes and failures in treatment of substance abuse: Treatment system perspectives and lessons from the European continent. *Nordic Studies on Alcohol and Drugs, 37*(4), 323–337.
Laing, R. D. (2018). *The politics of the family: And other essays*. Routledge.
Levine, B. E. (2022). *Profession without reason: The crisis of contemporary psychiatry—Untangled and solved by Spinoza, freethinking, and radical enlightenment*. AK Press.
Maiese, M. (2022). Neoliberalism and mental health education. *Journal of Philosophy of Education, 56*(1), 67–77.
Moncrieff, J., & Kirsch, I. (2015). Empirically derived criteria cast doubt on the clinical significance of antidepressant-placebo differences. *Contemporary Clinical Trials, 43*, 60–62.
Rogers, C. (1995). *On becoming a person*. Harper.
Roger, C. R. (2015). *On becoming a person: A therapist's view of psychotherapy*. Mariner Books.
Skott-Myhre, H. A. (2008a). *Youth and subculture: Creating new spaces for radical youth work*. University of Toronto Press.
Skott-Myhre, H. A. (2008b). Radical youth work and becoming youth: Creative force, resistance and flight. *Scottish Youth Issues Journal, 10*, 17–28.
Skott-Myhre, H. A. (2011). *Youth and subculture as creative force: Creating new spaces for radical youth work*. University of Toronto Press.
Skott-Myhre, H. A. (2020). *Post-capitalist subjectivity in literature and antipsychiatry: Reconceptualizing the self beyond capitalism*. Routledge.

Skott-Myhre, H. A., & Skott-Myhre, K. G. (2008). Radical youth work: Love and community. *Relational Child and Youth Care Practice, 20*(3), 48–57.

Skott-Myhre, K. (2016). Youth: A radical space of pilgrimage. In H. Skott-Myhre, V. Pacini Ketchabaw, & K. Skott-Myhre (Eds.), *Youth work, early education, and psychology* (pp. 179–193). Palgrave Macmillan.

Waldron, H. B., Kern-Jones, S., Turner, C. W., Peterson, T. R., & Ozechowski, T. J. (2007). Engaging resistant adolescents in drug abuse treatment. *Journal of Substance Abuse Treatment, 32*(2), 133–142.

Watts, A. (2017). *Psychotherapy east & west*. New World Library.

Part V

Sublation

13

Self-death as a Symbol of Radical Freedom

Farhan Shah

The Challenge of Goethe

"Suicide is an event that is a part of human nature. However much may have been said and done about it in the past, every person, must confront it for himself anew, and every age must come to its own terms with it" writes Johan Wolfgang von Goethe. What can Goethe's words reveal about our unique ability and unsettling potential to pronounce our own death sentence? Is self-destructiveness something we become possessed by? Is it an underlying psychopathology, a faceless and destructive force compelling us to take our own lives? Or, as the title of the eighth film in the *Conjuring* universe suggests, "The devil made me do it," is it, when rephrased in a secular-medical context, the depression that made me do it?

It cannot be overstated how crucial it is to give this Dionysian potential a mature language. The suicide statistics, for example, in Norway are telling. Currently, approximately six hundred people take their own lives

---

F. Shah (✉)
Center for Process Studies, Salem, OR, USA

© The Author(s), under exclusive license to Springer Nature Switzerland AG 2025
J. Hook, F. Gruba-McCallister (eds.), *The Revolutionary Psychologist's Guide to Radical Therapy*, The Politics of Mental Health and Illness,
https://doi.org/10.1007/978-3-032-02399-5_13

each year. In 2021 alone, 658 individuals committed suicide. Every week, about twelve people choose to end their lives. Considering that each suicide leaves behind ten bereaved individuals, 5000–6000 people are affected annually in Norway. Around three thousand people each year are directly impacted in Oslo and its surroundings alone, not to mention the extensive underreporting and unrecorded cases. As a society, are we prepared to recognize and attune ourselves to the unique and deeply personal nature of this leap toward self-destruction? Can we approach it in a way that humanizes rather than dehumanizes? Can we move beyond reducing human lives to mere numbers, reports, and statistics?

The crucial question we must explore is how we should talk about our death wishes and the allure of the abyss's dark depths. The way we approach this self-destructive capacity inherent in our humanity makes a significant difference. As philosopher Vigdis Songe-Møller (2021) asserts,

> Suicide is fundamentally a human act, not an atrocious act that we can simply distance ourselves from, even though for many of us it is difficult, or impossible, to understand that one of our loved ones chose death over life. Suicide may appear to be an unnatural act, but then we forget precisely this: that suicide is part of the human possibilities. (p. 25)

Vigdis' perspective is insightful and calls for a reflective process that encourages us to reassess our inherited dogmas, accepted truths, and entrenched thought patterns. One place to start is by critically examining conventional terminology. The word "suicide" or the phrase "to commit suicide" carries connotations of criminalization and sin, echoing the condemnatory views of ancient Greek philosophy (particularly parts of Aristotelian philosophy) and the medieval metaphysical dominance of Catholic theology, especially as articulated by Thomas Aquinas and Augustine. These orthodox views, like ghosts never fully exorcised, persist in our secular world. This is evident in the Norwegian government's action plan for suicide prevention, which includes the introduction of 'the zero vision for suicide.'

The Dark Sides of the Zero Vision

One of the dangers of the 'zero vision for suicide' is that, despite its honourable intentions, it symbolizes an omnipotent fantasy rooted in a paternalistic and moralistic attitude that implicitly assumes everyone must live. In preventive work, a fundamental question arises: Does someone genuinely want to live? And who ultimately decides the extent of suffering one should endure?

The dominant narrative asserts that everyone should live, regardless of life's quality or the individual's choices. Consequently, the 'zero vision for suicide'—with its invasive and authoritarian measures—can paradoxically hinder people from developing the will to live. In other words, this 'zero vision for suicide' can dangerously simplify and existentially amputate human life in a destructive pursuit of a utopia, an imaginary construct, which can cause as much pain and alienation as it seeks to alleviate.

Our vigorous efforts within the therapeutic apparatus and society-at-large to realize this imaginary ideal result in nothing less than the dehumanization of human beings. Armed with an arsenal of assessment procedures, evidence-based methods, medical treatments, and involuntary hospitalizations, we attack the ontological openness of human life—the inherent lack of existential fullness that defines our humanity and decisions. This approach creates a prophylactic hell. The criticism of this imaginary ideal pertains to its (mis)understanding, manifesting as an unwarranted belief in the medical paradigm and the treatment procedures that arise from anxiety about life's fundamental unpredictability, rather than the ideal itself. The dark side and dangerous consequence of this approach is that we end up opposing existence itself, negating the inherent nothingness and the rupture arising from our radical unspecificity and indeterminacy. Philosophers Gilles Deleuze and Félix Guattari (1977) capture this sentiment: "We no longer believe in the myth that there are fragments, like parts of an ancient statue, just waiting for the last piece to be found...We no longer believe in an original wholeness that once existed, or in a final wholeness that awaits us in the future" (p. 42).

The question that should be pursued further—taking the above into consideration—addresses whether we have truly developed the necessary critical distance from the worldview advocated by the zero vision. This vision functions as a kind of regressive fantasy and longing for a predictable, risk-free, and magical world. As psychoanalyst Julia Kristeva (1991) notes, "It is an extraordinary person who does not invoke an original refuge to compensate for personal confusion" (p. 8). Indeed, we are all guilty of creating individual and collective narratives and fantasies—both religious and secular—about an 'original refuge' to cope with the personal confusion, existential anxiety, and radical incompleteness of life. In the same vein, the 'zero vision for suicide', inspired by the zero vision in traffic safety, represents this regressive longing and pursuit of the 'great simplification'. That is, the belief that if we secure bridges, railway tracks, or access to deadly weapons, increase medical treatment for depressive disorders or involuntary hospitalizations/restraints in mental health care, remain vigilant, or introduce dialectical behaviour therapy nationwide, we can necessarily prevent suicide and ultimately achieve a utopian ideal (the zero vision). These are desperate attempts to keep confusion, risk, and anxiety about humanity's unique capacity to act 'unnaturally'—and the ontological rupture—at bay. Yet, despite these efforts, the consistently high suicide rate in Norway haunts us, revealing the limitations and dangers of this approach.

Is this what we want in a liberal democracy and humane society, where respect for individual dignity and the freedom to pursue one's own life projects—with the inherent risks—is fundamental? How does this align with Norway's ratification of the Discrimination Convention and the United Nation's call for a paradigm shift: moving from a focus on biomedical treatment procedures to psychosocial, humanistic, and recovery-oriented paradigms? These paradigms emphasize the importance of individuals' life stories about their suffering, recognizing them as meaningful and guiding the organization and provision of support in the mental health field.

The Reductionist-Naturalistic Approach

When it comes to terminology, expressions like 'to commit suicide' or 'to die by suicide' strip away agency and undermine the effort to understand the reasons behind our death wishes, reasons individuals ascribe to their own desires for death. These terms should be replaced with a language that respects and acknowledges persons' autonomy over their own existence—for better or worse. *For freedom inherently includes the possibility of using it against life.* Embracing a more mature perspective on the complexity of death wishes is crucial, as the medicalizing and psychiatric viewpoint is based on a naturalistic-deterministic paradigm that reduces humans to biochemical units. The issue does not necessarily lie in the scientific approach itself, which is valid, but in the excessive focus on reducing the breadth, diversity, and richness of human life to mere neurophysiological processes.

A biomedical explanatory model of human life pain entails an objectification of human life, where the status and agency of the human subject is stripped away in favour of the more quantitatively measurable. The primary focus becomes *causal explanation* rather than attempting to understand the *teleology* of human choices and actions. In other words, humans are not spectators in their own lives, but rather agents who choose and perform actions with reasons. Reasons pertain to motives, intentions, purposes, and telos, which cannot be captured in scientific classifications or arithmetical formulas.

One reason the suicide rates have remained consistently high for over two decades, despite new action plans, preventive efforts, and state funding, is the conflation of suicidality with mental illnesses like depressive disorder. In other words, the desire for death is often clinically conflated with hypothetical mental illness. This biomedical perspective can impede the development of a nuanced sensitivity towards individuals grappling with existential crises, where self-destruction appears as an appealing but also extreme solution. To effectively reduce the conditions where the desire to die overshadows the will to live, we must confront a significant, untapped challenge: moving beyond the myth of mental illness, questionable psychiatric diagnoses, bureaucratic inefficiencies, and naive reliance on the positive effects of psychiatric medications.

Non-Pathological Approaches

In my view, we need to prioritize non-pathological approaches, such as socio-diagnosis, which identify the sources of life's pain and unbearable fundamental states rooted in trauma, social exclusion, racism, physical and psychological violence, loneliness, economic hardship, and poverty. This approach can better encompass the complexity of suicidality than the empty category of 'mental illness'. As a society, we should move from a symptom- and diagnosis-centric language, which suggests that something is inherently wrong within individuals, to a more dynamic understanding of human life. Social psychologist, Arnulf Kolstad and Ragnfrid Kogstad (2019) noted, "We search for the causes of mental disorders in the wrong place; where medical science has prestige, in biology, but not where the sufferings actually arise, in interactions with other people and generally in the life we live or are subjected to" (p. 25). Kolstad rightly argued that we need to "develop a corrective to yesterday's gene and brain fetishism."

The core message is that the intense focus on biology and brain health detracts from critically examining the factors that sustain or even reinforce inequitable resource distribution in societal development, which are contributing causes of mental ill-health and suicidality. For instance, Norway's 'Action Plan for Suicide Prevention,'[1] with its sixty-one preventive measures, does not address the relationship between economy, debt, living conditions, and suicidality. This omission from the contextual field is concerning, raising critical questions about the dominant orthodox understanding of suicidality and preventive measures. Shifting the focus from the contextual and dynamic field—sensitivity to structural measures and systemic conditions—to the individual psychological level implies a psychologization and reductionism of human life, as laid out by the dominant medical paradigm. This collective illusion is convenient because it allows us to avoid addressing a society that is cold, hierarchical, normatively homogeneous, and exclusionary. That is, societal conditions that contribute to the problem and are not remedied by naive faith in risk

---

[1] https://www.regjeringen.no/no/dokumenter/regjeringens-handlingsplan-for-forebygging-av--selvmord-2020-2025/id2740946/

assessments, involuntary hospitalizations, epidemiology, or increased use of psychopharmaceuticals. Relying on the magic of medicine and psychopharmacology in the face of something as immensely complex and unpredictable as our own self-destructiveness represents a regression rather than openness to future possibilities.

Deaths of Despair

The reflections above do not imply that individuals grappling with existential crises should be abandoned or that society can no longer offer salvation. The value of meaningful communities, collective projects, and protective structural and civil measures is not underestimated. On the contrary, if we are to retain the concept of pathology, our focus should shift to socio-political pathology. Philosopher Arne Johan Vetlesen (2020) in his book entitled *Pain in Our Times* refers to this as *social suffering*, which includes socio-political and structural causes that foster despair, toxic stress, and alienation, rather than purely psychic pathology.

In American public health research, suicide is categorized alongside drug-related deaths and high alcohol consumption under the term "deaths of despair."[2] This perspective, which contrasts with more reductionist and biomedical approaches, underscores society's responsibility. We can all contribute to driving some individuals into desperation, despair, and hopelessness. There is little reason to believe these conditions do not also apply to Nordic countries. We can address this suffering through meaningful communities that recognize the constant fragility of human life, and through structural interventions such as political measures for better living conditions, equal opportunities, economic stability, and a predictable job market. In an era dominated by efficiency, productivity, and neoliberalism, society is organized in ways that reduce opportunities for qualitatively good and safe communities focused on care, belonging, and structural measures promoting healthy social-psychological living conditions. Despite material prosperity, contemporary times are

---

[2] 'Deaths of despair' are rising. It's time to define despair (sciencenews.org)

therefore painful, setting the stage for global epidemics of deaths of despair.

The late philosopher and sociologist Zygmunt Bauman (2000) describes the dark sides of *liquid modernity* and its accompanying continuous atomization and privatization in an apt manner when he notes that

> …if people fall ill, it is assumed that it happened because they were not determined and persistent enough to follow their training program; if they continue to be unemployed, it is because they have not learned how to handle a job interview, or they have not tried hard enough to find a job…How one lives becomes a biographical solution to systemic contradictions. Thus, life politics emerges, where illnesses are individual, and so is the treatment; worries are private, and so are the means to get rid of them. (p. 50)

This privatization of human suffering is what the dominant biomedical hegemony leads to. In this way, it (unintentionally) contributes to counteracting more ecological and holistic approaches, which recognize the complexity and multifaceted nature of human life, where the public sphere is just as important as the individual's will, responsibility, and choices.

The Ontological Incompleteness of Human Existence

An excessive focus on the objective, structure-oriented perspective can easily lead to structural and systemic fetishism, overshadowing the individual's meaning-oriented horizon. While we exist within contexts, we also have the capacity to transcend them. We possess a unique ability to envision an ontologically open future, allowing for both constructive and destructive change and creative transformation. This lack of fullness of being (manque-a-etre) that defines human life means that our agency transcends epistemological, scientific, and structural totalization.

The high incidence of false positives (those predicted to take their own lives but do not) and false negatives (those predicted not to take their own lives but do) in suicidology and preventive work highlights the radical uncertainty and unpredictability inherent in human life. Empirically and statistically, one might have all the right conditions for a safe and meaningful life yet still choose to end it. How can we understand these seemingly incomprehensible choices and radical leaps? Faced with an ontologically open future and humanity's unknown possibilities, including the capacity for self-destruction, we need epistemic humility that acknowledges our insufficiency and radical incompleteness. As psychiatrists Stangeland et al. (2018) note, we rightly fail "…to gain an overview of everything happening in a person's life. Suicide risk assessments identify many false positives, leading to intrusive measures for many in the hope of saving a few. It is unknown whether control measures reduce the incidence of suicide, and even more serious if the measure can have harmful effects" (p. 1). The debate concludes that our prediction models are too insufficient and superficial, with minimal clinical utility. Attempting to predict highly complex and uncertain human actions with reductionist and deterministic models is doomed to failure. We must learn to keep our narcissistic omnipotence and tendency to adopt an all-knowing attitude in check. By obscuring human possibilities, we create a false consciousness of the human potential.

The False Necessity Trap

The role of radical therapy should be, among other things, to expose the deception that instruments of certainty help maintain the illusion of certainty through a process of *naturalization*. This process, known as the false necessity trap, transforms human-made constructs, created by human activity and praxis, into seemingly necessary and essential arrangements. Similarly, the biomedical paradigm fosters essentialism by obscuring the fact that humans, through their choices and creative power, are the originators of social arrangements and institutions based on some meta-narratives and myths. This essentialism implies that systemic, institutional, and clinical routines, procedures, and conceptualizations—such as those related to suicidality and the a priori epistemic hegemony of clinical experts—appear inherently fixed and essential. However, in reality, they are the results of human decisions and knowledge production, which are inherently contingent, perpetually unstable, and changeable. Thus, they are always 'human-imposed'.

Human, All Too Human

These reflections should provoke and challenge us to strive continually for advancements in future knowledge development, proactive support services, politics, and society-at-large when addressing the topic of our death wishes. Can we envision a future where understanding human self-destructive capacity is liberated from the rigid confines of pathology and moralistic paternalism? We need to recognize that the act of self-death is not a deviation from normality or mental illness, nor an anomaly, but rather a fundamentally human act, rooted in life's constant instability and our radical freedom to choose either life or death. This freedom carries the seed of its own self-destruction. As long as we possess the ability to negate the most essential drive—the drive to continue living—every reference to any necessity seems misplaced, perhaps even evasive. The choice to end one's own life is the ultimate assertion of autonomy, a declaration that transcends the biological imperative to survive. It challenges the notion that our lives are bound by unalterable necessities, revealing instead a profound existential freedom and self-creativity.

In light of this, the narratives that rely on the assumption of inherent drives and predetermined paths, or those approaches that pathologize this all too human capacity and possibility, thus transferring it into the category of 'mental illness' and 'medical treatment,' appear inadequate. They fail to account for the ontological autonomy each of us holds; an autonomy that can defy even the most powerful of instincts. This capacity persuades us to confront the reality that human existence is perpetually a question for us. That is to say, human existence is not bound by necessity, but is instead a perpetual, uninterrupted exercise of freedom and choice emerging from the creative abyss from which all possibilities flow. Or as Jean-Paul Sartre (1977) puts it, "My freedom is perpetually in question of my being. It is not a quality added on or a property of my nature. It is very exactly the stuff of my being; and as in my being, my being is in question" (p. 439).

In the end, recognising self-death as a manifestation of our radical freedom calls us to reflect on the nature of our choices and the societal structures that shape and create them. It calls us to avoid the trap of false necessity by reimagining a world where the human spirit can navigate its profound freedom and its burden with dignity and support, rather than moralistic judgement and belittlement. This is not merely a task for mental health professionals, but a collective human endeavour—to hold space for the full spectrum of our common humanity, even in its most painful and terrifying expressions.

References

Bauman, Z. (2000). *Liquid modernity*. Polity Press.
Deleuze, G., & Guattari, F. (1977). *Anti-Oedipus: Capitalism and schizophrenia* (R. Hurley, M. Seem, & H. R. Lane, Trans.). University of Minnesota Press.
Kolstad, A., & Kogstad, R. (2019). *Medikalisering av psykososiale problemer [Medicalization of psychosocial problems]*. Abstrakt Forlag.
Kristeva, J. (1991). *Strangers to Ourselves* (L. S. Roudiez, Trans.). Columbia University Press.
Sartre, J. P. (1977). *Being and nothingness* (H. E. Barnes, Trans.). Washington Square Press.
Songe-Møller, V. (2021). Why suicide? Philosophical reflections. In D. Kari & V. Songe-Møller, (Eds.), *Nye Perspektiver på selvmord [New perspectives on suicide]* (pp. 14–30). Cappelen Damm Akademisk.
Stangeland, T., Hammer, J., Aarre, T. F., & Ryberg, W. (2018). We cannot predict, but we can prevent. *Journal of the Norwegian Medical Association: Journal of Practical Medicine, new series, 138*(2), 1.
Vetlesen, A. J. (2020). *Smerte i vår tid [Pain in our time]*. Dinamo Forlag.

14

How to Ruin Your Clients: Mindfulness as Cruelty

Glenn Wallis

"You're on Earth. There's no cure for that."
—Samuel Beckett, *Endgame* (1964)

Introduction

Can mindfulness meditation function as a radical practice, thereby serving the goals of a revolutionary psychologist? This is the two-part question driving this chapter. It is a pertinent question for two reasons. First, as I will show, mindfulness meditation has become all but ubiquitous in Western psychotherapeutic interventions. Second, "Mindfulness, Inc." has come under fierce criticism for functioning as "the perfect ideological

G. Wallis (✉)
Incite Seminars, 501(c), Philadelphia, PA, USA
e-mail: gw@glenwallis.com

supplement" to neoliberal capitalism, as Slavoj Žižek (2001, para. 1) puts it. Significant to my purposes here, the criticism goes further by showing that it functions as such by "presenting itself as the remedy against the stressful tension of capitalist dynamics, allowing us to uncouple and retain inner peace and *Gelassenheit*" (letting be) (Žižek, 2001). Indeed, mindfulness has been heartily embraced by the likes of corporations such as Google, Aetna, Beiersdorf, Bosch, General Mills, LinkedIn, Goldman Sachs, Intel, Royal Dutch Shell, and far beyond (Boston Consulting Group, 2018). Can a formation that has been fine-tuned as a means for increasing employee productivity and for growing already bloated shareholder profits, indeed, for *improving military resilience* (Myers, 2015), really be used as a practice for radical change? My answer is affirmative. Only one deviation from the current Mindfulness formation is required. This deviation, in turn, requires only that Mindfulness proponents *enable* a particular element that is, in fact, already lies dormant in mindfulness. Currently, this element functions as the repressed truth of Mindfulness, the unspeakable feature of the Mindfulness Real that threatens to tear asunder its positive psychology façade. The uncanny element is *disenchantment*.

American Colitis

I would venture a guess that Freud's famous "American colitis" resulted from more than the culinary "savages" cooking his meals during his 1909 visit to Clark University in Massachusetts. It had as much to do with the psychological brutes practicing his science. In America, his ideas were being blatantly sensationalized in the press and commercialized on the couch. As far as he could tell, American psychotherapy was wholly bereft of intellectual depth and creativity. All these foibles were visible in perhaps the worst "American tendency" of all, the propensity in the therapeutic session to "shorten study and preparation, and to proceed as fast as possible to practical application" (Freud, 1930, para. 3). I observed close up how mindfulness meditation slowly usurped the goals and practices of traditional Buddhist practice in the West. In a more secondhand way, I

14 How to Ruin Your Clients: Mindfulness as Cruelty

see mindfulness strategies having a similar effect on traditional therapeutic goals and practices.

Readers might wonder why mindfulness should even be discussed in serious conversations about psychology. There are good reasons. For instance, a recent study titled, "The evolution of mindfulness from 1916 to 2019," identifies nearly 16,000 relevant published accounts of "mindfulness" during that period (Baminiwatta & Solangaarachchi, 2021). The overall conclusion of the study is that the data reveals "a sharp increase in mindfulness research since 2000, a trend suggesting that research in this area has increased exponentially and may continue to do so for some time" (Baminiwatta & Solangaarachchi 2021, p. 1). Another study employing similar bibliometric methods identified some 16,581 publications on mindfulness between 1966 and 2021 alone (Baminiwatta & Solangaarachchi, 2021). Since 2006, the authors note, reported an explosive growth of publications treating the theme of mindfulness. It is significant to the purposes of the present volume that nearly 50% of the studies are found in psychology journals and over 20% in psychiatry journals.

Indeed, the "evolution" mentioned in the first study refers to the fact that interest in "mindfulness" shifted from consciousness-awakening practices to professionalized wellness interventions. In fact, the very term "mindfulness-based intervention" is now ubiquitous in contemporary Western wellness literature. MBIs, as they are referred to, are therapeutic approaches grounded in mindfulness that promote mental and physical health (Zhang et al., 2021). The most well-known interventions are mindfulness-based stress reduction, mindfulness-based cognitive therapy, dialectal behavior therapy, and acceptance and commitment therapy. Specific mindfulness techniques employed within these interventions include calming breath exercises, concentration and focusing practices, body scan meditations, and facilitator-guided imagery.

None of this would be a problem worth addressing, in my eyes at least, but for one crucial matter: mindfulness is not Mindfulness. Who can argue with those techniques per se? They engender the *Gelassenheit* that Žižek (2001) derisively invokes—a consciousness born of calm and composure. In a violent world of incessant distractions wrought by infernal technology that is all but fused to our bodies day and night, should we not be *celebrating* the "Mindful Revolution" (Pickert, 2014)? Like me, many readers, I imagine, know individuals who have reported physical, psychological, and emotional benefits stemming from MBIs. Great! But as one article scrutinizing the third-person observational article widely surveying the research concludes that "poor methodology associated with past studies of mindfulness may lead public consumers to be harmed, misled, and disappointed" (Van Dam et al., 2018, p. 1).

This is where we must recognize a crucial distinction, namely, that between "mindfulness" and "Mindfulness" as subject-creating ideological formation. The matter can be confusing because Mindfulness proponents regularly engage in an (unconscious?) equivocation of terms. The critique of mindfulness (lowercase) is not a critique of certain claims regarding human cognition. Perhaps the equivocation is baked into the whole thing. For, it is clearly present at the inauguration of the Mindfulness movement when founder Jon Kabat-Zinn proclaims that "Mindfulness is awareness that arises through paying attention, on purpose, in the present moment, non-judgmentally. It's about knowing what is on your mind" (2003, p. 145). Who would deny that the capacity of "paying attention" and all the rest is an important human trait? In reading the Mindfulness explications of what, precisely, constitutes such "mindful attention," however, it becomes obvious that an ideological edifice has been erected around that founding conceptual statement. In the most substantive critiques of mindfulness that I mentioned earlier, the term "mindfulness" itself refers to the value-laden *ideology*, not to the naked *mental quality*. When we fail to make this distinction, we lose sight of the identity of Mindfulness as a system of thought, one that is, moreover: (i) implicated in a very specific social-economic-political context, namely, neoliberal capitalism within the military-industrial-techno complex, and (ii) productive of a very particular subject and world. That is, in Simon Critchley's (2013) trenchant formulation, "in a world that is all too rapidly blowing itself to pieces…closes his eyes and makes himself into an island" (pp. 4–5), who "in the face of the increasing brutality of reality…tries to achieve a mystical stillness, calm contemplation" (pp. 4–5). Worse even, we lose sight of mindfulness (lower case) as a trainable cognitive capacity, a form of attentiveness from which our world might benefit.

Fortunately, given the family pedigree of Mindfulness, it will not be difficult for a therapist who seeks a revolutionary approach to shift away from Mindfulness as an ideological formation to mindfulness as a naturalistic awareness practice. All that is required is the addition of a postulate that is already at hand. Non-Euclidean geometry is an instructive example here. The difference between Euclidean and non-Euclidean geometry lies in the behavior of a line. Euclid's fifth postulate assumes the parallelism of lines. In upholding this postulate, along with the other four, Euclideans radically *limit* the field of possible forms. Rejecting his fifth postulate and preserving the other four), non-Euclidean geometry *enables* radical new possibilities; it permits elliptical and hyperbolic curvature. This result is significant because non-Euclidean geometry is now able more accurately to describe the actual state of spatial affairs. My suggestion is to follow this approach, but instead to *add* a postulate. The postulate, as I said, is already present in the earliest canonical sources of Mindfulness, though absent from its current formulation. It is, namely, *disenchantment*. Adding this postulate to mindfulness work within a therapeutic practice will serve the larger, and longer term, goals of a revolutionary psychologist. I should mention here that I take this goal to be, in general terms, the *ruination* of the client for the status quo, and I take the practice to be one that is unrelenting in its *cruelty*. I will say more about these two terms later. First, I must make the case for disenchantment as an essential feature of mindfulness and as a concealed feature of Mindfulness.

Primordial Sources

What I am suggesting is that Mindfulness be destroyed. I mean destruction in Heidegger's (1967) sense of *Destruktion*. This German neologism entails a simultaneous affirmation and negation, an embrace together with an undoing. In this sense, what is intended is closer to dismantling (*Abbau*) than to destruction per se (*Zerstörung*). In Heidegger's case, what is being dismantled is the edifice of *concealment* within the history of ontology that serves to obscure the original, Greek, sense of the meaning of *Being* as presence. In our case, we are dismantling the concealment within the tradition of Mindfulness that serves to obscure the original, Buddhist, premise that disenchantment is a fundamentally necessary, and perpetually fecund, feature of mindfulness practice, indeed, of human awakening. Once a concept or formation is thus dismantled, a re-description occurs that has serious consequences for the status quo tradition. In Heidegger's (1967) own words:

> A tradition that has become dominant renders that which it "transmits," first and foremost, so inaccessible that it rather becomes concealed. Tradition consigns to self-evidence that which has come down to us and blocks access to the primordial "sources" from which the transmitted categories and concepts have been, in part, genuinely created. Tradition even makes us forget that such an origin was the case. It fosters the lack of a need even to understand the necessity of returning to the sources. (p. 21)

If Mindfulness were not an adaptation of, indeed, genetically entangled with, Buddhist meditation and Buddhist psychological theory such a move would not be necessary. Mindfulness could simply be presented as yet another wellness application and go on its merry way, unmolested by critics like me. The fact, however, is that Kabat-Zinn takes great pains to establish Mindfulness within the lineage of Buddhism. He repeatedly states that his original intention was "to bring the ancient Buddhist meditation practice known as mindfulness" (Kabat-Zinn, 2024, para. 1) into the medical mainstream. Indeed, Mindfulness, is even *more* Buddhist than Buddhism: it is "the wisdom and the heart of Buddhist meditation without the Buddhism" (Kabat-Zinn, in Wallis, 2016, p. 502).

It is revealing that we can better understand the Mindfulness meditation that is the "base" of the various mindfulness-based interventions by teasing out the specifically Buddhist concepts functioning implicitly as their active ingredients. For instance, we could start with *sati* as the Buddhist concept behind "mindfulness" itself, and then go to *samatha* and *vipassana* as calming and insight, *papañca* as conceptual proliferation or mind-wandering, *paññā* as wisdom, and even *nirvāṇa* as perpetual letting go. These Buddhist concepts operate all but transparently in Mindfulness rhetoric. Of course, Kabat-Zinn's innovation was to transplant *sati*/mindfulness from a Buddhist framework to a medical one. In so doing, he transformed the very function of *sati*/mindfulness itself. In the Buddhist formation, the practice is oriented toward hyper-critical insights into the nature of self (as non-essentialized and non-centralized subjectivity), society (as the site of a conflagration of unredeemable pain), and the determinative relations between the two (resulting in unfreedom). In the Mindfulness formation, the orientation shifts toward insights that lead to conclusions that are individualist, prosocial, adaptive, accepting, curative. In the Buddhist formation, affects such as anxiety, disillusion, disgust, and pain itself, do important work. In the Mindfulness formation, "stress, anxiety, and pain" are problems to be remedied. The decisive difference in the ethos of each, again, lies in our repressed postulate of disenchantment. To see how its activation might work, we now turn to *cruelty*.

Cruel Therapy

The concept of disenchantment comes from the Buddhist Pali technical term, *nibbidā* (Wisdom Library, 2017). This is also translated as weariness, disgust with worldly life, tedium, aversion. My claim in this section is that the active employment of disenchantment as an ideological feature, coupled with the additional active ingredients of mindfulness meditation practice, transforms the therapeutic environment from a space of personal adaptivity and social acquiescence into one that "inspires us with the fiery magnetism of its images and acts on us like a spiritual therapeutics whose touch can never be forgotten" (Artaud, 2001, p. 70). This, in short, is Antonin Artaud's evocative description of what he terms "cruelty." For our purposes, it assumes a therapeutic space that is merciless, or at least will appear so in the context of our happiness-obsessed present. In this section, I will try to convey something of the spirit of cruelty in Artaud's sense. Then, I will offer some programmatic comments. My goal here is to show how mindfulness meditation can be transformed into a "cruel" practice and thereby become a catalyst for a client-subject not only *ruined* for our current capitalist formation, but *liberated* as an agent of change.

Where there is a stink of shit/there is the scent of being.
  —Antonin Artaud, *The Umbilicus of Limbo* (1989)

We can transpose a comment that Artaud made concerning the writing of a book to the practice of therapy: "I would like to practice a therapy that would drive clients mad, that would be like an open door leading them where they would never have consented to go; in short, a door that opens to reality" (Artaud, 1976, p. 59). For our purposes, what Artaud calls "reality" is better understood as "the Real." The concept of the Real enables us to talk about disavowed features of reality, features that threaten to sunder our constructions of order, sense, value, and meaning. The "Real" is also used to signify a facet of existence that is presupposed, yet untouched, by human symbolic systems, such as language and ideology.

Artaud employs a charged and idiosyncratic idiom to name an essential feature that marks the Real: "cruelty." The Real, in fact, is the definitive cruelty. (Artaud, of course, worked in the domain of theater. In what follows, it should not be difficult for the reader to transpose that term to "therapy.") He believed that the very purpose of theater is to *refract* this cruelty: theater should be *coextensive* with the Real. It should ensue *from* the Real, thus operate alongside it. And yet the theater of the 1920s aspired to be little more than a melodramatic retreat from the threats of modern life. It sought to *shield* its audience from the cruel Real. Artaud had a different vision. He saw in theater a practice that, to repeat, "inspires us with the fiery magnetism of its images and acts upon us like a spiritual therapeutics whose touch can never be forgotten." With this aspiration, he was up against no less than a popular institution that served, like the church and the police, the creation of a public submissive to an oppressive status quo. Artaud thus made it his mission to transmute this theater of complacency into an "immediate and violent" maelstrom, one that exposed its viewers to the primal truths of *their* lives. Only a theater that wakes up its audience's "nerves and heart," he believed, is worthy of the name. Such a theater must be built on the cruelty that is the Real, on those eschewed features of reality that, to evoke Artaud's wise words from the epigram to this section, stink. Such a theater must not shrink from the possibility that "extreme action, pushed beyond all limits" must ensue from its feral process. For, if not pushed with such intentional zeal, the machinations of delusion and self-satisfaction will overwhelm the vitality that is catalyzed by the lucid acknowledgment of the cruel Real. Taking Gilles Deleuze's evocative phrase about writers, we can say that the radical therapist is concerned "not [with] a system of demonstration, but [with] an ordeal in which the [client's] mind is given new eyes" (Ramey, 2012, p. 22). Therapy, like a literal theater, a *theatron*, thus becomes a space of "violent" (to the happiness-obsessed status quo), if perhaps cathartic, seeing. Therapy becomes a catalyst for the crushing, cruel, ordeal of human awakening.

Freud's colitis was in no small part due to the fact that he witnessed the Theater of Therapy lapsing into a refuge of comfort, into an institution of sleepy, complacent social conformity, into thought so sluggish as to mope its way into today's desert of Mindful, Inc. Recall, after all, his view that "much is gained if we succeed in transforming your hysterical misery into common unhappiness" (Breuer & Freud, 1895, pp. 273–274). I find three things about this statement significant for our purposes. First, this was Freud's imagined response to a general query, or perhaps an accusation, made by his patients. Second, it is interesting that, in the original German edition of 1895, the comment appears at the literal end of the book (it is the final paragraph on the final page). Should not the issue of psychotherapy's profound limitations in relation to "happiness" be at the forefront of a book titled *Studies on Hysteria*? After two world wars, Freud would devote much time to the relationship between unhappiness, society, and therapy. (He would also, not incidentally, come to see the failure of psychoanalysis as a cure.) But here, as early as 1895, I think we can glimpse his later theory in its nascence. Third, at least two of the five women whose therapies were the basis of this work, and indeed for the centrality of speech in the Freudian system, considered their analyses a complete failure. In any case, the entire passage is useful for our purposes.

> Whenever I promised to help my patients or to bring them relief through a cathartic cure, I repeatedly had to hear the objection: "You even say yourself that my suffering is probably associated with my relationships and fate, and that you cannot, of course, change any of that. In what way, then, do you want to help me?" To this objection, I have been able to answer as follows. — I do not, of course, doubt that fate would find it easier than me to

resolve your suffering; but you will become convinced that much is gained if we succeed in transforming your hysterical misery into common unhappiness. Against the latter, you will be better able to defend yourself with a recovered nervous system. (Breuer & Freud, 1895, pp. 273–274)

Is cruelty the very lifeblood of psychotherapy? Can "common unhappiness" be a vital name of the Real? If so, what a terrible irony! It means that psychotherapy possesses valuable resources—concepts, insights, strategies, practices—for helping us realize this intractable human truth for ourselves, and, perhaps, for the radical reformation of self and society. And yet psychotherapy functions as a conservative protector of the social status quo and as an ideological fortress producing subjects whose treasured goal appears to be to remain unscathed—in some sense or another—by life's inevitable vicissitudes. Paradoxically, however, it is from within the very desert of Mindfulness itself that we may recover the concealed element for a cruel therapy of "common unhappiness." It is to this matter that we now turn.

> First the body. No. First the place. No. First both. Now either. Now the other. Sick of the either try the other. Sick of it back sick of the either. So on. Somehow on. Till sick of both. Throw up and go. Where neither. Till sick of there. Throw up and back. The body again. Where none. The place again. Wherenone. Try again. Fail again. Better again. Or better worse. Fail worse again. Still worse again. Till sick for good. (Beckett, 1989, p. 101)

The therapist trains the client in several effective strategies and capacities. Let's consider some of these in a sequence that could conceivably be employed as part of a therapeutic program. I want to mention at the outset that none of this (from one to five) should be, in principle, unfamiliar to a practitioner or client of a mindfulness-based intervention. If the goal of therapy is the conventional one, namely, to treat an issue that is localized in the individual client, then these strategies may be quite useful. Specifically, these strategies may help to ameliorate symptoms around the ailments that MBIs address, such as stress, borderline personality, insomnia, addiction, depression, psychosis, pain, hypertension, weight control, cancer-related symptoms, and so on (Zhang et al., 2021).

14 How to Ruin Your Clients: Mindfulness as Cruelty

Maybe these strategies can also help to create the conditions for a more fruitful therapeutic session in general. The radical therapist, however, is not content to stop with these conventional strategies and outcomes. Why not? Because they function to foster a subject who upholds the status quo. My instructions are directed to the radical therapist, who asks how they might function *radically*, that is, how they might better enable the client to *bore to the root*.

1. *Instructions for calming.* "Now, breathing in and out, place your attention where the breath touches your nostrils and upper lip. Continuing in this fashion, allow yourself to settle. You are sitting calmly, *not* so that you may take refuge from your pain, but so that you may enter more fully into its clarifying presence. Sit, experiencing the effervescent charge of innate anxiety. This is anxiety born of being. This is the stress and tension born of the fusion of your body and the world into One. Sit, liberating cruelty."

    Commentary. The client learns methods for self-calming. In both our original source, Buddhism, and in MBIs, the natural breath is typically used as a focus for steadying the mind-body-emotion continuum, thereby attaining calm. In the cruel or radical formation, the breath also indexes the "naturalness" of the practice in that it remains unencumbered by ideological valuations, such as the breath as "healing," "sacred," "vital energy," and so on. Indeed, even the conceit of "naturalness" should be stripped away in the radical formulation. *Primordial sources* are *ānāpānasati*, immediate awareness of the in-breath and out-breath (note the following words employed: *sati*, which is the basis for the term "mindfulness;" *samādhi*, concentration, composure; *samatha*, calming; *pīti*, visceral effervescence. *Instructions for observing.* "Observe the cacophonous interconnecting swirl of thinking, ideation, mental imagery, internal voice, external sound, emotional tones, bodily feelings, scents, light, air, and beyond. *Feel* it all. Sit with equanimity within this roiling monstrosity of energetic flows.

    Commentary. The client is trained to notice the tendency of the mind to proliferate ideation and to wander indiscriminately, thereby arousing a tangled web of thoughts, emotions, feelings, and behaviors. We can name an instructive difference here: In the conventional therapist's view, these thoughts, etc., do not necessarily have a justification *in reality*. In the radical therapist's view, they are precisely co-constitutive with an inevitably self-fabricated "reality." Concomitant with this observation, is the realization that our subjective experience arises when the sensorium—eyes, ears, nose, tongue, body, and mind—makes contact with its respective phenomena—visual objects, sounds, scents, tastes, sensations, and thoughts. Unlike the Mindfulness and Buddhist formulations, in the radical or cruel formulation, none of these processes is viewed as being problematic in any way. They are not something to be altered or fixed; they are something to be observed. *Primordial sources* are *papañca*, conceptual proliferation; *saṅkhāra*, fabrication; and *vipassana*, insight, noticing; *khandha*, aggregates of subjective experience; *phassa*, touch, contact; *paṭiccasamuppāda*, interrelationality; *upekkha*, equanimity.

2. *Instructions for unbinding.* "Now, just sit, leaving everything as it is, observing and feeling everything as it is. Notice this interconnecting, agonistic, conflictual mutation of drives, instincts, desires, aversions, tensions, wishes, fantasies, realities—what happens when you *leave it alone*?"

   Commentary. The client learns to allow the ideations and fixations to disentangle themselves, at least temporarily. How? By leaving them alone, by not investing them with attentive energy. This can be expressed positively as *letting go* or *extinguishing*. As in the Buddhist tradition, cruel therapy can view *extinguishment* as having a short-term effect (on whatever complex or symptom), but one may lead eventually to a long term or even permanent effect. Unlike the Mindfulness and Buddhist formulations, in the radical or cruel formulation this process is not desired or celebrated; it is merely observed as being a possibility. *Primordial source* is *nirvāṇa*, unbinding, extinguishment.

3. *Instructions for acknowledging.* "Now, using the breath as an immediate example, acknowledge the inevitable dynamic arch of phenomena: *the breath arises, the breath persists, the breath dissolves, and the breath disappears.* Acknowledge this contour for any and all phenomena at hand or imaginatively. Acknowledge the pain, anxiety, stress, nervous-

ness, tension, disappointment, sadness, and so on, aroused by this intractable, cruel contour.

Commentary. The client learns to acknowledge the basic arc and characteristics of phenomena. The arc of everything that arises in the client's sensorium is: *arising, persisting, dissolving, and disappearing.* A bit more abstractly, in making this observation, the client is also observing three basic characteristics of phenomena, namely, that they (i) *lack* abiding substance, as is validated in their (ii) *impermanence*, which gives rise to their (iii) *distressfulness.* As in Buddhism and Mindfulness, in the cruel formulation, none of this is bemoaned. *Primordial sources* are *anatta,* insubstantiality, emptiness, lack; *anicca,* impermanence; and *dukkha,* distress, unsatisfactoriness, pain, ("common unhappiness"?).

4. *Instructions for wise unknowing.* "Now, see that your prior (conventional) ideological framework conceptualized the processes presented in 1–4 in ways not obviously given in the processes themselves. Sit, observing the unknowingness that attends to the vibrant, lived, experienced phenomena.

Commentary. Through all of this, the client is coming to a mature intelligence about the basic nature of the phenomenal-subjective world. The radical therapist doesn't want to contend that any of this constitutes *knowledge* of the world per se because, in the long term, it seems to entail the *impossibility* of anything like "knowledge." *Primordial source* is *paññā,* perspicuity, wisdom.

The revolutionary therapist does not stop here. To do so is to remain within the conventional. It is also, arguably, to remain subject to the critics' accusation of complicity in the perpetuation of the status quo. If nothing else, "revolution" implies profound disturbance of convention. (I want to mention that I can certainly sympathize with a conventional therapist who *nonetheless* persists in this limited approach. Perhaps my sympathy stems from observing the seemingly beneficial effects that my therapist-parents had on the lives of their clients.) By definition, the radical therapist is one who has exited the conventional ideology of positive psychology with its emphasis on healing, on the individual, and on the particular. For the radical practitioner, the localizable depression or addiction, etc., is but a miniscule prism in which is reflected a grander, more devastating, truth. So, in a very real sense, the radical therapist (I am using this term interchangeably with "the cruel therapist") is one who wants to *make things worse*. The radical therapist is one who wants the client to recognize that things are actually far more devastating than they ever imagined. Why? Because the particular pain is but an instance of a universal pain. The particular pain may prove amenable to treatment to some degree. We can strategize escapes, however temporarily. We can attitudinally manipulate particular pain, however superficially, even to the point of valorizing it as a teacher of life wisdom. But universal pain is an interminable conflagration of irredeemable vehemence from which there is no escape. It is a monster of energy discharging its fire millions-fold, literally every tick of the clock. It is this *regarding of* the Real of universal pain that stimulates disenchantment. I will say more in a moment. First, it might be useful to highlight the ways in which certain aspects of the above strategies serve as contributors to this regarding. I make the following sketchy remarks with the intention of stimulating further elaboration by the reader.

In observing *interrelationality*, for example, the client starts to wonder about the very location of their distress. They recognize that it is not *in* them. As Freud's critical patients observed, the distress is at the nexus between us and our relations to others and to the "world." In other words, the distress, say, "anxiety," is located in the continuum between us (our "nervous system") and our material conditions. As Freud's patients further observed, no therapist can change those conditions. Indeed, a client, too, can do little in that regard. From material relations there is no exit. Okay, I can imagine a skeptic saying, but can't we *improve* our material relations and conditions? A revolutionary psychologist must surely, at a minimum, believe in that possibility, right? The cruel therapist responds, well, unfortunately, our therapeutics has already engendered insight into the *distress, unsatisfactoriness,* and *pain* that obtains to all conditioned phenomena—and the client cannot shake the suspicion that within the category of "conditioned phenomena" is included *everything*. Distress, pain, at some register or another, is not something we *possess*, it is what we *are*. Subtract pain from the human, and you have done away with the human. So, where does that leave us in terms of action? It leaves us wherever Samuel Beckett's injunction to "fail again, fail better" leaves us. We should try to fix things with all the robustness we can muster, individually and collectively. But I ask the reader, doesn't all evidence suggest that we will fail? I agree that we should never cease thinking with the concept of utopia in play. But who really believes that it will ever be realized? Doesn't the history of the world, indeed, of a single human life, bear out the impossibility of our curative fantasies? Can we not accumulate a dreadful number of examples in which every fix comes with a new set of problems? To give a couple of obvious examples: with the solution to slow transportation, namely, the car, comes 51 million traffic injuries every year; over 1.2 million deaths; the leading killer of children, teenagers, and young adults aged 5–29 (World Health Organization, 2023); with the solution to physical pain relief, opioids, come over 600,000 overdose deaths every year (United Nations Office on Drugs and Crime, 2023), wrecked families, ravaged communities, and so on and so forth, to a sickening degree. But, our skeptic asks, what about the individual, is it not better to be treated for, say, an addiction, than not? I imagine that there must be cases where the symptom shields the client from an even more catastrophic outcome, like the inability to function, or even suicide. But, yes, let's grant the point. Nonetheless, the issue here is that the radical therapist is not content with this particular result.

With what then, is the radical therapist content? The radical therapist is content when the client is waylaid by disenchantment. When disenchantment becomes an *affect* permeating the client's view of himself and of the world, the therapist is satisfied. Disenchantment is not Nietzsche's "passive nihilism" of life-weariness. Neither is it his "active nihilism" of a redeeming value. Rather, the clients, regarding what they have now regarded about the phenomenal-subjective world, experiences his/their very "distress" as interminable tedium. He/They experiences the claims of positive psychology, of the wellness industry, of all those who are supposed to know, not to mention the whole crass, bloated spectacle of consumer society with its endless bellowing of BETTER! RICHER! NEWER! THINNER! HEALTHIER! IMPROVED! MORE YOUTHFUL! MORE BEAUTIFUL! MORE DESIRABLE! MORE! MORE! MORE! as asininely shallow and nauseatingly tedious. This does not mean that the clients haves cured themselves *of* their distress. Nothing is cured, nothing is solved, nothing is fixed or alleviated. The client is no longer enchanted by promises to heal "anxiety," "depression," "stress," and so on. That's all. The client has become disenchanted with the entire worldview within which such terms even function as self-evident descriptors of actual conditions. If, as the client now suspects, anxiety is precisely *constitutive* of the human being, should we not form a far less antagonistic relation to it, if not a complete revaluation? When clients become weary of themselves as needing to be fixed, when they becomes deadly bored with the tedium of "depression" or of a "failed" marriage or of "trauma," when they feels aversion to all "solutions," when they experiences disgust with the improvers of humankind, then the cruel therapist is content.

To be revolutionary, must a formation not first reject, then forcefully challenge, the dominant status quo? Must a revolutionary psychology not unreservedly endeavor to ruin the client for the prevailing ideology? Might such a cruel approach as sketched here help to create subjects that contribute to that goal?

References

Artaud, A. (1976). *Selected writings* (S. Sontag, Ed.; H. Weaver, Trans.). University of California Press. (Original work published 1938)
Artaud, A. (2001). The theater and its double. In S. E. Gontarski (Ed.), *The Grove Press reader 1951–2001* (pp. 70–75). Grove Press.
Baminiwatta, A., & Solangaarachchi, I. (2021). Trends and developments in mindfulness research over 55 years: A bibliometric analysis of publications indexed in Web of Science. *Mindfulness, 12*(9), 2099–2116. https://doi.org/10.1007/s12671-021-01681-x
Beckett, S. (1989). *Worstward Ho.* John Calder Ltd.
Boston Consulting Group. (2018). *Unleashing the power of mindfulness in corporations.* https://www.bcg.com/publications/2018/unleashing-power-of-mindfulness-in-corporations
Breuer, J., & Freud, S. (1895). *Studien über Hysterie.* Vienna, Austria. https://archive.org/details/StudienZurHysterie/mode/2up?q=ungluck
Critchley, S. (2013). *Infinitely demanding: Ethics of commitment, politics of resistance.* Verso.

Freud, S. (1930). Introduction to the special psychopathology of number. In J. Strachey (Ed. & Trans.), *The standard edition of the complete psychological works of Sigmund Freud* (Vol. 21, pp. xx–xx). London: Hogarth Press. (Original work published 1930)

Heidegger, M. (1967). *Sein und Zeit* (Original work published 1927). Max Niemeyer Verlag.

Kabat-Zinn, J. (2003). Mindfulness-based interventions in context: past, present, and future. *Clinical Psychology Science and Practice*, https://doi.org/10.1093/clipsy.bpg016

Kabat-Zinn, J. (2024). About. *Jon Kabat-Zinn: Personal website.*. https://jonkabat-zinn.com/about

Myers, M. (2015). *Improving military resilience through mindfulness training*. U.S. Army. https://www.army.mil/article/149615/Improving_Military_Resilience_through_Mindfulness_Training

Pickert, K. (2014, January 23). The mindful revolution. *Time*. https://time.com/1556/the-mindful-revolution

Ramey, J. (2012). *The hermetic Deleuze: Philosophy and spiritual ordeal*. Duke University Press.

United Nations Office on Drugs and Crime. (2023). *World drug report 2023*. https://www.unodc.org/unodc/en/data-and-analysis/world-drug-report-2023.html

Van Dam, N. T., van Vugt, M. K., Vago, D. R., Schmalzl, L., Saron, C. D., Olendzki, A., Meissner, T., Lazar, S. W., Kerr, C. E., Gorchov, J., Fox, K. C. R., Field, B. A., Britton, W. B., Brefczynski-Lewis, J. A., & Meyer, D. E. (2018). Mind the hype: A critical evaluation and prescriptive agenda for research on mindfulness and meditation. *Perspectives on Psychological Science, 13*(1), 36–61. https://doi.org/10.1177/1745691617709589

Wallis, G. (2016). Criticism matters: A response to Rick Repetti. In R. Purser, D. Forbes, & A. Burke (Eds.), *Handbook of mindfulness* (pp. 502–520). Springer. https://doi.org/10.1007/978-3-319-44019-4_33

Wisdom Library. (2017). Nibbidā. *Wisdom Library*. https://www.wisdomlib.org/definition/nibbida

World Health Organization. (2023). *Global status report on road safety 2023*. https://www.who.int/publications/i/item/9789240086517

Zhang, D., Lee, E. K. P., Mak, E. C. W., Ho, C. Y., & Wong, S. Y. S. (2021). Mindfulness-based interventions: An overall review. *British Medical Bulletin, 138*(1), 41–57. https://doi.org/10.1093/bmb/ldab005

Žižek, S. (2001). From Western Marxism to Western Buddhism: The Taoist ethic and the spirit of global capitalism. *Cabinet*. https://www.cabinetmagazine.org/issues/2/zizek.php

15

Facing the Abyss: Daoist Contemplative Psychology as Old/New Paradigm

Louis Komjathy 康思奇

The abyss has nine names and I have shown him three.
—*Húzǐ* 壺子 *(Gourd Master)*

Beyond Capitalist Meditation

Capitalism appropriates and assimilates, commodifies and domesticates. Like the production, sale, and purchase of N.W.A. records and Che Guevara t-shirts, it consistently and perpetually alienates workers from the products of their/our labor, with ever greater profits for management, owners, and shareholders. Simply consider the present book, potentially neutralizing revolutionary potential. Debt-slavery and wage-slavery. As the pseudonymous British street-artist and unapprehended international

---

L. Komjathy 康思奇 (✉)
Daoist Foundation, 501(c), Chicago, IL, USA
e-mail: lkomjathy@daoistfoundation.org

© The Author(s), under exclusive license to Springer Nature Switzerland AG 2025
J. Hook, F. Gruba-McCallister (Eds.), *The Revolutionary Psychologist's Guide to Radical Therapy*, The Politics of Mental Health and Illness,
https://doi.org/10.1007/978-3-032-02399-5_15

criminal Banksy has commented, "You are an acceptable level of threat and if you were not you would know about it" (Potter, 2019).

"Capitalist meditation" refers to forms of meditation that conform to, support, and perpetuate the consumerist status quo. Buy meditation; sell meditation; process meditation bought and sold. Most forms of meditation practiced in mainstream American society are capitalist meditation, involving anesthetization, exploitation, and oppression of workers. They would not be known, taught, or learned if they were not. That is, if they represented an actual alternative, with socio-political consequences, they would be suppressed. As systematically discussed in my chapter on modern therapeutic meditation in the edited volume *Contemplative Literature* (Komjathy, 2015), it is no coincidence that meditation in general and so-called "mindfulness" in particular have become psychologized and medicalized (see also Rieff, 1966; Imber, 2004; Purser, 2019). Largely representing domesticated and reconceptualized Buddhist meditation, they place emphasis on "health" and "wellness," with the supposed promise of greater resiliency to stress and illness through increased relaxation (conformity and compliance)—instances of branding and marketing. That is, rather than address and alter structural inequalities, such forms of meditation help to make "better workers" with increased productivity and profitability. This is not just about profiteering; it also is about control. While therapeutic meditation may assist in the (Buddhist) alleviation of suffering, it does not assist in the (Buddhist) aspiration for universal liberation. How might Socially Engaged Buddhism (SEB) actually respond to the Military-Industrial-Prison-Slaughterhouse Complex (MIPSC)? (And this is to say nothing of the Tibetan Buddhist missionization project or Buddho-neuroscientific careerism and clinical psychological hegemony in meditation studies.) As the Bright Eyes song goes, "Don't be a criminal in this police state—You better shop and eat and procreate." Capitalist meditation is yet another means to anesthetize the general population and to reproduce mainstream capitalist society. The latter includes meditation as commodity and industry.

For readers of the present volume, including those committed to and aspiring for actual freedom and flourishing, various issues emerge from the engagement with (rejection/subversion of) capitalist meditation. First, what are the informing values, framing metaphors, and situational contexts (see, e.g., Sontag, 1978; Lakoff & Johnson, 1980)? The latter include the associated illness/wellness narratives (see, e.g., Kleinman, 1988), ideally beyond the normativity of allopathic medicine, the pharmaceutical industry, and the insurance system. In terms of power and oppression, who offers the diagnosis, and which treatments are recognized, approved, and funded (see, e.g., Laing, 1967)? Does meditation just become yet another exercise in the production of pathological egoists and the formation of malignant narcissists (see, e.g., Vitz, 1994 [1977]; Heelas, 1996)? Is it really just coincidence that so many spiritual celebrities and prominent meditation teachers are so utterly unconvincing as human beings? Power, corruption, and lies. And worse still.

In truly revolutionary meditation, meditation as revolutionary activity, one sees through the veils of delusion, overcomes social conditioning and personal habituation, and rejects (works to overthrow?) any and all systems of oppression. This includes recognizing, renouncing, and remedying one's own conformity and complicity (see, e.g., Komjathy, 2020c, 2023d, 2024c). How dangerous will we dare to be (e.g., Kripal, 2010; Giroux, 2015)? As an emerging contemplative response, perhaps representing an alternative form of social engagement, one works to become liberated and to liberate others from acquisitive, exploitative, and oppressive modes of being. One becomes part of a new (old) contemplative counterculture, resistance movement, and spiritual underground.

Daoist Contemplative Psychology

"Daoist contemplative psychology" refers to psychological views informed by and informing Daoist contemplative practice and contemplative experience. Here I use "psychology" as a comparative and cross-cultural category referring to discourse on, study of, or theories about *psyche*. The latter is a Greek term that may refer to consciousness, emotion, mind, soul, spirit, thought, and so forth. Thus, herein "psychology" does not refer to the modern Western social scientific discipline and/or therapeutic profession ("Psychology"). Rather, it relativizes the latter by raising issues, questions, and insights related to culture-specific and tradition-specific views, approaches, and modalities, with Daoism being the primary focus of the present chapter. It thus also might be understood along the lines of "indigenous" and "decolonial psychology."

As a "new" form of psychological investigation, "contemplative psychology" is a phrase coined by the Dutch psychologist Han de Wit (b. 1944) in his book *Contemplative Psychology* (1991). As stated by de Wit, "In using the term *contemplative psychology*, we are referring to the *psychological* insights, knowledge and methods that we find *within contemplative traditions* themselves" (p. 1, italics in original)[1] Moreover,

> The term *contemplative psychology* refers rather to the psychological insights and beliefs that are often implicitly present in the vision of religions, and that become concretized in the authentic religious practices of individuals. (p. 12, italics in original)

He continues,

> This brings us to the main purpose of this introductory study in contemplative psychology: to make explicit and clarify the nature and position of the psychological *know-how* that contemplative traditions contain….The clarification of the psychological aspects of contemplative traditions may also contribute to *a general understanding of the value of contemplative traditions and their psychological perspectives*, both from a practical and from a scientific psychological or methodological point of view. (p. 14, italics in original)

For de Wit, contemplative practice utilizes and activates a special set of psychological states or conditions. It involves a specific type of knowing ("contemplative epistemology"), which includes first-person experience. However, this is not uncritical adherent discourse, that is, the discourse of apologetics and dogmatics; rather, it is a more systematic investigation of one's life through experiences within contemplative practice. The goal,

---

[1] In contrast to some humanistic and transpersonal psychologists, de Wit uses the phrase "contemplative traditions" in explicit connection with religion, specifically adherents and communities committed to contemplative practice and spiritual development. See Komjathy (2015, 2018). In pre-modern religious practice, this usually would be the purview of the religious elite, often ascetics, clerics, and monastics.

ideally, is to become more conscious, integrated, and, from one perspective, realized. De Wit identifies this as a path to that which religious traditions identify as enlightenment, liberation, fulfillment, emancipation, salvation, and so on. This relates to contemplative practice as located in and expressions of soteriological systems, that is, a way of life oriented towards something larger, including an "ultimate purpose." For de Wit, an existential and psychological shift occurs through contemplative practice. Such shifts are documented in the psychological views of religious traditions. Contemplative psychology in turn attempts to map the "higher" levels of human functioning. Thus, "contemplative psychology" is especially relevant for investigating and understanding contemplative experience. It has certain parallels with tradition-based psychology (i.e., psychological views and insights derived from and utilized within religious traditions), but the latter is located *within* religious traditions and in the perspectives of adherents. Contemplative psychology, on the other hand, draws insights from religious traditions in an effort to create an integrated psychological system focusing on spiritual development (cf. Wilber et al., 2008). In this way, contemplative psychology tends to be comparative, inter-religious, and syncretic. For present purposes, we will investigate "Daoist contemplative psychology" in terms of both its contextual meaning *and* its potential contemporary relevance, including the ways in which it might challenge, qualify, and even subvert received (assumed) views.

Along these lines, and as systematically discussed in my books *Contemplative Literature* (2015) and *Introducing Contemplative Studies* (2018), "contemplative practice" is a broader category for distinct practices and approaches more commonly referred to as "meditation" and "prayer," but also including certain forms of art, dance, movement awareness, photography, theatre, and so forth. Contemplative practice thus may be religious, spiritualist, secular, or ecumenical. Possible connective strands or family resemblances include attentiveness, awareness, interiority, presence, silence, transformation, and a deepened sense of meaning and purpose. From my perspective, it is important not to reduce contemplative practice to mere technique. Rather, we must be attentive to various dimensions (e.g., community, ethics, place) and more encompassing and integrated lifeways. "Contemplative experience" designates experiences that occur within the parameters of contemplative practice, are associated with particular contemplative practices, and/or are deemed significant by contemplatives and their associated communities.

Applying these insights to our current topic, we will focus on classical Daoist apophatic and quietistic (emptiness-/stillness-based) meditation, with particular attention to the technical specifics and informing views. This was the primary form of contemplative practice utilized in the inner cultivation lineages (ICL) of classical Daoism (see Komjathy, 2013, 2023c; also Roth, 1999, 2015, 2021),[2] even to the point of representing quasi-orthopraxy and the community's shared (and assumed) practice repertoire. Such attentiveness assists one in making sense of the widespread misrepresentation and misinterpretation of classical Daoism as so-called "philosophy". There is systematic ignorance or neglect of the praxis-based contemplative approach and characteristics. The associated training regimen, in turn, utilized a specific contemplative psychology, which I refer to as "cartographies of Daoist contemplative experience." In terms of classical Daoism, some of these include the "Three Externalizations," "Three Pivots," "Four-Sixes," and various Daoist "Beyond/Non-States," which are beyond the confines of the present chapter. Such are maps of human potential, flourishing, and transformation. They offer an alternative and radical vision of human being and experiencing.

A Praxis-Based View and Approach

The previous points about "contemplative practice" and "contemplative experience," including "contemplative psychology," relate to my broader theory of "praxis" (see Fig. 15.1; also Komjathy, 2015, 2018, 2023e).

---

[2] "Classical Daoism" is referred to as so-called "philosophical Daoism" in outdated colonialist and Orientalist constructions of Daoism. Reference to the latter should be taken *ipso facto* as ignorance and misunderstanding concerning Daoism. For my revisionist interpretive framework and accompanying critiques of received views, including contexts of reception and interpretive legacies, see Komjathy (2013, 2023c). The former, focusing on the "Seven Periods and Four Divisions," is increasingly becoming accepted as the standard revisionist view.

15 Facing the Abyss: Daoist Contemplative Psychology...

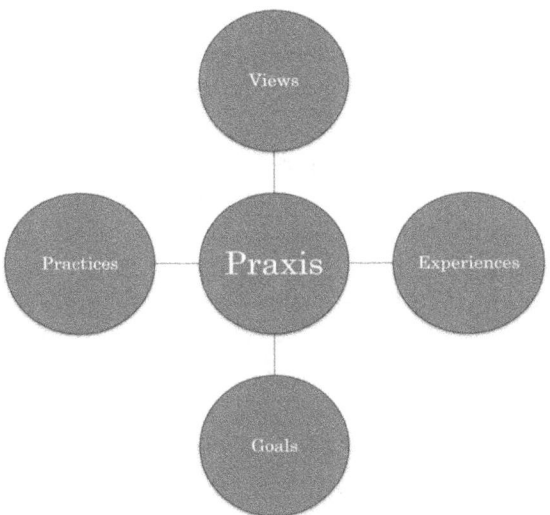

Fig. 15.1 Dimensions of (religious) praxis

Here "praxis" is used in a more technical, theoretically sophisticated sense. It draws attention to the interrelated and mutually informing dimensions of view, practice (or method), experience, and goal in a given approach or system. Specific views inform and are informed by specific practices; specific practices inform and are informed by specific experiences; specific experiences and goals inform and are informed by specific views and specific practices; and so forth. What this means in terms of applied and lived/living contemplative practice is that it is possible to extract a given practice from the associated views, including soteriology (ultimate purpose) and theology (ultimate concern), thus resulting in decontextualized and reconceptualized practice. In the present case, Daoist techniques uninformed by Daoist views, Daoist experiences, and Daoist goals are not Daoist praxis.[3] The views are integral to practice and

---

[3] Readers should note that the vast majority of popular teachers of and publications on "Daoist/Taoist practice/meditation" are just that: They lack a deep and sophisticated understanding of actual Daoist approaches, perspectives, views, and so forth. This is not to mention any formal affiliation with the religious tradition which is Daoism.

experience, and intact/integrated Daoist praxis may result in radically different effects. On some level, one inhabits a different world and different reality.[4] Investigation of the latter in terms of similarities and differences with other systems, including potential compatibility and reconcilability, is the work of comparative theology.

One key point here, and this cannot be overemphasized, is that the texts of the classical Daoist corpus, with the two most well-known and influential being the *Lǎozǐ* 老子 (Book of Venerable Masters; abbrev. LZ; a.k.a. *Dàodé jīng* 道德經 [Scripture on the Dao and Inner Power]; abbrev. DDJ) and *Zhuāngzǐ* 莊子 (Book of Master Zhuang; abbrev. ZZ),[5] are *rooted in and assume familiarity with* the source-practice of Daoist apophatic and quietistic (emptiness-/stillness-based) meditation. That is, it is almost impossible to understand the associated views and perspectives ("philosophy") without familiarity with said practice, even if only through historical and textual reconstruction. In fact, the elders and teachers of classical Daoism advocate for a practice-based and experience-based approach, beyond rigid doctrine and without accompanying dogma. This is so much the case that one of the classical Daoist names for "Daoism" is *bùyán zhī jiào* 不言之教 ("Teaching beyond/without Words") (LZ 2 and 43, also 56; ZZ 5 and 22) (see Komjathy, 2023c). This relates to various Daoist "beyond/non-states," which I will discuss momentarily.

Considering classical Daoist contemplative practice in general and classical Daoist apophatic and quietistic meditation in particular, there are various, associated indigenous Chinese Daoist technical terms (see Table. 15.1). To begin, there are two larger umbrella terms that encompass the various method-specific designations. They are *dàoshù* 道術 ("techniques of the Dao"; also translated as "arts of the Way") and *xīnshù* 心術 ("techniques of the heart-mind"; also translated as "arts of the

---

[4] This relates to my "radical pluralistic" view of religion, which involves a generalized quasi-polytheism. Interested readers may consult my published work.
[5] These are anonymous or pseudonymous works consisting of historical and textual materials dating from the fourth to second centuries BCE. They contain teachings and practices associated with various elders of the inner cultivation lineages of classical Daoism. For guidance, see Komjathy (2023c). The present chapter uses traditional Chinese characters with Pinyin Romanization of "Mandarin" pronunciations. Unless otherwise indicated, all translations are my own. Numbers for Daoist texts follow my *Title Index to Daoist Collections* (2002). For additional guidance, see the Alternate Homepage of Dr. Louis Komjathy (www.louiskomjathy.com/taoïsme).

Table 15.1 Classical Daoist technical terms designating "apophatic meditation"

bàopǔ 抱樸 ("embracing simplicity")	shǒumǔ 守母 ("guarding the Mother")
bàoyī 抱一 ("embracing the One")	shǒuyī 守一 ("guarding the One")
guīgēn 歸根 ("returning to the root[s]")	shǒuzhōng 守中 ("guarding the Center")
jìngxīn 靜心 ("stilling the heart-mind")	xīnyǎng 心養 ("mind-nourishment")
shǒucí 守雌 ("guarding the feminine")	xīnzhāi 心齋 ("fasting the heart-mind"; heart-fasting/mind-retreat)
shǒujìng 守靜 ("guarding stillness")	zuòwàng 坐忘 ("sitting-in-forgetfulness"; seated-forgetting/forgetful-sitting)[a]

[a] Note that in her otherwise reliable translation of the eighth-century CE *Zuòwàng lùn* 坐忘論 (Discourse on Sitting-in-Forgetfulness; DZ 1036; ZH 992), Livia Kohn (2010) has problematically rendered *wàng* 忘 as "oblivion." In addition to distorting the verbal sense of the character, this rendering obscures the connection with emptiness and stillness and further implies obliviousness, which is the opposite result of the practice. Kohn's (mis)translation also has infiltrated popular discussions (and commodifications) of the classical Daoist practice and the later text. Cf. Komjathy (2022). See also below

heart"), or "Way-Arts" and "Heart-Techniques" for short. From a comparative and cross-cultural perspective, these may be understood as "spiritual exercises," "transformative techniques," and "techniques of self" (see Hadot, 1995; Komjathy, 2007, 2015, 2018, 2023e; Martin et al., 1988; Murphy, 1992). *Dàoshù* appears in chapters six and thirty-three of the *Zhuāngzǐ*, while *xīnshù* is derived from the four so-called "Xīnshù 心術" (Heart-mind Techniques; abbrev. HMT or THM) chapters (chs. 36–38 and 49) of the *Guǎnzǐ* 管子 (Book of Master Guan; abbrev. GZ). As appearing therein,

> Fish thrive in water; humans thrive in the Dao. For those who thrive in water, dig a pond and they will find nourishment enough. For those who thrive in the Dao, don't bother about them and their lives will be secure. So it is said, fish forget (*wàng* 忘) each other in rivers and lakes; humans forget each other through the techniques of the Dao. (ZZ 6)

The techniques of the heart-mind involve practicing non-action (*wúwéi* 無為) and regulating the apertures [senses] (*zhìqiào* 制竅). ("Xīnshù shàng 心術上" [Heart-mind Techniques I]; GZ 36)

Thus, these Daoist methods aim at realizing the Dao 道 (Tao/Way), the sacred and ultimate concern of Daoists. From a classical and foundational Daoist perspective, the Dao has four primary characteristics: (1) Source of everything (*yuán* 元/原); (2) Unnamable mystery (*xuán* 玄); (3) All-pervading sacred presence (*líng* 靈; also *qì* 氣); and (4) Universe as transformative process (Nature) (*huà* 化). The primary Daoist theology ("Daology") is monistic (one impersonal reality [Reality]), panentheistic (sacred in and beyond the world), and panenhenic (Nature as sacred). Daoism is, in turn, one of the more world-affirming and body-affirming contemplative systems and traditions. As discussed momentarily, the associated meditative methods also focus on stilling the heart-mind, the psychospiritual center of human personhood from a traditional Chinese and Daoist perspective. This involves disengagement and deconditioning.

Moving into the method-specific terms, with each referring to stillness-based meditation, one first observes that each consists of a two-character phrase, with the majority being verb/noun constructions. Daoist adepts engaging in this form of meditation "embrace," "forget," "guard," "hold," and "return." Here a note on the corresponding etymology may be helpful. *Bào* 抱 ("embrace") consists of *shǒu* 手/扌 ("hand") and *bāo* 包 ("enwrap/enwomb"), with the latter originally depicting a fetus (*sì* 巳) inside the womb (*bāo* 勹), or a swaddled baby. *Guī* 歸 ("return") consists of *duī* 𠂤 ("mound"; here probably *shī* 師 ["troops"]) and *zhǒu* 帚 ("broom/sweep"), thus suggesting clearing space and removing opposition, after which an area is returned to peace and harmony and/or one returns home. *Shǒu* 守 consists of *mián* 宀 ("roof") and *cùn* 寸 ("hand"; also "inch" and "pulse"), suggesting keeping watch over something inside a room or residence. From an applied and lived Daoist perspective, *cùn* also invokes the later Daoist term of *fāngcùn* 方寸 ("Square Inch"), which is an esoteric designation for the heart region. Finally, *wàng* 忘 ("forget") consists of *wáng* 亡 ("extinguish/lose") and *xīn* 心 ("heart"). In terms of Daoist contemplative practice, it points towards the dissolution of ordinary consciousness states and suspension of ordinary perceptual and cognitive modes. One also is advised to "center" (*zhōng* 中) and "fast" (*zhāi* 齋). These various characters suggest that Daoist apophatic and quietistic meditation involves seclusion and withdrawal, both physical and psychological. In such psychosomatic isolation, one is able to guard and protect that which is precious in/as/through one's being, namely, stillness as sacred connection with the Dao. In fact, in chapter sixteen of the *Lǎozǐ*, "returning to the root" is defined as stillness, which in turn clarifies one's life-purpose (*mìng* 命). Along these lines, the character *jìng* 靜 ("stillness"), also translated as "tranquility," is interesting: It consists of *qīng* 青 ("green/young/pure") and *zhēng* 爭 ("contend/contention"). Although the latter is often understood as a phonetic, from a Daoist perspective the character suggests the purification of contention, and thus invokes the Daoist beyond/non-state of *wúzhēng* 無爭 ("non-contention") (see, e.g., LZ 81; also below). One forgets ordinary concerns and extraneous matters, including various forms of psychological agitation, confusion, and distortion.

Such inner cultivation allows practitioners to connect to and be pervaded by the Dao as Ancestor, Beginning, Center, Ground, Mother, Mystery, One, Root, and Source. This is what I refer to as "theologically-infused contemplative practice"; there is a sacred orientation in which one aligns and attunes with something else and sometime more. "Compelled to name it, we call it 'Dao'." The more than merely human. By adopting a "yin mode" characterized by open receptivity and acceptance, here designated by *cí* 雌 ("female/feminine"), one enters the contemplative state of "forgetful**ness**" (*wàng* 忘) and "still**ness**" (*jìng* 靜), which are closely related to "empti**ness**" (*xū* 虛).[6] Along these lines, "heart-fasting" is defined as "*xū*-emptiness" in ZZ 4, while "forgetful-sitting" is defined as "great pervasion" (*dàtōng* 大通) in ZZ 6 (see also ZZ 11 and 33). Here we

---

[6] The gendered language has led some modern interpreters to claim quasi- or proto-feminist characteristics. In fact, the related terms are only loosely gendered, and not as conventionally assumed. "Mother" points to the Dao-as-Source, as that which births and nourishes all beings without discrimination or preference. As an impersonal, amoral process, the Dao itself is fundamentally genderless; it is no more a mother than a father. *Cí* 雌, like *pìn* 牝 ("female/feminine"), does not refer to female humans. The character contains *zhuī* 隹 ("short-tailed bird/sparrow"). Contextually speaking, it invokes yin, which is the privileged mode for *both* female and male Daoists in classical and foundational Daoism.

also note an apparent paradox or tension: One seems to be encouraged to undertake various actions while following a contemplative path rooted in *wúwéi* 無為 ("non-action/effortlessness"). One response is that these are *preliminary* gestures, movements, or positionings for creating the atmosphere and establishing the setting for the practice. One makes space for the deeper dimension of the practice to unfold: The dissolution of self in emptiness, forgetfulness, and stillness. There is an accompanying Daoist oral transmission (*kǒujué* 口訣): Sit and forget until even forgetting is forgotten. This is contemplative absorption and mystical (non)union.

There are a wide variety of classical Daoist textual passages that provide technical specifics on the associated meditation method (see Komjathy, 2023c; also Roth, 2021). Two of the most important and highly influential passages derive from an imaginary dialogic exchange between the Ruists ("Confucians") Kǒngzǐ 孔子 (Master Kong; "Confucius"; ca. 551-ca. 479 BCE) and his senior (and impoverished) disciple Yán Huí 顏回 (Zǐyuān 子淵; ca. 521-481 BCE) as appearing in the *Zhuāngzǐ*.

> You must fast! I will tell you what that means. Do you think that it is easy to do anything while you have a heart-mind? If you do, the luminous heavens will not support you…Unify your aspirations (*yīzhì* 一志)! Don't listen with your ears; listen with your heart-mind. No, don't listen with your heart-mind; listen with qi 氣. Listening stops with the ears, the heart-mind stops with joining (*fú* 符), but qi is empty and waits on all things. The Dao gathers in emptiness alone. Emptiness (*xū* 虛) is the fasting of the heart-mind (*xīnzhāi* 心齋). (ZZ 4; see also LZ 42 and ZZ 22)[7]

> I'm improving…I can sit and forget…I smash up my limbs and body, drive out perception and intellect, cast off form, do away with understanding, and make myself identical (*tóng* 同) with Great Pervasion (*dàtōng* 大通).

---

[7] Note that Watson, in his generally excellent translation, mistranslates qi as "spirit." This has led to misunderstanding and mischaracterization on the part of Western popularizers without knowledge of the Chinese original. It also is instructive on how one poor translation choice, like *de* 德 as "potency" (John Major et al.), qi as "breath" and "breathing" by extension (Harold Roth), and *zuòwàng* as "sitting in oblivion" (Livia Kohn), can taint an otherwise reliable work. This is especially the case in terms of reconstructed and/or lived Daoist practice. For guidance, see Komjathy (2022). I will discuss the "energetics of Daoist practice and experience" in due course.

This is what I mean by sitting-in-forgetfulness (*zuòwàng* 坐忘). (ZZ 6; see also ZZ 11 and 19)[8]

Significantly, in the parallel passage in chapter twenty-two of the *Zhuāngzǐ*, it is the legendary Lǎo Dān 老聃 (Elder Dān; a.k.a. Lǎozǐ 老子 ["Master Lao"]) who instructs Kǒngzǐ on the practice of heart-fasting (see Komjathy, 2023c). As is the case with many forms of meditation, one begins by disengaging sense perception and then stills excessive emotional and intellectual activity, especially in the form of habituated psychological patterns and reactivity. One moves through progressive states of relaxation to the point of (not)attaining emptiness and numinous pervasion. This involves abstaining from concerns that disturb the heart-mind and forgetting distractions. One sits and forgets, until even forgetting is forgotten. This is the state of *forgetfulness*, which is largely parallel to emptiness and stillness. Interestingly, the first passage involves Kǒngzǐ instructing Yán Huí, while the second involves Yán Huí instructing Kǒngzǐ. That is, it is *dialogic and inter-relational*. Through intensive, dedicated, and prolonged meditation practice, the disciple becomes the master. In addition, read contextually, the first installment of the practice results in Yán Huí (and the dedicated Daoist practitioner by extension) losing his ordinary self ("Before I heard this, I was certain that I was Huí. But now that I have heard it, there is no more Huí") while the second results in complete absorption in the Dao ("If you're identical with it, you must have no more likes! If you've been transformed, you must have no more constancy [*wúcháng* 無常]!").[9] This relates to various other contemplative states, including emotionlessness (*wúqíng* 無情) and formlessness (*wúxíng* 無形). The *Zhuāngzǐ* in turn speaks of clearing out the "underbrush of the head" and "brambles of the heart-mind" (*péng zhī xīn* 蓬之心; ZZ 1) as well as making the body like "withered wood" (*gǎomù* 槁木) and heart-mind like "dead ashes" (*sǐhuī* 死灰) (ZZ 2, 22, 23, and 24). I

---

[8] *Zuòwàng* also appears in ch. 12 of the early second-century BCE *Huáinánzǐ* 淮南子 (Book of the Huainan Masters; DZ 1184; ZH 978), significantly the LZ commentary chapter. For individuals who are interested, I have prepared "Contemplative States in the *Zhuāngzǐ*" as part of the Daoist Foundation Self-Study Guides series.

[9] Although Daoism tends to privilege "constancy" (*cháng* 常), here non-constancy relates to dissolution, formlessness, and pervasion as important contemplative and mystical experiences, often indicating practice efficacy.

take the latter phrases to refer to a deep state of meditative absorption, a trophotropic condition characterized by extremely low levels of physiological activity (see Fischer, 1980; Forman, 1990). This is so much the case that it appears that the practitioner has ceased breathing. Respiration has so slowed, deepened, and lengthened to become imperceptible. The later Daoist tradition refers to this as "embryonic respiration" (*tāixī* 胎息).

One key dimension of Daoist apophatic and quietistic meditation, and a Daoist quietistic lifeway more generally, centers on *qì* 氣, which I prefer to leave untranslated, but which has been variously rendered as "subtle/vital breath," "energy," and even "pneuma." This involves the traditional Chinese and Daoist view that a subtle current or vapor animates and circulates through universe, world, all beings, and oneself (myself and yourself). While there are many types of qi, here we may simply note that Daoists are primarily interested in more primordial, less differentiated forms, which the later Daoist tradition refers to as the "qi of the Dao" (*dàoqì* 道炁; or "Way-Energy" for short). This has some connection with Daoist understandings of "original qi" (*yuánqì* 元氣) and "perfect/real/true qi" (*zhēnqì* 眞氣). In any case, the key point is that this is both a cosmological and theological view, associated with the previously mentioned "numinous presence" of the Dao, and an energetic (qi-based) view of being and experiencing. It is a psychosomatic view that helps to bridge conventional mind-body dualisms, as everything is a manifestation of qi charted along a spectrum from the most material (rocks, for example) to the most rarified (primordial vapors, for example). It also leads to or at least awakens a different existential and ontological mode, although some may dismiss this as "archaic vitalism." Interestingly, there also appears to have been a contemporaneous intra-Daoist debate about the deepest dimensions of self and levels of practice. For example, the anonymous, probably mid-fourth century BCE *Nèiyè* 內業 (Inward Training; GZ 49; abbrev. NY; see Komjathy, 2023b, I.1; also Roth, 1999) identifies the "four alignments" (*sìzhèng* 四正), also referred to as "fourfold aligning."

(1) Aligning the body (*zhèngxíng* 正形)
(2) Aligning the four limbs (*zhèng sìtǐ* 正四體/*zhèng sìzhī* 正四肢)
(3) Aligning qi (*zhèngqì* 正氣)
(4) Aligning the heart-mind (*zhèngxīn* 正心)

Thus, while the *Zhuāngzǐ* identifies qi as the deepest dimension of human personhood, the *Nèiyè* points to the heart-mind (see below). One potential resolution involves understanding these as related, with different emphases. The former emphasizes a form of energetic listening, while the latter emphasizes expanded consciousness, with a stronger connection to (apparently transpersonal) spirit (*shén* 神). "There is a spirit naturally residing in the body./One moment it leaves, the next it arrives" (NY 13). In addition, the *Nèiyè* speaks of a "heart-mind within the heart-mind" (NY 14). This is pure consciousness beneath/within/beyond ordinary psychological patterns. There are, in turn, diverse intra-Daoist views about the degree to which one can conceal the emergent energetic pattern and other transformative effects, which is beyond the purview of the present discussion.

Ultimately, then, classical Daoist apophatic and quietistic meditation informs and is informed by *wúwéi* 無為, which is one of the most (over?) emphasized, appropriated, and misunderstood Daoist technical terms. In addition to supposedly "doing nothing" (try releasing *all* of the tension in your body), popular misinterpretations include following one's own selfish desires ("going with the flow") and reproducing habituation. This also relates to passivity to the point of atrophy, a common misconception related to "quietism." *Wúwéi* literally means "without acting/doing" and is translated more technically as "non-action" and "effortlessness." It is a classical and foundational Daoist commitment, practice, principle, state, and value. It relates to other, related principles and practices, including "embracing simplicity" (*bàopǔ* 抱樸) and "decreasing desires" (*guǎyù* 寡欲), with *pǔ* translated more technically as "unhewn simplicity/uncarved block," invoking gnarled trees (*mù* 木), and associated with innate nature (*xìng* 性) (see below). On a practical level, one does the least required to do something well; on a more theological level, one stops doing everything that prevents one from being what one is. As expressed in LZ 48, "Decreasing and again decreasing (*sǔn zhī yòu sǔn* 損之又損), one arrives at non-action." This is twofold decreasing (*chóngsǔn* 重損) in which one returns to the ground (*tǔ* 土) of one's being, abiding in the twofold mystery (*chóngxuán* 重玄) of the Dao (see LZ 1).[10] One does nothing extra.

---

[10] Given the widespread adherence to cultural relativism, hyper-historicism, pseudo-postmodernism ("deconstructionism"), secular materialism, social constructivism, and the like, I am aware that

Wúwéi may be further understood as effortless activity, and non-interference and non-intervention by extension. A key point here, and this cannot be overemphasized, is that *wúwéi* is *rooted in and assumes* the practice of apophatic meditation. This is so much the case that I would suggest that it is basically equivalent with contemplative deconditioning. Like the misinterpretation of classical Daoist texts as "philosophy" (disembodied ideas for intellectual rumination), it also helps to explain the widespread "non-Daoist" confusion: We are largely observing ordinary mind and habituated consciousness trying to understand original mind and realized consciousness. It is an attempt, perhaps unknowingly, to domesticate and neutralize the potential for radical freedom. As a principle, then, *wúwéi* is applied and actualized through Daoist practice-realization. The practice is, in turn, contentless, non-conceptual, and non-dualistic. It is ultimately beyond. Beyond naming, thinking, and knowing.

On Realizing Nothing

By way of/around conclusion, I would like to offer some insights and reflections about Daoist apophatic and quietistic meditation from a lived/living Daoist perspective. This involves critical subjectivity, specifically what I refer to as a "scholar-practitioner approach" (SPA) and "critical adherent discourse" (CAD) (see Komjathy, 2015, 2018, 2023a, 2023e). As discussed, explored, and advocated in my earlier publications, this is an intellectual and scholarly form of first-person and possibly second-person discourse that is open to other-investigation and other-debate. It is *not*, and in fact challenges and rejects, apologetics, confessionalism, dogmatism, evangelism, insularity, sectarianism, uncritical belief, and similar tendencies. One issue in terms of conventional academic approaches, although possibly less so with respect to the present edited volume, is the "taboo of subjectivity" (Wallace, 2000; see also Forman,

---

many readers presumably will baulk at Daoist expressions of essentialist and originalist views. One response is that the practices result in such realization. One also might point towards alternative interpretive frameworks (projections and filters) as forms of social conditioning and habituated modes.

1990; Ferrer & Sherman, 2008). This relates to the "insider/outsider question" ("problem") (see, e.g., Komjathy 2016). Conventional Sinological Daoist Studies largely represents a form of nineteenth-century Orientalism, in which Daoism is engaged as historical artifact through textual reconstruction (see Komjathy, 2013, 2022, 2023b). Its primary purpose is to appease the Orientalist gaze and to advance academic careerism, including power, prestige, and privilege. It involves uncritical adherence and conformity to mandated approaches and models (cf. Komjathy, 2022, 2024b). Religious Studies emerged out of and in contradistinction to Theology (Christian Theology), so it has attempted and largely continues to distance itself from the latter by excluding lived adherence, experience, practice, and the like.

Thus, perhaps somewhat surprisingly, both disciplines and fields exclude participation in their objects of study.[11] They cling to problematic and unconvincing claims to "objectivity." This helps to explain many interpretive deficiencies, including the disempowerment, erasure, exclusion, and marginalization of more radical voices and approaches. The approaches I advocate for (SPA and CAD) have certain parallels with the approaches taken by Daoist authors of the classical and medieval periods, albeit with a modern sensibility, whose texts are often appropriated and domesticated in insular academic discourse communities in a manner paralleling the capitalist meditation industry. Politicians and technicians masquerading as scholars and intellectuals. But perhaps I still have too much attachment to the academy's promise (cf. Bourdieu, 1988; Komjathy, 2018, 2022; Wilderson, 2020).

In terms of my own lived contemplative practice and religious affiliation, briefly, I formally "converted" to Daoism in 1993, when I was twenty-two years old, although I began training two years earlier; I have been practicing Daoist Quiet Sitting (*jìngzuò* 靜坐; also referred to as "tranquil sitting") since that time; I am an ordained Daoist priest (*dàoshì*

---

[11] Of course, some religious adherents (e.g., Christians, Jews, Muslims, and increasingly Buddhists, Jains, and Sikhs) get a pass on the "adherence question." From my perspective, this is because, unlike Daoism, these traditions, at least conventionally (re)presented and engaged, are more doctrinal and philosophical. It also is because few scholars of Daoism are trained in or located in Religious Studies. Again, recall the Orientalist fiction, fabrication, and fantasy of so-called "philosophical Daoism."

道士; ord. 2006) in the Huàshān 華山 (Mount Hua) lineage (26th-generation) of Quánzhēn 全眞 (Complete Perfection) Daoism; and I am the founding Co-director and senior teacher of the Daoist Foundation 道教基金會 (est. 2007), through which I have taught Daoist meditation practice in various contexts and venues.[12] While here I will briefly discuss Daoist Quiet Sitting, I should mention that I engage in and teach holistic and integrated Daoist training, or "full-spectrum Daoist practice" if you prefer. "Quiet Sitting" is the primary contemporary name for Daoist apophatic and quietistic meditation, although it is sometimes referred to as "guarding the One" and "sitting-in-forgetfulness" (see above). It is a form of what I refer to as religiously-committed, tradition-based, and theologically-infused contemplative practice. That is, it is a *Daoist* practice, recalling the integral relationship between view/practice/experience/goal. As such, it is orientated toward the Dao as sacred, with the ultimate (non)goal of realizing the Dao, and, as such, from a tradition-based Daoist perspective there is no form of Daoist practice that is not theologically-infused.

As I have been trained and as I teach, Quiet Sitting primarily relies on oral commentary on the above-cited "heart-fasting" passage in chapter four of the *Zhuāngzǐ*. Emphasis is placed on "listening to/with qi" (*tīngqì* 聽氣). However, it also utilizes the (later) Daoist view of the navel region (Qìhǎi 氣海 [Ocean of Energy]) as the lower "elixir field" (*dāntián* 丹田), the primary storehouse of qi in the body. This means that the primary layer of the practice is quietistic, while the secondary layer is alchemical (see Komjathy, 2013; Komjathy & Townsend, 2022). The practice is, in turn, located in a larger quietistic approach and path, which is rooted in the previously discussed Daoist principle of *wúwéi*. In terms of practical specifics, one simply allows thoughts and emotions to dissipate naturally. One simply sits in stillness. Again, from a Daoist perspective, this involves the view of innate nature as stillness, which is the Dao-as-Stillness. As one's practice deepens, one moves from "minor

---

[12] While sociologically and perhaps phenomenologically speaking I am technically a "Euro-American Daoist convert," I do not view myself in this manner. In addition to a variety of relevant experiences (e.g., meditative absorption, mystical union, recollection), my (perhaps pre-conversion) Daoist identity has been confirmed by various senior Daoists. My primary Daoist name is Xiūjìng 修靜 (Cultivating Stillness), while my Huàshān lineage name is Wànruì 萬瑞 (Myriad Blessings).

stillness" to "major stillness." The latter corresponds to "absorption" (*dìng* 定), with the character also translated as "concentration" and "stability." Interestingly, this character was used to translate the Indian and Buddhist *samādhi* (cf. *jhāna/dhyāna*).

Ultimately, the boundaries of ordinary identity dissolve; consciousness expands; and one disappears into the Dao in a (non)state of mystical union. In my own experience, there is much overlap with the abovementioned "Daoist contemplative cartographies," including Gourd Master's "layers of the Abyss." That is, there are a variety of forms of emptiness (see Komjathy, 2024b). One issue that comes up in lived/living Daoist practice, which may be pertinent for the present volume, is the question of dissociation. While a potential danger and legitimate concern, Daoist Quiet Sitting reveals ordinary personhood as a construct and an illusion. Although sometimes potentially helpful for daily existence, from a Daoist perspective, it is an obstacle to perceiving and experiencing one's innate nature, which is impersonal and transpersonal. This is one's original and inherent connection with the Dao as sacred. It reveals a context of energetic embeddedness and interrelationality, which is the nature of reality from a Daoist perspective. A tradition-based Daoist might even subvert this quasi-telos by noting that one already is the Dao. In the words of the anonymous eighth-century CE *Qīngjìng jīng* 清靜經 (Scripture on Clarity and Stillness; DZ 620; ZH 250), "Although we call this 'attaining the Dao' (*dédào* 得道),/In truth there is nothing to attain."

In terms of the relevance and applicability of this old/new paradigm of Daoist contemplative psychology to alternative psychological approaches, it offers a radically different vision of human potential and spiritual realization. This is the possibility of overcoming habituation and disorientation, of returning to original being and sacred connection. Daoist Quiet Sitting involves a process of deconditioning, of overcoming inherited and habitual stories of who we are and who we might be. It is a "wellness narrative," beyond conventional "illness narratives," found in the Diagnostic and Statistical Manual and International Classification of Disease. However, it also is beyond "wellness," and thus beyond the totalizing purview of the so-called "wellness industry."

As such, it represents a counterculture, underground, and even resistance movement to capitalist, including spiritual capitalist, appropriation, banalization, commodification, and domestication. It challenges current constructions of "meditation as medicine" and "meditation as therapy." Daoist practice-realization is fundamentally atherapeutic and perhaps even untherapeutic. It offers a vision of and method for realizing something beyond ourselves narrowly perceived. In reconnecting with the Dao, one may discover a well-being that is completely untouched by the drive to consume goods and make oneself a fitter, happier, more productive and obedient wage-slave. The Daoist contemplative approach is anti-self-help in that when we discover our innate (trans)wellness, neoliberal self-improvement projects may (will?) finally come to an end.

For those of us committed to, involved in, and advocating for radical psycho-ontological alternatives and new socio-political models,[13] Daoist Quietism represents a perhaps unfamiliar source for inspirational and visionary possibilities. We may investigate, challenge, and transform received structures of constraint and bondage, whether cognitive or physical. The primary Daoist response centers on personal cultivation and grassroots community in potential solidarity with anarchistic and socialistic movements: It suggests that change is possible based on our own commitments and that we may form affinity groups and intentional communities with other like-minded individuals. The "contemplative approach and mode" involves inquiry, observation, discernment, and insight. We "perceive beyond." This relates to our deeper aspirations, dreams, and longings, perhaps beyond the previously known and dreamt. For this, Daoist Quietism encourages us to awake up in the true sense: "Someday there will be a great awakening, when we realize all of this is a great dream" (ZZ 2). As outlined above, classical Daoism in turn provides a contemplative methodology:

> Appear plain and embrace simplicity;
> Lessen selfishness and decrease desires.

---

[13] While my primary identity centers on Daoist adherence and affiliation, I am anarchist on politics (grassroots self-determination); Marxist on economics (worker control of the means and products of labor); Rilkean on human nature (possibility/actualization, including the importance of beauty and poetry); and Weberian on academia (kleptocracy [perhaps kakistocracy] and technocracy masquerading as meritocracy).

(LZ 19)

By embracing voluntary simplicity, by living through what is essential, through "enough" (zú 足), we lay bare the ground of our being and lives, and we discover authentic meaning and purpose. We come to appreciate the "taste of blandness," perhaps analogous to mountain spring water in a summer afternoon. We also (re)gain the energetic and spiritual vitality, including resiliency and discernment, to understand what a given relationship or situation requires for transformation. Then, perhaps, we may become fully human in a Daoist sense as biological, cosmological, and geographical beings. Body, community, place. In awe and wonder. And we further understand and ideally work to enact contexts wherein all beings, both human and "non-human," may be free to flourish on their own terms. Such is one "great dream" that emerges from one "great awakening."

Then, perhaps inspired by this Daoist contemplative vision, we may face the Abyss, which reveals an expansive field beyond the known and knowing. This is freedom beyond conformity, complicity, and fear-based modes. It reveals a context of embodied being, energetic participation, and relational embeddedness. It opens portals into fuller aliveness, connection, and subtlety. This is reality as a revelatory mystery even more mysterious than mysteriousness.

References

Andresen, J., & Forman, R. C. (Eds.). (2000). *Cognitive models and spiritual maps*. Imprint Academic.

Bourdieu, P. (1977). *Outline of a theory of practice* (R. Nice, Trans.). Cambridge University Press.

Bourdieu, P. (1988). *Homo academicus* (P. Collier, Trans.). Stanford University Press.

Cardeña, E., Lynn, S. J., & Krippner, S. (Eds.). (2000). *Varieties of anomalous experience: Examining the scientific evidence*. American Psychological Association.

de Wit, H. (1991). *Contemplative psychology* (M. L. Baird, Trans.). Duquesne University Press.

Deikman, A. J. (1982). *The observing self: Mysticism and psychotherapy*. Beacon Press.
Ferrer, J., & Sherman, J. (Eds.). (2008). *The participatory turn: Spirituality, mysticism, religious studies*. State University of New York Press.
Fischer, R. (1980). A cartography of the ecstatic and meditative states. In R. Woods (Ed.), *Understanding mysticism* (pp. 286–305). Image Books.
Forman, R. C. (Ed.). (1990). *The problem of pure consciousness*. Oxford University Press.
Foucault, M. (1999). *The history of sexuality* (R. Hurley, Trans., Vol. 3). Vintage.
Giroux, H. (2015). *Dangerous thinking in the age of the new authoritarianism*. Routledge.
Goldman, M. (2012). *The American soul rush: Esalen and the rise of spiritual privilege*. New York University Press.
Hadot, P. (1995). *Philosophy as a way of life: Spiritual exercises from Socrates to Foucault*. Blackwell.
Heelas, P. (1996). *The New Age movement: The celebration of the self and the sacralization of modernity*. Blackwell Publishers.
Imber, J. (Ed.). (2004). *Therapeutic culture: Triumph and defeat*. Routledge.
Kleinman, A. (1988). *The illness narratives: Suffering, healing, and the human condition*. Basic Books.
Kohn, L. (1987). *Seven steps to the Tao: Sima Chengzhen's Zuowanglun*. Monumenta Serica.
Kohn, L. (1989). Guarding the One: Concentrative meditation in Taoism. In L. Kohn (Ed.), *Taoist meditation and longevity techniques* (pp. 125–158). Center for Chinese Studies, University of Michigan.
Kohn, L. (2010). *Sitting in oblivion: The heart of Daoist meditation*. Three Pines Press.
Kohn, L., & LaFargue, M. (Eds.). (1998). *Lao-tzu and the Tao-te-ching*. State University of New York Press.
Komjathy, L. (2007). *Cultivating perfection: Mysticism and self-transformation in early Quanzhen Daoism*. Brill.
Komjathy, L. (2011). Field notes from a Daoist professor. In J. Simmer-Brown & F. Grace (Eds.), *Meditation and the classroom: Contemplative pedagogy in religious studies* (pp. 95–103). State University of New York Press.
Komjathy, L. (2013). *The Daoist tradition: An introduction*. Bloomsbury Academic.
Komjathy, L. (Ed.). (2015). *Contemplative literature: A comparative sourcebook on meditation and contemplative prayer*. State University of New York Press.

Komjathy, L. (2016). Möbius religion: The insider/outsider question. In J. Kripal (Ed.), *Religion: A next-generation handbook for its robust study* (pp. 305–323). Palgrave Macmillan.
Komjathy, L. (2017). *Taming the wild horse: An annotated translation and study of the Daoist horse taming pictures.* Columbia University Press.
Komjathy, L. (2018). *Introducing contemplative studies.* Wiley-Blackwell.
Komjathy, L. (2020a). Contemplative studies: A new vision. Alternate Homepage of Dr. Louis Komjathy. Retrieved March 1, 2024, from www.louiskomjathy.com/kontemplacja.
Komjathy, L. (2020b). Daoist body-maps and meditative praxis. In G. Pati & K. Zubko (Eds.), *Transformational embodiment in Asian religions: Subtle bodies, spatial bodies* (pp. 36–64). Routledge.
Komjathy, L. (2020c). Daoist meditation. In S. Newcombe & K. O'Brien-Kop (Eds.), *Routledge handbook of yoga and meditation studies* (pp. 189–211). Routledge.
Komjathy, L. (2021). Daoist meditation: From 100 CE to the present. In M. Farias, D. Brazier, & M. Lalljee (Eds.), *The Oxford handbook of meditation* (pp. 310–331). Oxford University Press.
Komjathy, L. (2022). *Primer for translating Daoist literature.* Purple Cloud Press.
Komjathy, L. (2023a). *Dàodé jīng* 道德經: *A contextual, contemplative, and annotated bilingual translation.* Square Inch Press.
Komjathy, L. (2023b). Further explorations of/in Daoist embodiment. In Y. Greenberg & G. Pati (Eds.), *Routledge handbook of religion and the body* (pp. 377–394). Routledge.
Komjathy, L. (2023c). *Handbooks for Daoist practice* (Twentieth Anniversary Edition. Vol. 3). Square Inch Press.
Komjathy, L. (2023d). On being mindful: The promise and perils of the 'mindfulness movement'. Alternate Homepage of Dr. Louis Komjathy. Retrieved March 1, 2024, from www.louiskomjathy.com/kontemplacja
Komjathy, L. (2023e). Praxis. In N. Lowen & A. Rostalska (Eds.), *Diversifying philosophy of religion: Critiques, methods and case studies* (pp. 194–204). Bloomsbury Academic.
Komjathy, L. (2024a). The impact of contemplative studies on research paradigms. In B. Flanagan & K. Clough (Eds.), *Routledge handbook of research methods in spirituality and contemplative studies* (pp. 361–371). Routledge.
Komjathy, L. (2024b). *Dàodé jīng: A Daoist contemplative translation.* Square Inch Press.

Komjathy, L. (2024c). *Traces of a Daoist immortal: Chén Tuán 陳搏 of the Western Marchmount*. Brill.

Komjathy, L., & Townsend, K. (2022). *Entering stillness: A guide to Daoist practice*. Square Inch Press.

Kripal, J. (2010). *Authors of the impossible: The paranormal and the sacred*. University of Chicago Press.

LaFargue, M. (1992). *The Tao of the Tao Te Ching*. State University of New York Press.

Laing, R. D. (1967). *The politics of experience*. Pantheon Books.

Lakoff, G., & Johnson, M. (1980). *Metaphors we live by*. University of Chicago Press.

Martin, L., Gutman, H., & Hutton, P. (Eds.). (1988). *Techniques of the self: A seminar with Michel Foucault*. University of Massachusetts Press.

Maslow, A. (1999/1968). *Toward a psychology of being*. Wiley.

Mauss, M. (2006). *Techniques, technology and civilization* (N. Schlange, Ed.). Berghahn Books/Durkheim Press.

Murphy, M. (1992). *The future of the body: Explorations into the further Evolution of human nature*. Penguin Putnam.

Potter, P. (2019). *Banksy: You are an acceptable level of threat and if you were not you would know about it*. Carpet Bombing Culture.

Purser, R. (2019). *McMindfulness: How mindfulness became the new capitalist spirituality*. Repeater Books.

Rieff, P. (1966). *The triumph of the therapeutic: Uses of faith after Freud*. Harper and Row.

Roth, H. (1999). *Original Tao: Inward training (Nei-yeh) and the foundations of Taoist mysticism*. Columbia University Press.

Roth, H. (2015). Daoist apophatic meditation: Selections from the classical Daoist textual corpus. In L. Komjathy (Ed.), *Contemplative literature* (pp. 89–143). State University of New York Press.

Roth, H. (2021). *The contemplative foundations of classical Daoism*. State University of New York Press.

Sells, M. (1994). *Mystical languages of unsaying*. University of Chicago Press.

Sontag, S. (1978). *Illness as metaphor*. Farrar, Straus & Giroux.

Vitz, P. (1994/1977). *Psychology as religion: The cult of self-worship* (2nd edn). Wm. B. Eerdmans.

Wallace, B. A. (2000). *The taboo of subjectivity: Toward a new science of consciousness*. Oxford University Press.

Wilber, K., Engler, J., & Brown, D. (Eds.). (1986). *Transformations of consciousness: Conventional and contemplative perspectives on development*. Shambhala.

Wilber, K., Patten, T., Leonard, A., & Morelli, M. (2008). *Integral life practice: A 21st-century blueprint for physical health, emotional balance, mental clarity, and spiritual awakening*. Integral Books.

Wilderson, F. (2020). *Afropessimism*. Liveright.

Young, D., & Goulet, J. (Eds.). (1994). *Being changed by cross-cultural encounters: The anthropology of extraordinary experience*. University of Toronto Press.

Part VI

Concluding Thoughts

16

To Arms! Psychotherapy as Class Warfare

Jon Hook

> "The weapons with which the bourgeoisie felled feudalism to the ground are now turned against the bourgeoisie itself."
> —(Karl Marx and Friedrich Engels, *The Communist Manifesto* (1848))

Psychotherapy as Religion

Mainstream psychotherapy holds significant and growing influence over workers in industrialized society. Sociologists have documented the increasing use of psychological terms in everyday life over the past 50 years (Cohen, 2016, p. 76). The psychologization of everyday life spreads quickly through social media. One can scroll through TikTok, YouTube, Instagram, Reddit, and numerous other platforms and see for themselves

J. Hook (✉)
Counter-Psych, Chicago, IL, USA

just how easily once obscure terms reserved for the psychiatrist's office spill easily from the lips of young people everywhere. The problems of modern life are increasingly understood to be the result of a disordered mind not our disordered society.

As a system of ideological reproduction psychotherapy is clearly hard to beat. The only cultural power that comes close is religion and even here there is a tendency for religious and spiritual authorities to defer to psychiatrists and therapists when a person's problem lies outside the bounds of spiritual or reflective healing. Note how the Catholic Church trains its exorcists to distinguish between the actual presence of demons and the delusion of presence (Bauer, 2022) or the tendency of spiritual self-help books to disclaim that the reader should seek professional help if they believe themselves to be truly mentally ill (Hanson, 2009, p. 13). In moments of the most acute distress, like when a person panics on a meditation retreat, it is called a psychotic break and the sufferer is sent not a monk or nun, but to a psychiatric facility (Chatterjee, 2024).

The closer one looks, the more the lines between therapy and religion blur. Here and throughout this chapter, I use the term "religion" as a heuristic for a practice-worldview that addresses human suffering. Religion is a notoriously broad and fraught term, one that resists easy definition and evokes a web of connotations. As a worldview, religion can be superstitious or scientific and both at the same time. As a practice, religion can be oppressive and liberatory and both at the same time. In spite of—and indeed because of—its vagueness, the heuristic of religion is useful for understanding the structure and function of psychotherapy especially its tendency to oppress and its potential to liberate. The comparison of psychotherapy to a religion is not just metaphorically useful, but historically valid.

In her book "In Therapy We Trust" (2001) historian Eva Moskowitz traces the origin of modern American psychotherapy back to the theistic spiritual self-help movement ignited by Phineus Quimby (1802–1866). Quimby claimed that God has given us the tools to be happy and that all diseases, mental and physical, could be cured by what we now call counseling (Moskowitz, 2001, pp. 15–16). Predating Cognitive Behavioral Therapy by a century, his method was to sit with the patient showing them compassion and rooting out their mistaken beliefs about themselves which have prevented their emotional development (Moskowitz, 2001, p. 16). Although widely derided by skeptics in his day, Quimby was reported to have cured numerous diseases in thousands of patients with his Mind Cure (Moskowitz, 2001, p. 11) and his views eventually entered the mainstream where they were reborn as the New Thought Movement (Moskowitz, 2001, p. 18). William James himself reported benefiting from mind cure healing (Duclow, 2002) and when the talking cures of the gilded age were incorporated into psychology formally, they jettisoned God, but retained their spiritualist roots (Moskowitz, 2001, p. 29). Today this trend continues.

Thirty years ago, Buddhist meditation was considered a purely religious practice, while today it is ubiquitous in psychotherapeutic circles (Moloney, 2016). Prior to the mindfulness revolution, cognitive behavioral therapy was developed from a whole smattering of religious and philosophical concepts drawn from sources as various as Daoism and Stoicism (Diaz & Murguia, 2015). The view that psychotherapy is closer to a religious ritual than a medical intervention is not only a matter of historical interest, but a scientific description of the way it works.

Psychotherapy As Science

Clinical psychology has traditionally viewed mental illness and its treatment through the lens of twentieth century medical disease models in which mental diseases are matched to appropriate medical interventions (Wampold & Imel, 2015). While at face value the taxonomy of mental illnesses and development of viable treatments would appear to be a useful starting point, this approach has faced strong criticisms for its lack of scientific depth (Hofmann & Hayes, 2019) and limited impact on real world treatment efficacy (Neimeyer et al., 2009). Although a full review of the evidence is beyond this chapter's scope, three key points should be understood by all contemporary therapists. First, specific therapeutic interventions have far less impact on client outcomes than overall skill of a therapist, which predicts three to eight times more variance in outcome than the specific techniques used (Baldwin & Imel, 2013; Barkham et al., 2017). In other words, it is not so much what the therapist does, but how well they do it that most impacts their outcomes. Second, despite the explosive increase in therapeutic techniques, scientific studies, and therapy schools over the past 30 years, average psychotherapy outcomes have not increased (Miller et al., 2013). Finally, therapists with more knowledge, training, and education in psychotherapy do not achieve better outcomes on average than those with less (Goldberg et al., 2016).

If psychotherapy were merely about delivering X treatment to Y disorder, then one would expect that specific treatments would drive outcomes, the accumulation of techniques would have improved therapy over time, and therapists with more knowledge of these interventions would have better outcomes. Yet, despite being almost nothing like a medical science, such as cardiology, psychotherapy in fact achieves outcomes comparable to cardiac interventions (Lipsey & Wilson, 1993). In other words, therapy generally works at improving people's well-being at least up to a point (Duncan et al., 2010).

As against the medical illness model, the Contextual Model of psychotherapy provides a far more reasonable and empirically supported view of how psychotherapy works by identifying three pathways to psychotherapeutic healing: the client-therapist relationship, client expectations, and finally the specific interventions used (Wampold, 2013). From this perspective, it is a caring relationship with a charismatic healer that is responsible for the outcomes that psychotherapists obtain (Bacon, 2018). Regarding the role of specific ingredients in therapy, contemporary behavioral scientists convincingly argue that psychotherapy and related healing practices are effective not because a specific cure is delivered to a specific ailment, but because the client-therapist dyad activates overarching healing behavioral processes innate to human repertoires (Hofmann & Hayes, 2019). The most convincing evidence of this comes from the fact that the hundreds of unique psychotherapy schools all achieve similar outcomes (Wampold et al., 2017). Returning to religion as a comparison, a pastor may speak of God's providence and love while a therapist provides psychoeducation on neuroplasticity, but both inspire hope in the human being. Both the parishioner and the client leave their respective temples feeling somehow renewed.

The critical question, then, is not whether psychotherapy makes people feel better, but how it does. It is the fact that one stoops to enter church doors that concerns the critic of religion, not the sweet-smelling incense they find inside. No serious psychologist denies that churches, ashrams, and temples have certain norms, beliefs, aesthetics, and ideological commitments, but how many see psychotherapy this way? Rather than being seen as another cosmos of values, norms, postulates, practices, and aesthetics, psychotherapy is often viewed as a sterile natural science like geology (Hamilton, 2013). So unquestioned and widespread is the status of psychology as a fundamental common sense that it has become the "monotheistic ontology of late modernity" (Madsen, 2018, p. 16). In our age, psychotherapy is religion disguised as medicine. Given its proliferation and diversity of thought, perhaps it is fairer to say that psychotherapy is not a religion in disguise, but many religions in one disguise. Like American Protestantism, psychotherapy is a big tent movement that plays an eerily similar role in society to religions of the past.

Psychotherapy As Ideology

Consider the following thought experiment:

> You are a practicing psychotherapist, and you hear a knock at your door. You open it to be greeted not by your typical client, but by a medieval peasant woman named Elinor. She is from the year 1388 and lives in a small village in England. Elinor reports that she has come to you to be rid of what she calls "melancholia" and "the vapors". You gather that in contemporary terms, she means that she experiences depressive moods and panic attacks. What's more she has excruciating headaches, fearful dreams, and an overall sense of malaise. Elinor loves her family and her village, but feels something is deeply wrong with her.

What might we tell Elinor? Given what you know about her, what is her presenting concern, the cause of her distress, her diagnosis, and the recommended treatment? Surely it is not to rid her of a demon, as her priest suggests. Nor is it to let her blood, demand she abstain from sex, or eat spicier foods as physicians using medieval medicine might have suggested (Siraisi, 2009). We know these treatments simply won't do, because unlike her contemporaries we know that Elinor is not suffering from being possessed by demons or from an imbalance in her humors. Unlike her priest and unlike her physician, we know that Elinor is suffering from being a medieval peasant.

Any therapist with Google can determine that in 1388 English Peasants were quite unhappy. They had recently suffered from an outbreak of the Black Death which devastated their families and their King, Richard II, was exacting extreme taxes on Elinor's people to pay for a war with France (Ormrod, 1990). In about two years from Elinor's time, peasants will revolt leading to much bloodshed and a failed revolution. No doubt Elinor's diet, daily routine, and habits of mind contribute to her melancholia and vapors, but they are not the sole or primary cause. We may not have ready answers for Elinor at session zero, but is there any doubt that we would see her oppression as the cause of her illness? Would it be so reckless to ask Elinor to imagine a better world in which she is not the slave of her landlord, but an equal? Elinor herself may even balk at the suggestion, such is the extent of her indoctrination at the hands of her church, but with enough love and support she may come to a broader view. We may not demand she revolt, but we would effortlessly weave the values of our post-feudal society into our conversations with her. In fact, we would do so by total accident. Perhaps we may even decide to bite our tongue about social justice and help her deal with the day or the week ahead, but we would never do so while insinuating that she existed in a God-given natural order.

Now imagine Elinor is not a peasant, but a retail worker and imagine that the year is not 1388, but 2024. There is no plague, but there was a pandemic that never ended. She is not owned by her landlord, but rented by her boss for all the best hours of the day and he takes the lion share of her wages for his profit all the same. Elinor is not taught to believe in humor imbalances, but chemical ones despite the scant evidence for either (Lacasse & Leo, 2015). She blames not her soul, but her brain for her distress and asks you to purify it. What would we tell this version of Elinor? The modern clinician is not so different from the medieval soothsayer. Where one searches entrails for a sign and portents, the other searches childhoods for lost memories of trauma. Where a good friend may question your treatment at work, a good clinician will question your irrational beliefs. Just as few priests would dare question medieval Elinor's existence as a peasant, few therapists now dare question modern Elinor's role as a wage slave.

Under capitalism, discussion of someone's working conditions, the very basis of their survival, is acceptable only if it can be construed as a sign of their mental dysfunction rather than the cause of their dysfunction and never in terms of freedom or oppression. According to James Davies, references to work-related dysfunctionality have proliferated as a criterion for mental illnesses across editions of the Diagnostic and Statistical Manual of Mental Disorders (DSM) (Davies, 2017; Cohen, 2022). The message of the DSM and the industry that relies on it is clear: people are healthy in as much as they are willing and able to perform the work that the capitalists offer them. In the medieval era, a priest could repeat Christ's invocation that the meek shall inherit the earth all he liked, so long as it was clear that Jesus didn't mean this literally. In our time, capitalist therapists are free to mend the client in any way they like and even commit themselves to talk of social justice so long as they do not contradict the values of the ruling class; so long as they repair the worker so that they go back to work.

Such false freedom echoes the other false freedoms of capitalist society. We have a free market, but here freedom means freedom for the owner and wage slavery for the worker. You may vote for anyone you like in elections, so long as it is for one of two preselected imperialist stooges. If we, the working people, fail to produce a good leader, fail to survive on low wages, and develop severe psychological distress as a result, we may at least rest assured that this was because we were free to do so. When capitalism bursts at the seams, spilling over with contradictions, the capitalist therapist sews these seams closed. But mainstream psychotherapy is not merely a needle and thread. As part of the complex machinery of capitalism, it is a cudgel for the ruling class to beat down the working class (Lenin & Chretien, 1917/2015). Of course, like their medieval counterparts, mainstream therapists may do many things other than merely distract and repress. Therapists may compassionately address a whole host of issues, some of which are biological, developmental, and universal to the human species, but let us not mince words or make obscurations. A cudgel with a smiley face is a cudgel, nonetheless. If psychotherapy exists as the repressive religion of capitalism, then we must do more than simply practice it more effectively. We must call into question the conditions that give rise to the need for psychotherapy and turn the cudgel around.

To Cull the Living Flower

In the Introduction to his "Critique of Hegel's Philosophy of Right," Marx (1843) briskly cuts through the metaphysical illusions that religion provides, but not in an unsympathetic light. His voice on the matter is best expressed verbatim.

> Religion is the sigh of the oppressed creature, the heart of a heartless world, and the soul of soulless conditions. It is the opium of the people. The abolition of religion as the illusory happiness of the people is the demand for their real happiness. To call on them to give up their illusions about their condition is to call on them to give up a condition that requires illusions…Criticism has plucked the imaginary flowers on the chain not in order that man shall continue to bear that chain without fantasy or consolation, but so that he shall throw off the chain and pluck the living flower. (Marx, 1843, para. 4)

As the "monotheistic ontology of late modernity" psychotherapy has replaced religion as the contemporary flower of the chain of capitalist suffering (Madsen, 2018, p. 16). Yes, at its worst it has been used to deliberately confuse and abuse, but this is an obvious (and notably boring) point to make. We, like Marx, should be concerned about what psychotherapy does even at its best. At best, the institution of psychotherapy is a revolving door that creates its clientele by ignoring the system that causes preventable psychological suffering in the first place. At the same time, we must also recognize that psychotherapy is not just an illusion, but an inevitable one in a world requiring illusions.

In his critique of religion Marx continues,

Thus, the criticism of Heaven turns into the criticism of Earth, the *criticism of religion* into the *criticism of law*, and the *criticism of theology* into the *criticism of politics*. (Marx, 1843, italics in the original, para. 7)

Marx argues that religion is not to blame for dividing people or providing false hope and illusory consolation. Rather, it is society which makes religious illusion necessary that is to blame. Like Marx, we must turn the criticism of psychotherapy into the criticism of politics. Capitalist society is the problem we must solve, not religion and not psychotherapy. This is precisely why folding one's arms and walking away simply won't do. If psychotherapy were merely abolished, as some one-sided critics suggest it should be, something new and ever more beguiling would take its place. It is not for want of pain that people smoke opium, after all. Perhaps the call to abolition would be more convincing if there were any real efforts to make it so rather than to merely study the issue academically. It is with similar reason that Marx and Engels famously compared philosophy to masturbation saying,

One has to 'leave philosophy aside,' one has to leap out of it and devote oneself like an ordinary man to the study of actuality…Philosophy and the study of the actual world have the same relation to one another as masturbation and sexual love. (Marx & Engels, 1846/1976, p. 236)

Whatever it is we do about psychotherapy, we must descend from the ivory tower and actually do it. We must labor for actual people in actual clinics in the actual world. With a widespread contingent of young and early career therapists growing suspicious of the status quo, it is time for critics of our profession put away childish things and get to work.

Consider again the case of peasant Elinor. What would happen if in her time a committed segment of clergy and physicians concluded that feudalism was the problem she faced? What if they incorporated this view into their practice and saw no difference between love and justice? As it happens, many clergy and physicians did come to such a conclusion and, alongside peasants, rejected the status quo entirely. What resulted was not the end of medicine nor the end of spirituality, but the end of feudalism.

We moderns must take the same stand our ancestors did and make one step further out of the darkness of history.

Turning Therapy On Its Head

Under capitalism, psychological suffering is pathologized as a personal failing or disorder, diverting attention away from the systemic issues that contribute to such distress and that prevent the sufferer from creatively addressing it. A Marxist socialist view, in contrast, reframes psychological suffering under capitalism as a causal response to material conditions and the limited power one has to address them.

From a Marxist perspective, while capitalism represented a significant advance over feudalism in terms of generating and distributing resources, it has also produced new and unexpected forms of psychological alienation (Marx, 1844, p. 30). Under capitalism, workers are alienated from the products of their labor and the creative process of laboring itself. By being forced to maximize their labor time irrespective of how much sense it makes, they are further alienated from their own human potential and the potential of our human species. By transforming labor from a process into a commodity, capitalism disconnects people from the creative, purposeful activity that Marx saw as fundamental to human nature (Eagleton, 2017). This alienation strips individuals of their sense of purpose and autonomy, reducing them to mere cogs in the machine of capital. This psychological toll of capitalism is a double poison that not only exploits workers but also disconnects them from their potential for addressing their suffering in creative or meaningful ways. This is why the radical must turn therapy on its head by addressing the society within the individual, not just the individual within society, until a new symbiosis is achieved.

In eliminating the private ownership of the economy and placing the economy in the hands of the people, socialism brings alienation to an end (Marx, 1844, pp. 34–35). Instead of being treated as mere commodities, people would be valued for their individual contributions and creativity and work would become a source of fulfillment for all. People would reconnect with their work, their communities, and their own potential, restoring the sense of meaning that capitalism stripped away. Work life would begin to attain to something closer to what Joseph Campbell called Bliss (2004). Through the collective ownership of resources, individuals would no longer compete for survival but instead work cooperatively for the mutual benefit of all. Whether capitalism is the root cause of all oppressions from racism and sexism to transphobia and patriarchy, it is clearly the system that keeps them "in business" (Eagleton, 2012, p. 166). The end of oppression and opening of a new world of possibility is what is meant by liberation in the Marxist tradition. Compared to the toothless gestures and symbolic reforms of liberal politics, socialism carries the bite to cut the structural roots of oppression at once.

The promise of socialism is not a utopia free of suffering, however. There is no question that psychological pain will continue in a world without capitalist exploitation because joy and sorrow are two sides of the same coin. As Terry Eagleton remarks, under socialism there will still be "lethal jealousies, overweening ambitions, tasteless trousers, and inconsolable grief" (Eagleton, 2012, p. 101). Quite to the contrary, socialism is the promise of new and better problems. Freed from the need to labor meaninglessly, human beings under socialism will be able to address the ever so subtle, ever so grand troubles of the human condition.

Prior to capitalism in medieval Elinor's time, the "mad priest of Kent" John Ball was executed for suggesting that in the Garden of Eden there were no ruling monarchs (Chisholm, 1911, p. 263). Like so many revolutionaries of history, John Ball turned the propaganda tool of the ruling class against the ruling class famously asking, "When Adam delved and Eve span, Who was then the gentleman?" (Dobson, 1970, pp. 373–375). Like fourteenth century Catholicism, twenty-first century psychotherapy is a stockpile of weapons that we must dismantle, reinvent, and reappropriate for the realization of socialism.

The Weapons of Liberation

At its core, this book is aimed at answering a question that has followed me for years: "What, specifically, is radical therapy?". This is an extraordinarily difficult question for two reasons. First, psychotherapy is a relatively limited practice. Yes, therapy addresses society's psychospiritual shortcomings and hence is ripe for making change, but it cannot do everything. One might be as reasonable to ask by what means plumbers may bring about anarchism. Of course, not everything is as abstruse as it seems. If the plumbers of the world unite and stop fixing everyone's toilets, humanity will find the motivation for establishing a whole new society as fast as it can. Second, only after socialism has finally and totally replaced capitalism will we really know what methods work to bring it about. At present we only know what works to bring about socialism under certain circumstances. In this respect, at least we are not in the infancy of the movement. In fact, it may be that socialism struggles most because it is adolescent. For all the glory of its rebelliousness, it is tempestuous, arrogant, and after all these years it is still living on its parents' dime. On the specific methods which would bring about the end of capitalism, Marx said,

> Communism is for us not a state of affairs which is to be established, an ideal to which reality [will] have to adjust itself. We call communism the real movement which abolishes the present state of things…We do not anticipate the world with our dogmas but instead attempt to discover the new world through the critique of the old one…This is why we do not indulge in writing recipes for the cook-shops of the future. (1846/1976)

For a deterministic materialist like Marx, communism (and its prerequisite, socialism), is not a fixed idea that the world must be beaten into, but a natural evolutionary process that must be discovered for us to participate in its creation. Yes, human agency builds socialism, but the material world itself determines and constrains human agency. We are the world itself. Engineers invent more fuel-efficient vehicles not by praying to pictures of concept cars, but by learning the physics which necessitates their invention and then gradually building them through trial and error. Likewise, the conditions which give rise to socialism are dependent on the context in which we find ourselves. What we now call psychotherapy is a vast and evolving menagerie of concepts, theories, and interventions. What we do today will be as unrecognizable to the therapists of the 2100s as Quimby's Mind Cure is to us and hence we cannot write psychotherapy manuals for the clinics of the future.

While we cannot predict what psychotherapeutic methods will assist in bringing about socialism, we can identify general principles to guide the evolution and maintenance of new methods. Doing so is strategically critical not only because socialism is a moving target, but because resistance to capitalism is so easily captured by reformist movements like woke capitalist rainbow imperialism. As Mark Fisher (2009) points out, "Capitalist realism involves the pre-emptive formatting and shaping of desires, aspirations, and hopes by capitalist culture itself, ensuring that any attempt at resistance is already enfolded within its operations" (p. 13). What follows, then, are four necessary, but not sufficient principles to guide the transformation of mainstream capitalist psychotherapy into a radical practice.

Principle 1: Develop a Radically Contextual Worldview

Stephen Pepper (1942) contrasts mechanistic and contextual worldviews as distinct ways of understanding reality. The mechanistic worldview, which relies on the metaphor of a machine, views the world as composed of divisible parts that interact with each other in a predictable fashion (Pepper, 1942, pp. 186–231). The mechanistic worldview has been incredibly useful scientifically for fields like classical physics and engineering, but has limitations in fields that study interacting parts of much greater complexity, interactivity, and evolution. In psychotherapy, the machine metaphor mutates under capitalism into understanding of mental health issues as individual dysfunctions, akin to broken machine parts, which can and should be fixed in isolation from broader causal influences.

By contrast, the contextual worldview takes as its root metaphor the "act in its context" (p. 233) and emphasizes the interconnectedness of phenomena within a given situation (Pepper, 1942, pp. 232–279). The application of contextualism to psychotherapy allows one to see human beings not as isolated machine parts, but as active and evolving entities in an unfolding and interacting event. This is precisely what is meant by the word "history" in Marxist thought, not a past occurrence but an ongoing event that manifests here and now. Hayne Reese (1993) identifies Marxism as a fundamentally contextualist worldview because of Marx's emphasis on human activity as the core truth criterion and his belief in the dialectical evolution of the material world.

On a scientific level, contextualism rejects the one-sided distinction between empiricism and social action. Not only does contextualism provide a solid theoretical foundation for mental health and social justice, but it is far more scientific and useful in its application with the complex systems approach to mental health (Borsboom, 2017) and idionomic statistics (Sanford, 2022) as two prominent contemporary examples. Historically, Soviet psychologists were ahead of the curve with their study of human behavior as a complex and emergent social phenomenon (Lethbridge, 1992). Radical therapists must pick up the study of what Boris-Lomov called the "individual-society relations" (1977, as cited in Lethbridge, 1992, p. 45).

Historically, Marxism stands as the oldest and most successful resistance traditions to capitalism. Where Marxism failed, materially or morally, it did so because it stood against impossible odds and gargantuan enemies (Eagleton, 2012, pp. 12–29). Despite all of this, Marxism's successes far outweigh its failures. Beginning with the October Revolution of 1917, socialists relying on Marx and Engel's created a state that founded itself on a worker's democracy (Turovtsev, 1973). Like any country, the USSR had its shortcomings and material limitations, but even so the Soviet state was the first in history to prioritize universal healthcare, free education, women's rights, anti-racism, and guaranteed employment—all of which dramatically improved its citizens' living standards (Keeran & Kenny, 2010, p. 2). Western readers wary of Marxism due to its supposed totalitarian past should note that contemporary liberal scholars increasingly challenge Cold War-era narratives on the USSR (Ryan & Grant, 2020). Much of the mainstream history written over the past 50 years is now seen as wildly exaggerated if not entirely fabricated (Ryan & Grant, 2020, p. 9). The famous Black American singer Paul Robeson summed up the ethos of the USSR during a visit in 1934 saying, "Here, I am not a Negro, but a human being for the first time in my life… I walk in full human dignity." (King, 2011, para. 4). As demonstrated in the book *Red Star Over the Third World*, Marxism has since inspired movements across Asia, Africa, the Caribbean, and Latin America, offering a robust theoretical base and practical strategies for liberation with China being the most prominent and most paradoxical example (Prashad, 2017). Regarding the global north, the development of advanced social democracy in the Nordic and European countries was heavily influenced by the geopolitical pressure exerted by the Soviet Union (Rasmussen & Knutsen, 2022). America's New Deal was strongly influenced by coalition socialists (McGuire, 2019) and was in some ways an effort to fix the economy or risk socialist revolution. Stepping down from its lofty political implications, a radically contextualist worldview carries with it certain ethical assumptions and aspirations or values that suffuse the day-to-day life of the clinician.

Principle 2: Maintain Uncompromising Radical Values

Whether psychotherapy changes the client a little or a lot, these changes are shaped by values rooted in our worldview (Hamilton, 2013). Just as radical priests challenged feudalism, radical therapists today must confront capitalist values embedded within themselves and replace them with liberatory ones. Our values guide our actions, often without us realizing why we do things or to what end. Values are not abstract—they shape our experiences and inform the actions we take and vice versa. Many of us act in ways that make us miserable because we have internalized the values of the rich and powerful. Think of the times in your life when you have felt undue pressure, guilt, or shame in a workplace even when no one imposed this feeling on you. This is internalized capitalism and the primary purpose of ideology. No capitalist needs to force you to do something when you instinctually obey.

Though it's impossible to provide an exhaustive list of radical values, anti-capitalism is central to all of them. Anti-capitalism rejects the unjust arrangement where a small group—the capitalist class—controls the means of production, while the majority must sell their labor to survive. This is not just about rich and poor; it's about the absence of true democracy. From clinics where private practice owners exploit their employees' wages to academic trainers who maintain total control over students' career aspirations, our environments are so capitalistic that is scarcely possible to imagine an alternative. This is why talk of social justice in therapy circles rarely goes beyond the superficial thoughts, feelings, and words contained within interpersonal interactions. The values of liberalism are not and can never be radical, but remain folial; like faded flower arrangements on a grave. This is where alternative spaces and sources of inspiration are critical. Until we spend time in spaces that counter our conditioning, we will not even be aware of what our values are much less will we be able to change them. One surefire way to inculcate oneself with the values of liberation is to consume a steady diet of leftist literature and media and to spend time discussing these with other radicals. When these sources of nourishment are properly digested, they fortify an emancipated psyche and become a natural expression of one's acts and speech. It is not until the foundation of our lives is human that we can become human.

The radical therapist cannot be mealy mouthed or wishy washy on this or any values. Our commitment must be as firm in rejecting wage slavery as others are in condemning past systems like serfdom or slavery. There are no two sides to genocide. Nonetheless, the enactment of these values in therapy must comport with the client's worldview and with what is effective for them at the time. Peasants cannot be asked to walk off their farms if they starve in doing so, nor is it the goal of the radical therapist to preach socialism to people. We must simply acknowledge how we see the world and let clients decide for themselves if we are being reasonable; therapists of any ideology can and should be value-transparent.

One major and immediate advantage of reassessing one's values is that it allows the therapist to access their innate nature and allows therapy to become a creative expression of the self. Therapy may come to resemble something like the brilliance and madness of Jodorowskys' Psychomagic (2010), a method compassionate healing totally unbound by the conventions of White professional managerial culture.

Psychotherapy carries a reputation for being difficult emotional labor and like all work it can become a dour, solemn obligation. No doubt negative emotions play an important role in healing, but we must reject psychotherapy's Victorian obsession with inner turmoil. It should be clear to any thinking person that sitting in a windowless room talking about one's emotional pain is not the only path to healing. Radical psychotherapy must be distinguished by its subversive joys. It must involve no small degree of humor and ease. Embracing the good things in life for their own sake is a particularly Marxist value because it is precisely the need to become efficient and frugal accumulators of capital that prevents us from living life directly,

> The less you eat, drink and buy books; the less you go to the theatre, the dance hall, the public house; the less you think, love, theorise, sing, paint, fence, etc., the more you *save* – the *greater* becomes your treasure which neither moths nor rust will devour – your capital. The less you are, the less you express your own life, the more you *have,* i.e., the greater is your *alienated* life, the greater is the store of your estranged being. (Marx, 1844, italics in the original, para. 7)

By far the best way to enact the values of radicalism is to address the conditions that bring our clients to us in the first place.

Guideline 3: Work in Systems

Working within systems is a natural extension of maintaining a radically contextualist worldview. This is both the most effective and most difficult thing to do. It requires building relationships outside of the clinic and in communities with other like-minded people. Often our allies in other circles will be very different from us and we will need to navigate competing worldviews and interests to help our clients flourish. Any sufficiently radical clinic must be one among many intersecting circles of care. Therapy should be the second or third choice to meet people's needs in other ways, coming after they have secured housing, healthcare, legal aid, community belonging, and so on.

The naive and myopic critic may remark that the individual client is much more malleable than their society, so it is inefficient to criticize, much less address, social systems. But this view misses the point entirely. Therapy is shaped by history, not nature, and was originally designed to prioritize the individual over the group. We must address both the individual within society and the society within the individual. Rather than diminishing individual agency, the radical therapist's role is to increase it by helping remove obstacles to individual and collective growth.

While systems work is critical, it is important to make one thing clear: our goal is not systemic reforms, but the wholesale transcendence of the system. What we need more than focus groups and advocacy networks is an internationalist political movement capable of dismantling capitalist societies, one by one (Lenin, 1935). Still, radical therapists and the people they serve cannot choose between tomorrow and today. The present and the future must enfold each into a single evolving whole expressed in the very life of radical therapists themselves.

Guideline 4: Cultivate Resistance as a Lifeway

Here I offer an admonition rarely heard elsewhere: it is your revolutionary duty to live a full and happy life. In a world driven by fear and promises of future reward or punishment, the most subversive act is to pursue joy and peace in the present. The radical therapist must embody the message of "The Revolution of Everyday Life" echoing Raoul Vaneigem (1967/2012) when he wrote,

> People who talk about revolution and class struggle without referring explicitly to everyday life, without understanding what is subversive about love and what is positive in the refusal of constraints, such people have a corpse in their mouth. (p. 11)

Your regular old daily life is the battleground for our collective liberation. From our hourly habits to the relationships we hold, all of our behaviors have been influences by people no smart nor saner than us. Having been so made, our lives may be remade.

The audience of this book may come from imperialist countries and feel guilty about their happiness. This is rooted in puritanical and neoliberal values (Teo, 2018) that teach us to believe happiness is a finite resource. But this is an illusion—happiness, like joy, grows the more it is experienced and the more it is shared. While we uphold the sanctity of the individual, toxic one-sided individualism must be avoided at all costs. It is not the isolated actions of individuals that will bring about meaningful change, but the collective struggle of the working class to transform the economic base of society (Marx & Engels, 1848). Unsurprisingly, cooperation across racial, ethnic, sexual, and gender lines does not easily come about through shame and guilt, but rather through mutual beneficence and collective joy. We resist the divide and conquer strategies of the capitalists and remain one working class as part of one human species on one living planet (Marx & Engels, 1848).

Ultimately, the commitment to a radical life means seeing through the illusory separation between self and other. The radical therapist must take this journey and follow it to its end whether through intellectual reflection, meditative contemplation, somatic movement, or other means. Through these means the self of the therapist may well dissolve altogether and thereby may come the end of suffering for one and all.

In addressing only the symptoms of capitalism, mainstream psychotherapy offers a way of life out of a cure. You may have your anxiety alleviated or your depression allayed, but only so that you may go on living as you were. What radical psychotherapy must offer instead is a cure out of a way of life. It must, of course, reduce suffering, but what's more essential is that it opens up the possibility of living. And may we offer a thousand paths to that splendid fullness. Let a referral to a radical therapist be not a call to find another coping mechanism, but an invitation to begin a new way of life. Let it function as a freely chosen, freely rejected cosmos of values, relationships, methods, and aesthetics. Above all, let it aspire to have no leaders, only communities of care. Let it prophesy the future by prefiguring it here and now.

The Future of Healing

Expand your imagination and consider the following thought experiment:

> You knock on a therapist's door. When it opens a healer from a distant future greets you. You share your troubles, and they explain that in their time, true economic democracy and genuine freedom have been estab-

lished—there are no races, classes, or houselessness. Every form of personhood permeates society at every level. Yet, even in this future, pain persists, and healers are still needed. Sensing you need more than a promise of future salvation, they have just the right thing to say.

What this future healer says, we can't possibly predict but must discover in ourselves. From Ursula K. Le Guin, the Strugatsky's, and Gene Roddenberry, science fiction abounds with promising futures where our present troubles have been solved by scientific and social technologies. But the optimism of science fiction is not about advanced technology nor the absence of problems. Consider the simple fact that we are already living in the future. We become bored while flying, watch videos beamed from distant planets, and speak to machines which, to the astonishment of all, have begun to speak back. Despite these advances, very few people run around in a constant state of stupefied awe. What is astounding about science fiction, then, is that it presents us with new possibilities of living. In science fiction futures people work not for their bosses, but for themselves with their friends toward the betterment of the whole human, animal, and ecological world. Space travel may indeed be grand, but the trip that science fiction takes us on is one in which our alienation has been dissolved and we are free to become human. It is precisely this future that radical therapy must become a clarion for.

The belief that a better world is possible is not a naive hope that comes from imagining the future, but a certitude that comes from studying the past. We radical therapists are not manufacturing new dreams against the nightmares of history. We are waking up and dreaming with our eyes open. For too long therapists have whispered, "I will break you the way the world is broken." Instead let us cry, "We shall mend together and together mend the world!" We may not transcend capitalism tomorrow, but the seeds we plant today will grow and their roots will crack the machine altogether. As our planet dies, we cannot help but call one another to life. The season of sowing is upon us. The time for radical therapy has come.

References

Bacon, S. (2018). *Practicing psychotherapy in constructed reality: Ritual, charisma, and enhanced client outcomes.* Lexington Books.

Baldwin, S. A., & Imel, Z. E. (2013). Therapist effects: Findings and methods. In M. J. Lambert (Ed.), *Bergin and Garfield's handbook of psychotherapy and behavior change* (6th ed., pp. 258–297). Wiley.

Barkham, M., Lutz, W., Lambert, M. J., & Saxon, D. (2017). Therapist effects, effective therapists, and the law of variability. In L. G. Castonguay & C. E. Hill (Eds.), *How and why are some therapists better than others?: Understanding therapist effects* (pp. 13–36). American Psychological Association. https://doi.org/10.1037/0000034-002

Bauer, N. M. (2022). The devil and the doctor: The (de)medicalization of exorcism in the Roman Catholic Church. *Religions, 13*(2), 87.

Borsboom, D. (2017). A network theory of mental disorders. *World psychiatry, 16*(1), 5–13.

Campbell, J. (2004). *Pathways to bliss: Mythology and personal transformation* (D. Kudler, Ed.). New World Library.

Chatterjee, R. (2024, March 31). Meditation and mental health: Can Vipassana be dangerous? *NPR.*

Chisholm, H. (Ed.). (1911). Ball, John. In *Encyclopædia Britannica* (11th ed., Vol. 3, p. 263). Retrieved from Encyclopædia Britannica database.

Cohen, B. M. Z. (2016). *Psychiatric hegemony: A Marxist theory of mental illness.* Palgrave Macmillan.

Cohen, B. M. Z. (2022). Psychiatric expansion and the rise of workplace mental health initiatives. In M. Harbusch (Ed.), *Troubled persons industries: The expansion of psychiatric categories beyond psychiatry* (pp. 129–145). Palgrave Macmillan.

Davies, J. (2017). Political pills: Psychopharmaceuticals and neoliberalism as mutually supporting. In J. Davies (Ed.), *The sedated society: The causes and harms of our psychiatric drug epidemic* (pp. 189–225). Palgrave Macmillan.

Diaz, K., & Murguia, E. (2015). The philosophical foundations of cognitive behavioral therapy: Stoicism, Buddhism, Taoism, and Existentialism. *Journal of Evidence-Based Psychotherapies, 15*(1), 37–50.

Dobson, R. B. (1970). *The Peasants' Revolt of 1381.* Pitman.

Duclow, D. F. (2002). William James, mind-cure, and the religion of healthy-mindedness. *Journal of Religion and Health, 41,* 45–56.

Duncan, B. L., Miller, S. D., Wampold, B. E., & Hubble, M. A. (2010). *The heart and soul of change: Delivering what works in therapy* (2nd ed.). American Psychological Association.
Eagleton, T. (2012). *Why Marx was right* (Reprint ed.). Yale University Press.
Eagleton, T. (2017). *Materialism*. Yale University Press.
Fisher, M. (2009). *Capitalist realism: Is there no alternative?* Zero Books.
Goldberg, S. B., Rousmaniere, T., Miller, S. D., Whipple, J., Nielsen, S. L., Hoyt, W. T., & Wampold, B. E. (2016). Do psychotherapists improve with time and experience? A longitudinal analysis of outcomes in a clinical setting. *Journal of Counseling Psychology, 63*(1), 1–11.
Hamilton, R. (2013). The frustrations of virtue: The myth of moral neutrality in psychotherapy. *Journal of Evaluation in Clinical Practice, 19*(3), 485–492.
Hanson, R. (2009). *Buddha's brain: The practical neuroscience of happiness, love, and wisdom*. New Harbinger. Publications.
Hofmann, S. G., & Hayes, S. C. (2019). The future of intervention science: Process-based therapy. *Clinical Psychological Science, 7*(1), 37–50.
Jodorowsky, A. (2010). *Psychomagic: The transformative power of shamanic psychotherapy*. Inner Traditions.
Keeran, R., & Kenny, T. (2010). *Socialism betrayed: Behind the collapse of the Soviet Union*. iUniverse.
King, G. (2011, September 13). What Paul Robeson said. *Smithsonian Magazine*. https://www.smithsonianmag.com/history/what-paul-robeson-said-77742433/
Lacasse, J. R., & Leo, J. (2015). Antidepressants and the chemical imbalance theory of depression: A reflection and update on the discourse. *The Behavior Therapist, 38(7)*, 206–212.
Lenin, V. I. (1935). *What is to be done?* Wellred Books.
Lenin, V. I., & Chretien, T. (2015). *State and revolution: Fully annotated edition*. Haymarket Books.
Lethbridge, D. (1992). *Mind in the world: The Marxist psychology of self-actualization*. MEP Publications.
Lipsey, M. W., & Wilson, D. B. (1993). The efficacy of psychological, educational, and behavioral treatment: Confirmation from meta-analysis. *American Psychologist, 48*(12), 1181–1209.
Madsen, O. J. (2018). *The psychologization of society: On the unfolding of the therapeutic in Norway*. Routledge.

Marx, K. (1843). *Introduction to a contribution to the critique of Hegel's philosophy of right*. In Marxists Internet Archive. Retrieved August 20, 2024, from https://www.marxists.org/archive/marx/works/1843/critique-hpr/intro.htm

Marx, K. (1844). *Economic and philosophic manuscripts of 1844* (M. Milligan, Trans.). Progress Publishers. https://www.marxists.org/archive/marx/works/download/pdf/Economic-Philosophic-Manuscripts-1844.pdf

Marx, K., & Engels, F. (1846/1976). *The German ideology*. In *Collected Works* (Vol. 5, p. 236). Lawrence and Wishart.

Marx, K., & Engels, F. (1848). *The communist manifesto*. In *Marx/Engels Internet Archive*. Translated by S. Moore in cooperation with F. Engels. https://www.marxists.org/archive/marx/works/1848/communist-manifesto/

McGuire, J. T. (2019). Social justice feminists and their counter-hegemonic actions in the post-World War II United States, 1945–1964. *Politics & Gender, 15*(4), 971–990.

Miller, S. D., Hubble, M. A., Chow, D. L., & Seidel, J. A. (2013). The outcome of psychotherapy: Yesterday, today, and tomorrow. *Psychotherapy, 50*(1), 88–97.

Moloney, P. (2016). Mindfulness: The bottled water of the therapy industry. In R. E. Purser, D. Forbes, & A. Burke (Eds.), *Handbook of mindfulness* (pp. 269–286). Springer.

Moskowitz, E. S. (2001). *In therapy we trust: America's obsession with self-fulfillment*. John Hopkins University Press.

Neimeyer, G. J., Taylor, J. M., & Wear, D. M. (2009). Continuing education in psychology: Outcomes, evaluations, and mandates. *Professional Psychology: Research and Practice, 40*(6), 617.

Ormrod, W. M. (1990). The Peasants' Revolt and the government of England. *Journal of British Studies, 29*(1), 30–49.

Pepper, S. C. (1942). *World hypotheses*. University of California Press.

Prashad, V. (2017). *Red star over the third world*. Pluto Press.

Rasmussen, M. B., & Knutsen, C. H. (2022). *Reforming to survive: The Bolshevik origins of social policies*. Cambridge University Press.

Reese, H. W. (1993). Contextualism and dialectical materialism. In S. C. Hayes, L. J. Hayes, H. W. Reese, & T. R. Sarbin (Eds.), *Varieties of scientific contextualism* (pp. 71–105). Context Press.

Ryan, J., & Grant, S. (Eds.). (2020). *Revisioning Stalin and Stalinism: Complexities, contradictions, and controversies*. Bloomsbury Academic.

Sanford, B. T. (2022). *An idiomatic network analysis of psychological processes and outcomes* (Doctoral dissertation). University of Nevada, Reno. http://hdl.handle.net/11714/8222

Siraisi, N. G. (2009). *Medieval and early Renaissance medicine: An introduction to knowledge and practice.* University of Chicago Press.

Teo, T. (2018). Homo neoliberalus: From personality to forms of subjectivity. *Theory & Psychology, 28*(5), 581–599.

Turovtsev, V. (1973). *People's control in socialist society.* Progress Publishers.

Vaneigem, R. (2012). *The revolution of everyday life* (D. Nicholson-Smith, Trans.). PM Press.

Wampold, B. E. (2013). *The great psychotherapy debate: Models, methods, and findings.* Routledge.

Wampold, B. E., Flückiger, C., Del Re, A. C., Yulish, N. E., Frost, N. D., Pace, B. T., Goldberg, S. B., Miller, S. D., Baardseth, T. P., & Laska, K. M. (2017). In pursuit of truth: A critical examination of meta-analyses of cognitive behavior therapy. *Psychotherapy Research, 27*(1), 14–32.

Wampold, B. E., & Imel, Z. E. (2015). *The great psychotherapy debate: The evidence for what makes psychotherapy work* (2nd ed.). Routledge.

Index

A

Activism, 123, 129, 233
Agency, 25, 102, 104, 129, 213, 237, 255
Alienation, 27, 100, 107, 119, 123, 136, 139–140, 183, 253, 257
Anti-capitalism, 27, 78, 135, 142
Anti-colonialism, 138–140
Anti-psychiatry, 244
Aphanipoesis, 240
Artaud, A., 269–271
Authoritarianism, 218

B

Bateson, G., 239
Bateson, N., 238–240
Biomedical model, 255, 258

Body, 152, 158, 186–187, 192, 215–216, 218, 223–224, 298
Bourdieu, P., 78
Buddhism, 108, 268–269, 282

C

Capitalism, 22, 25, 27–28, 37–38, 77, 99, 108, 120, 139, 144, 281
Capitalist meditation, 282–283, 297
Class, 18, 77–78, 104, 143
Climate change, 33, 116
Clinical gaze, 38, 41
Co-collaboration, 232, 234–236, 242
Colonialism, 117–118, 186
Comas-Diaz, L., 45–46

Commodification, 44, 138, 300
Communism, 143–147
Community, 27, 65, 98, 119, 123, 129, 164, 212, 216, 224, 232
Compassion, 17, 19, 23, 100, 123–125, 127, 129, 169, 225
Consumerism, 22, 117, 120–121, 277
Contemplative practice, 17, 123, 129, 266, 284–288, 291–292
Contemplative psychology, 283–286, 299
Contemplative role, 17, 24
Contextualism, 48, 60, 239, 245, 256
Contradiction, 23, 25, 145, 147, 258
Counter-hegemony, 23, 83, 91
Critical consciousness, 23, 28, 48–49, 122–123, 126, 130, 233
Critical ethnopsychiatry, 193
Critical-Liberation Psychotherapy (CLP), 44–49
Critical psychology, 18, 25–26, 55, 57–58, 66, 98–100, 102, 107, 135, 150, 159, 164
Cruelty, 267, 269–271
Cultural capital, 78
Cumulative deprivation, 104
Cushman, P., 37, 108, 120

Daoist Contemplative Psychology, 283–286
Daoist meditation, 296–301
Davies, J., 98, 150

de Wit, H., 284–285
Deaths of despair, 257–258
Decolonial therapy, 127, 131, 181, 194, 196
Dehumanization, 101, 242, 244, 253
Deleuze, G., 242–244, 253, 271
Depression, 39, 105, 120, 124, 215, 217, 275
Depth psychology, 121, 126
Development, 102–105, 235, 240, 285
Dialectic, 100, 146, 181, 192
Direct knowledge, 19, 22
Disciplinary power, 40, 165
Discourse, 37, 41, 54–57, 61–64, 101, 145, 296
Disenchantment, 264, 267–268, 277–278
Disillusionment, 22, 25, 28, 107

Eagleton, T., 23
Ecosocial theory, 105
Ego, 103, 120, 124, 129, 157, 169, 190, 237
Ego, problem of the, 108
Embodiment, 99, 105, 158, 192, 197
Empty self, 119–120, 123, 128–129
Epistemology, 61, 64, 284
Ergotherapy, 189, 191, 193
Essentialism, 193, 259
Eternal Strength, 232, 237
Existential anxiety, 100, 107, 254
Existentialism, 46, 48, 100, 108, 122, 185, 257

Index

F
Fanon, F., 138, 179–197
Fear, 21, 26, 100, 107, 301
Feminism, 38, 45, 139
Flourishing, 20, 23, 27, 103, 115, 282, 286
Foucault, M., 37–44, 54, 56–57, 62
Freedom, 25, 27, 97, 155, 187, 214, 255, 260–261, 296
Freud, S., 136–137, 160, 207, 271, 276
Friere, P., 20, 23, 101
Fromm, E., 22, 106, 108

G
Gramsci, A., 18, 77, 83
Greed, 23, 28, 99, 108, 117, 119, 123
Grief, 45, 120, 125–127
Guattari, F., 242–244

H
Hegemony, 18–20, 25, 28, 47, 97, 106
Heidegger, M., 100, 267
Herman, J., 211–213
Holism, 97, 100, 106, 109, 119, 163, 171, 232, 298
Hook, D., 37–39
Humanism, 36, 91, 185, 237, 245
Hyper-science, 54, 60

I
Ideology, 21–24, 37, 77–78, 81, 98, 101–102, 107, 120, 136, 145, 263, 266–267
Imperialism, 77, 142
Indigenous, 131, 135, 190, 284
Individualism, 19, 25, 28, 37, 97–99, 118–120
Inequality, 24, 27, 49, 98, 103–105, 219, 282
Institutional psychotherapy, 189–191
Integrated cycle of social injustice, 150, 221
Interconnection, 47, 55, 59, 100, 118–119, 123–125, 238–239
Internalization, 18–19, 39, 101, 117, 167, 220
Internalized oppression, 20–22, 106, 123
Internationalism, 142, 147

J
Justice, 17, 19, 27, 29, 75, 209, 212, 219

K
Kabat-Zinn, J., 266, 268

L
Laing, R. D., 21, 244–245
Lenin, V., 77, 83
Liberalism, 209–210
Liberation, 17–19, 22–23, 47–49, 67, 110, 121–125, 140, 196, 282, 285
Liberation psychology, 46, 65–66, 76
Liquid modernity, 258

Marmot, M., 104–105
Marx, K., 88, 92, 139
Marxism, 77, 88
Maslow, A., 91
Materialism, 45, 99, 107, 119, 154
Materialist value orientation, 107
Medicalization, 145, 188, 244, 255, 282
Mental illness, 186, 244, 260
Merleau-Ponty, M., 187
Methodologism, 58–59, 61, 64
Mind-body, 100, 273, 294
Mindfulness, 127, 263–269, 272–275, 282
Mystification, 21–22, 97, 106

Narcissism, 25, 108, 123
Neoliberalism, 22, 26, 43, 58, 61, 77, 98, 119–120, 160, 264
North African Syndrome, 188

Objectification, 38, 47, 48, 255
Oppression, 48, 67–68, 75–78, 101–102, 117–118, 122–123, 145, 283

Pandemic, 26, 142
Panopticon, 39–40
Pastoral power, 42
Patriarchy, 137
Positivism, 59–62, 64

Postmodernism, 32–33
Poverty, 76, 104, 256
Power, 18, 21, 24–25, 28, 37, 39, 42, 45, 46, 54–58, 64–65, 79, 91, 99, 101–102, 136, 138–139, 216, 283
Power-Threat-Meaning Framework, 171
Practices of the self, 43
Preliminary concern, 109
Prilleltensky, I., 24, 61, 65, 98, 101, 122
Prophetic role, 17, 23, 25
Psychiatry, 38, 55, 138, 145, 167, 194, 204, 255
Psychoanalysis, 48, 126, 140–142, 144, 187, 271
Psychological humanities, 66
Psychologization, 77, 256
Psychopolitical validity, 65
Psychotherapy, 31, 34, 37, 39, 42–44, 49, 75, 85, 91, 99, 143, 217, 264, 272
Psychotherapy, effectiveness of, 78–81
Psy disciplines, 41

Racism, 63, 76, 77, 139, 142, 184, 186, 192, 256
Radical, 179–181, 197, 260, 296
circle, 83–89
research, 55, 64–66
therapy, 21–26, 31, 46, 49, 54, 67–68, 78, 82, 91, 141–148, 188–190, 259, 272–278
youth work, 233–237, 240

Rawls, J., 103, 209
Real, the, 270–272
Red Clinic, 141–143
Reductionism, 238, 256
Reflexivity, 39, 64–65, 68
Relationship, 26, 36, 46–49, 65, 153, 167, 222, 237, 243
Religion, 58
Resistance, 48, 101, 107, 140, 241, 283, 299
Revolution, 24, 88, 135–136, 139–141, 181, 245, 267, 275, 278, 283
Rogers, C., 91, 237

Sartre, J-P., 260
Schizoanalysis, 244
Self-deception, 18, 20–21, 118
Selfhood, 31, 34–35, 40, 43, 46
Self practices, 44–45, 48
Sexism, 45, 77, 139, 142
Skott-Myhre, H., 234, 240
Social character, 22, 106, 108
Social construction, 32–35, 83
Social determinants, 104
Socialism, 27–28, 76, 82, 87, 91
Social Justice Oriented Interventions, 150, 221
Social practice, 18, 32, 116
Social suffering, 257
Societal change, 116, 121, 125, 127
Societal nature, 22, 99–100, 102
Socio-therapy, 190
Somatic work, 122, 128
Spirituality, 17, 19, 100, 103, 108, 129, 207, 299

Stress, 105, 152, 164, 213, 216, 257, 269, 282
Stress reduction, 265
Structural transformation, 174
Suffering, 19, 24, 28, 36, 44, 47, 75, 77, 91, 97, 101–109, 120–125, 142, 254, 258, 282

Taylor, C., 34, 36, 37
Teo, T., 54, 57–61, 63, 66, 106–107, 109
Tillich, P., 108
Tosquelles, F., 189–191
Transcendence, 17, 100, 129
Transformation, 18, 19, 28, 31, 42, 65, 109, 116, 130, 141, 189, 289
Transformative experiences, 129
Transformative psychologies, 121
Transformative therapies, 126
Transformative validity, 65
Transpersonal psychology, 100, 107
Trauma, 26, 101, 122, 127, 129, 152, 210, 211, 214, 215, 256

Ultimate concern, 108
Unconscious, 20, 22, 106, 117, 126, 136, 179, 187, 266

Values, 18, 23, 27, 28, 45, 83, 180, 190
Vicious cycle, 108, 158, 214

Watts, A., 108
Wellness, 61, 65, 118, 265, 268, 277, 282, 299

Young, I. M., 208, 210–211, 213

GPSR Compliance

The European Union's (EU) General Product Safety Regulation (GPSR) is a set of rules that requires consumer products to be safe and our obligations to ensure this.

If you have any concerns about our products, you can contact us on

ProductSafety@springernature.com

In case Publisher is established outside the EU, the EU authorized representative is:

Springer Nature Customer Service Center GmbH
Europaplatz 3
69115 Heidelberg, Germany

www.ingramcontent.com/pod-product-compliance
Lightning Source LLC
LaVergne TN
LVHW021336080526
838202LV00004B/194